Extraordinary Actors

Tel:

To be returned

Extraordinary Actors

Essays on Popular Performers

Studies in honour of Peter Thomson

edited by

Jane Milling and Martin Banham

UNIVERSITY
of
EXETER
PRESS

First published in 2004 by
University of Exeter Press
Reed Hall, Streatham Drive
Exeter EX4 4QR
UK
www.ex.ac.uk/uep/

British Library Cataloguing in Publication Data
A catalogue record for this book is available
from the British Library.

ISBN 0 85989 735 4

Typeset in 10pt Plantin Light
by XL Publishing Services, Tiverton

Printed in Great Britain by Antony Rowe Ltd, Chippenham

Contents

Illustrations

Preface

Leslie du S. Read in talking about acting has suggested that 'the uncanny power of performance springs from an ambiguous tension between what is actual and what is fictional'.[1] It is, of course, the actor who inhabits—to continue the paradox—what one might call the dynamic limbo between reality and the imagination, and it is a dangerous place in which to find oneself. The contributors to this book have all engaged with performers who, in one way or another, put themselves at risk in attempting to keep the audience's attention. Why they do so is implicit in much that follows, but it may be hinted at in a term used by Peter Thomson, to whose humane scholarship these essays are dedicated. As he describes in the introduction to *On Actors and Acting*, he relishes actors who 'are in discernible ways outrageous'.[2] Thomson, we suggest, uses 'outrageous' in the sense of 'takes your breath away', 'audacious', 'daring', 'astonishing' and, like all flesh and blood creatures, prone to the most spectacular 'misbehaviour'. He uses the word to express delight and astonishment, not anger or reproof. The actor, in other words, exists precariously and survives through courage, obstinacy, wit, vanity, charisma, luck and sheer bloody-mindedness. What drives the actor is a mix of courage and foolhardiness, hunger and joy. What else can one expect from a person prepared night after night to step out in front of an audience that always has the power to turn its collective thumb down? And yet, curiously, he or she does it all on our behalf, so that we may the better bridge the gap between the curiosity of our minds and the limits of our experience.

We invited the contributors to this book to talk about the 'extraordinary' in the world of performance, and to celebrate actors who exhibit that most extraordinary of theatrical talents—survival. We use the term 'popular' to indicate not a particular style but the impact the performers had or have. In three chronological sections, we run the gamut from dangerous (Alexander Leggatt on Richard Burbage) to wonderful (Martin White on Mark Rylance 'working wonders' at the New Globe), and from those whose performance we can only reconstruct from historical or textual sources (and the application of appropriate imagination) to actors whose work is 'live' for us via the stage, film, radio or television.

In offering a volume of essays to honour and celebrate, on the occasion of his retirement, the extraordinary contribution Peter Thomson has made to theatre scholarship, we could have focused on a number of matters dear to his heart and illuminated through his writing—the life and works of Shakespeare and Brecht being particular examples. (Or we could, of course, have concentrated entirely on cricket: it is surely no coincidence that the county that offered him a trial in 1956 was Shakespeare's—Warwickshire.) Our eventual decision to explore the world of actors reflects that enthusiastic interest in and concern for people that makes Peter Thomson's work as a teacher and a scholar so vital, shrewd and generous. He has an overwhelming curiosity (he would have made a brilliant detective) that brings any subject of his study fully and triumphantly to life. He happily accommodates rigorous and innovative research (as, for instance, in his *Shakespeare's Professional Career*[3]) together with a cheerful interest in odd conjunctions (witnessed, for instance, by the discussion of 'Murdered actors' in *The Everyman Companion to the Theatre*[4] or the consideration of 'Bigamy and theatre' in *On Actors and Acting*). Thomson's witty and wise company, on the page or in person, is unambiguously good for one. He built at the University of Exeter a Drama Department shaped by a passionate belief in the importance of the subject and distinguished by teaching and research initiatives that have influenced and inspired the subject nationally and internationally. And all this within a context of democracy and humanity.

The editors are delighted that this collection of essays by Peter Thomson's friends and colleagues is published by the University of Exeter Press. Despite his critical and close involvement with the creation of the series Exeter Performance Studies we hope and believe that until publication he knew nothing of this volume! We would like to thank Simon Baker, whose enthusiasm and wisdom has made this project a delight to work on, and the generous support of all at the University of Exeter Press. We also wish to place on record the significant initiative of Chris McCullough in the development of this project and his substantial authorial contribution to the introductory material within the volume. Our warm thanks go to him and to all the contributors who responded so positively to our invitation to mark the academy's affection and respect for Peter.

Martin Banham
Leeds, 2003

SECTION ONE
The Idea of Acting

SECTION ONE

The Idea of Acting

Introduction

Jane Milling

In the seventeenth and eighteenth centuries across Europe attention was turned to the theatre and to actors in a way it had never been before. Once courtly and household troupes began to establish commercial playing places and stable touring routes, alongside the popular troupes of the commedia and the itinerant performers of fairgrounds and booths, the professionalization of the player became inevitable. These newly professional actors performed in a variety of venues and styles. It is not easy to separate out strictly courtly or popular forms, as the commercial imperatives of competition and survival developed an entertainment market-place throughout Europe. Michael Bristol usefully describes the ironies of the blending of 'popular' and 'commercial' fields:

> The success of the theatre as a freestanding cultural institution during the early modern period has traditionally been described in terms of the development of a fully achieved, durable public art form from folkloric practices, literary experiments, and a wide range of amateur forms of theatricality . . . A less affirmative account might describe these events as the gradual alienation of traditional practices of narrative representation and performance from the diverse patterns of communal life in which they had previously been embedded.[1]

It is in this field of 'alienated' public art that the three sets of performers of this section are considered. The newly commercial theatre, in which Burbage, Betterton and commedia players like Tomasso Ristori, Pietro Mira and Antonio Sak performed, showed evidence of the cross-European influence of travelling troupes through shifts in repertoire, acting style and scenic innovation. The impact of these European influences was noted, in anecdote, by many cultural commentators. Heywood was impressed with the performance of 'all the Doctors, Zawneys, Pantaloones, Harlekeenes, in which the French, but especially the Italians, have been excellent'.[2] When an English troupe toured the German states the audience 'flocked wonderfully to see their gesture and action',[3] and as Laurence Senelick's chapter shows here, the courtly visits by commedia companies in Russia had a long-term effect on the popular iconography of the Russian clown. Exacerbated by the language barrier, what seems to have drawn audiences' attention to these foreign innovations in the commercial theatres, (as had also been the case for native performance modes) were the bodies and the performance skills of the actors.

At moments when the theatre achieved its greatest commercial success, the religious and philosophical outbursts against the actors tended to increase dramatically.[4] During the seventeenth and eighteenth centuries clerics and reformers were preoccupied with the threat of religious or moral anarchy that the stage might induce, through its contaminating mimicry. Whatever the moral precepts of a play, 'the life of Actors and Actrices, their gestures, actions, carriage and whatsoever else is in them, joyned to the bad inclinations of the generality of spectators, will quite hinder any good effect'.[5] It was not only the content of the plays that was of concern, but also the powerful influence of the players themselves. It is in this nexus that the chapter on Betterton seeks to place the dangerous potential of his actorly presence. Matthew Wikander notes that this anxiety about the actors was reproduced in the playwrights' own work and surfaces in reflections on acting within playtexts themselves, as Alexander Leggatt's study of Burbage exemplifies here.

The Renaissance rediscovery of classical rhetoric and the ancients had rejuvenated the idea of performance and acting as a metaphor for social and political behaviour. Beyond the notion of the two bodies of the monarch, and an acceptance of the inevitable importance of Machiavelli's advice for the princely, the crisis of acting as a metaphor for social interaction had slid through the social boundaries to apply just as regularly to the citizen. Jean Bellegarde reflected in 1696 that:

> Sincerity is the Soul of Commerce and Civil Society, and yet 'tis a very uncommon Vertue in so refining an Age as this we live in, 'tis an Art and a Trade to disguise the Sentiments . . . [religious hypocrites and con-men] bear a great resemblance to Comedians, who act several Characters in Masks, and change their Habits according to the Parts they play.[6]

This anxiety about actorly hypocrisy and sincerity was perhaps to find fullest expression in Rousseau's crisis of the inauthentic self in his *Letter to M. d'Alembert.*[7]

As a direct result of this concern with acting as a social metaphor during this period, we see the idea of acting itself, as opposed to interest in the theatrical or the playtext, become a subject of serious scrutiny. There was a shift in the language used to describe performance, and the word actor, rather than player, appeared with increasing regularity.[8] Peter Thomson has argued that on the Shakespearean stage, 'beyond the immediate ken of the audiences, and in ways imperfectly understood by the players themselves, a predominantly presentational style of acting was being shifted towards the representational'.[9] He goes on to identify the distinction between modes of playing that might be called presentation, personation and representation and to ponder some of the repercussions of this for the actors themselves. As the seventeenth and eighteenth centuries wore on this interest in acting evolved into the conception of different *styles* and *modes* of performance, and contemporaries debated about when, where and how an actor might appropriately use these diverse modes. Acting manuals were born, developing out of advice on rhetoric and oratory, and moving beyond general discussions of the purpose of the stage. Discussions of the problematics of acting by actors, as well as critics or philosophers, circulated widely throughout the eighteenth century, in such pamphlets as Garrick's *Essay on Acting* or Hill's *The Actor* or the debate in France which saw the eventual publication of Diderot's *Paradoxe*. It is with these paradoxes and nascent definitions of performance that the chapters on Burbage and Betterton wrestle.

Burbage, Betterton, Sak and Mira were accorded a popular status in the culture that surrounded them, entering the field of everyday cultural life. Cheaply circulating images such as *luboks*, cartoons and broadside elegies on actors' deaths abound in the period. Anecdotes and accounts of the actors' work and of their lives became interwoven into histories of the stage, periodical commentary and pamphlets. There was a plethora of satiric poetry and scandalous prose, in print and manuscript, which linked the protean body of the performer to a protean, excessive and threatening sexuality.[10] In the essays that follow, the authors have attempted to explore how and why these particular performers played such a significant role in the development of the idea of acting as a social metaphor and a professional skill, and thus what marked them as extraordinary performers.

CHAPTER ONE

Richard Burbage: A Dangerous Actor

Alexander Leggatt

As Shakespeare's leading man, creator of the tragic roles that have tested other actors' claims to greatness ever since, Richard Burbage piques our curiosity. We have reports of what Garrick, Kean and Irving did with those roles. For Gielgud and Olivier we have not only reports but memories and in some cases a record on film. For Burbage, we have only the most generalized contemporary tributes. The task of evoking him seems hopeless. Yet we can turn our problem the other way around: are we really that much better off with more recent actors? Reports are contradictory and can be clouded by the writer's own agenda; memories betray; and the filmed record can be the most treacherous of all. Olivier's Othello survives on film, with the external details of the performance intact but nothing like the impact of the living original, since what worked brilliantly on stage is too big for the screen. Future students of theatre will be deceiving themselves if they imagine, having seen this film, that they know what it was like to watch Olivier play Othello. There is such a thing as having too much information. It creates a misplaced confidence that can actually block our understanding, when tentativeness and a willingness not just to speculate but to admit we are speculating might get us closer to the truth. As for the treachery of memory, Peter Thomson gives an example from his own recollection of Donald Wolfit in *The Master of Santiago*: 'When the curtain rose, he was standing upstage with his back to us, dimly silhouetted against a large window (this is my true memory—Michael Kilgareff tells me that Wolfit entered slowly ten minutes in). He held his pose for a meaningful while before turning to walk down.'[1] The disparity can hardly be accounted for by a night-to-night change; it would require a significant rewriting of the script. Yet through the difference in detail there is a constant: the charismatic effect of a slow first appearance. The two memories differ on detail; on the spirit of the performance they agree.

This—the spirit—is what, without reviews, without film, and with only general memories from long dead writers, we can recover for Richard Burbage. We can begin, with some initial confidence (the reservation is important), to note the general impact he had. An elegy on his death calls him 'England's great Roscius, for what Roscius/Was more to Rome than Burbage was to us?'[2] Roscius was proverbial for the Elizabethans as the leading actor of Rome; the identification is a shorthand way of declaring Burbage's eminence. Writing shortly after Burbage's death, John Gee calls him 'the flower and life of his company, the loadstone of the auditory, and the Roscius of the stage'.[3] Burbage himself was proverbial within his lifetime: in Jonson's *Bartholomew Fair* (1614) Cokes asks the puppet-master Leatherhead, 'Which is your Burbage now? . . . Your best actor.'[4] If you wanted to add bite to a joke about acting by picking a name, the name you picked was Burbage. John Chamberlin wrote to Dudley Carlton (17 July 1617): 'The Lord Coke and his lady hath great wars at the council-table . . . she . . . declaimed bitterly against him, and so carried herself, that divers said Burbage could not have acted better.'[5]

We know of the public impact of the deaths of Garrick and Irving. With the news media in their infancy in Burbage's time, there was less in the way of public life as we understand it. But there is a contemporary report that the mourning for him exceeded that for James I's wife, Queen Anne, who had died a few days earlier.[6] The Earl of Pembroke wrote to a friend that he was in no mood to see a play 'so soon after the loss of my old acquaintance Burbage'.[7] The aforementioned elegy declares that his parts died with him (second version, 180). In *Iter Boreale* (1647) Richard Corbet describes a host 'full of ale and history' guiding visitors around the Battle of Bosworth:

> Where he mistook a player for a king.
> For when he would have said, 'King Richard died
> And called, "A horse! A horse!"' he 'Burbage' cried.[8]

We do not have to take the tale literally to get the point: Burbage did not just play Richard III, for his generation he *was* Richard III.

Another story that sounds too good to be true (but that might just be true), and that identifies Burbage with Richard, appears in the lifetimes of the parties concerned, in the diary of John Manningham of the Middle Temple:

> Upon a time when Burbage played Richard 3, there was a citizen grew so far in liking with him that before she went from the play she appointed him to come that night unto her by the name of Richard the 3. Shakespeare, overhearing their conclusion, went before, was entertained, and at his game ere Burbage came. The message being brought that Richard the 3 was at the door, Shakespeare caused return to be made that William the Conqueror was before Richard the 3.[9]

The punch line is a demonstration of Shakespeare's wit; but the set-up is a confirmation of the splendidly demoralizing power of the stage, regularly denounced by its enemies, and a tribute to the erotic impact of one actor in particular. Burbage, by this account, had sex appeal, and not just when he was playing Romeo. In Richard's seduction of Lady Anne, the language does something, but Richard achieves his real breakthrough when he bares his breast and invites Anne to stab him to death, giving her the choice: kill me or love me. The impact of the moment may depend not just on Anne's natural human inability to kill but also on the sexual magnetism of Richard's presence—which is the actor's presence. The breast-baring can be flagrant or discreet; the point is, Anne has to get close to him. (We see the magnetism at work in Olivier's film version; here for once the spirit of the performance does communicate.) If Burbage played Bertram in *All's Well that Ends Well*, the first audience may have understood Helena's desire for him better than we do; the answer came when Burbage walked on to the stage. The plot of Massinger's *The Roman Actor* (1626) hinges on the sex appeal of the title character, Paris. At the Emperor's command he and his fellows act a play called *The Cure of Avarice*, on the theory that it will cure a miser in the audience. The play fails (so much for generations of theorizing about the moral power of theatre) but the Emperor's mistress falls in love with the leading actor. I remember one production of *As You Like It* in which, when the actors playing Orlando and Charles took off their shirts for the wrestling match, there was a palpable buzz of excitement in the audience. A woman of my acquaintance later confessed, 'Those two haunted my erotic fantasies for weeks'. The citizen in Manningham's story was not content with fantasy, and true or not, the story provides an image of a recognizable audience response. Her successors greet the performances of favourite singers by throwing panties and hotel room keys on to the stage.

In more respectable ways, Burbage had impact. The elegy reports that his death scenes convinced the spectators he was really dead (178). The parts that died with him include 'young Hamlet' and 'old Hieronimo' (second version, 180), the author noting, not that both are avengers, but that Burbage could play a range of ages. A late report, Richard Flecknoe's *Discourse of the English Stage* (1664), likewise stresses his versatility as well as his absorption in his roles. Flecknoe calls him 'a delightful Proteus, so wholly transforming himself into his part, and putting off himself with his clothes, as he never (not so much as in the tiring house) assumed himself again until the play was done'.[10] We sense here the chameleon quality we can associate in our own time with Alec Guinness, Peter Sellers and Robert de Niro. The elegy also credits Burbage with that much-valued principle, decorum:

> How to the person he did suit his face,
> How did his speech become him and his pace
> Suit with his speech. Whilst not a word did fall
> Without just weight to balance it withal. (178)

The author may be recalling Hamlet's advice to the players, 'Suit the action to the word, the word to the action' (III ii 16–17).[11]

That raises a question: is Shakespeare putting in Burbage's mouth a description of Burbage's own acting style? Or was it a crafty way of getting him under control? (The Manningham story hints at the ancient rivalry of actor and playwright.) Burbage, we can imagine Shakespeare thinking, is not going to be able to go over the top if I make him say things like, 'Nor do not saw the air too much with your hand, thus, but use all gently, for in the very torrent, tempest, and as I may say whirlwind of your passion, you must acquire and beget a temperance that may give it smoothness' (III ii 4–7). Could Burbage say those lines with a perfectly straight face, given that they described his own acting, while the audience nodded sagely? Or (this being *Hamlet*) is there something more devious going on? The prince's advice on decorum is embedded in a passage that balances the warning against overacting with an equally decorous warning against underacting: 'Be not too tame, neither; but let your own discretion be your tutor. Suit the action to the word, the word to the action, with this special observance: that you o'erstep not the modesty of nature' (III ii 15–18). The passage is in fact a little unbalanced: it is the warning against overacting that has to be reiterated. The problem is built into the role: Hamlet goes so far over the top with Rosencrantz and Guildenstern that the latter has to give him a taste of his own advice: 'Good my lord, put your discourse into some frame, and start not so wildly from my affair' (III ii 282–83). Throughout the play Hamlet himself, driven by wild bursts of passion, has to call himself to order. Hamlet, arguably Burbage's greatest part, exemplifies not just the decorum of a theatre settling into realism after the extravagance of Marlowe and his leading actor Edward Alleyn, but the tension between the explosive energy of a charismatic actor and the control that harnesses that energy, for the sake not just of decorum but of sharper focus. Quiet and dangerous can be more compelling than loud and dangerous.

By linking Burbage and Hamlet, my argument itself has entered into dangerous territory, but it is necessary to do so. There is a problem with the tributes in the elegy and the other non-dramatic sources I have quoted. If you had to praise a famous actor, whose acting you had never seen, and knew nothing about, what would you say? You would turn on the automatic tributes: the conviction he brought to his roles, his ability to immerse himself in his part, his range, his ability to suit the word and the action, his power over the audience. All this the elegy does; all this any elegy to any notable actor might do. This is not to say that we should disbelieve the tributes; rather that if we want a sense of what Burbage was like as an actor we need something more specific. Kean, Garrick and Irving were highly, sometimes controversially, individual. Where is the evidence for the individuality of Burbage? The risk I shall be taking for the rest of this essay is to seek it in the parts we know he played, drawing on the Shakespearean tragic leads and on Ferdinand in

The Duchess of Malfi. The objection is obvious: these are in the first instance the effects of the script, not of the actor, and Burbage's successors would have had to play them as he did. But Shakespeare was a colleague, and knew his man; and Webster wrote at a time when Burbage's acting had been long familiar to anyone concerned with the theatre. If we can spot some recurring qualities, we may be in touch with what both playwrights, Shakespeare especially, thought of as Burbage effects—things he could play well, touches his audience would look for. We can spot W.S. Gilbert writing for the qualities of the most distinctive Savoy performers, writing George Grossmith parts, Rutland Barrington parts, Jessie Bond parts. There are surprises and exceptions (even Savoy casting was not rigidly predictable) and we must certainly allow for those in imagining Shakespeare's relationship with Burbage. We should also think of a two-way process: Richard III, we have seen, was a part strongly identified with Burbage, but the play's dating limits of *c.*1592 to 1594 could mean that it predates Burbage's emergence as the leading actor of the Chamberlain's Men (1594). Another actor could have played the role first. Burbage, when he took it over, may have done more than put his stamp on it: responding to what Shakespeare had written may have helped the emerging actor shape his own style. As Shakespeare, from this point on, wrote for Burbage, Burbage acted for Shakespeare, and Shakespeare may have helped to make him the actor he was. One thing the rest of this essay will suggest is that there is a surprising amount of Richard in Burbage's later roles. There are reasons for caution; but it is possible to see continuities, and those continuities I want to explore. In the words of Peter Thomson, 'I doubt very much whether . . . Burbage ever consciously did more than speak Shakespeare's lines (those he could remember) according to the impulses he sensed in them'.[12] What were those impulses?

An ability to command the stage by sheer personality was one of them. Othello can stop a street brawl with one line, 'Keep up your bright swords, for the dew will rust 'em' (I ii 60). Any leading actor should be able to command the stage, of course; the distinctive features here (to which we shall return) are speed and a certain dry wit. (Compare the difficulties the Prince of Verona, speaking much more solemnly, has in getting his subjects to stop fighting.) Asked what he sees in Lear's countenance worthy of obedience, Kent replies, simply, 'Authority' (I iv 27). That countenance, according to the elegy, included an expressive eye: the author describes Burbage as a lover leaping into a grave 'with so true an eye/That there I would have sworn he meant to die' (177). Reporting an effect few modern actors would risk, Desdemona tells Othello, 'I fear you, for you're fatal then/When your eyes roll so' (V ii 39). Olivier, in an interview I cannot now trace, claimed that as an actor he would rather lose his voice than his eyes. I recall him as Solness in the last scene of *The Master Builder*, heading off-stage to climb the tower and measuring the height of the tower with a quick upward movement of his eye.

That Burbage had a voice and knew how to use it we may infer from the demands Shakespeare made on it, from the patterned laments of Richard II to the quick-cutting of Macbeth, some of whose speeches are like verbal equivalents of a rock video. The elegy reports:

> Had'st thou but spoke to death, and used the power
> Of thy enchanting tongue, but the first hour
> Of his assault, he had let fall his dart
> And charmed been by thy so charming art.
> This he well knew and to prevent such wrong
> First cunningly made seizure of thy tongue. (178)

(Is this a clue to the cause of Burbage's death—a stroke that deprived him of speech before it took his life?) Is the Duke's comment on Othello's great set-piece, 'I think this tale would win my daughter, too' (I iii 170), not just one character's tribute to another but Shakespeare's tribute, not just to his own rhetoric, but to the performance he knew he was going to get?

Burbage was remembered as a tragic actor; there are no tributes to his Orlando or Orsino, if indeed he played them. The elegy declares that from this point playwrights should stick to comedy: the tragic parts have died (178). That a tragic role is a greater test is still a common assumption: more is at stake for an ambitious actor in his first Hamlet than in his first Orlando. But Shakespeare's contemporaries praised his gift for comedy (the preface to the Quarto *Troilus and Cressida*, a notably neglected piece of early Shakespeare criticism, is a good example—he comes across as the Noël Coward of his time). Many of Burbage's successors, from Garrick through to Gielgud, have been brilliant comic actors, and their gifts have been duly noted. Burbage's vein was tragedy. If we can talk of 'Burbage moments' many of these are moments of violence. Richard, bombarded with messengers bringing bad reports, suddenly explodes and strikes one of them (IV iv 438–39). In the middle of a scene about state business, his private feelings boiling over, Othello cries 'Devil!' and strikes Desdemona (IV i 235). Lear strikes Oswald (I iv 73). Violence is the stock in trade of tragedy, of course: what stands out about these moments is that they are sharp, sudden, unexpected. Caught in the slow, deliberate rhythm of Othello's summing-up of his life, we do not expect the burst of violence on which it ends. And we certainly do not expect Richard II, whose response to adversity has been to deliver long, mannered speeches, to beat the servant who brings him food, much less to seize a weapon and start killing his assailants. Benvolio's account of Romeo's fight with Tybalt should probably be taken as a guide to staging: 'to't they go like light-ning, for ere I/Could draw to part them was stout Tybalt slain' (III i 166–67). It is tempting to prolong the swordplay; but what the text suggests is that Romeo, who at first would not fight at all, not only strikes fast but kills fast.

So does Hamlet when he hears a noise behind the arras.

When the prince breaks from hiding on the words, 'This is I,/Hamlet the Dane' (V i 241–42), the character is declaring himself, and so is the leading actor, with a signature effect—the sudden, surprising burst of energy. By one reading, the elegy describes what happens next:

> Oft have I seen him leap into a grave
> Suiting the person (which he used to have)
> Of a mad lover, with so true an eye
> That there I would have sworn he meant to die. (177)

Other versions read 'sad' for 'mad'; but if this is an account of *Hamlet* the madness fits, the gleam in the eye is dangerous. It is worth noting that the elegy's first specific memory is of a moment of sudden action. Other Burbage roles show a tendency to hit the ground: Romeo flings himself to the stage floor (III iii 68–70); Othello falls in an epileptic fit, and flings himself on Desdemona's bed; Ferdinand throws himself to the ground in an attempt to throttle his own shadow (V ii 31–41).[13] (Does the grotesque comedy of Gloucester's leap include a parody by a secondary actor of a Burbage effect?)[14] The sudden burst of energy takes the form of unexpected running exits for Hamlet and Lear. Sometimes the energy is throttled. Richard gnaws his lip (IV ii 28); so does Othello (V ii 46).

Such effects are not peculiar to Burbage's roles, but the way they accumulate is suggestive. We may imagine regular playgoers picking up echoes from one performance to another. If we do not think of Romeo and Lear together, one reason may be that chances to see the same actor play the two in rapid succession are rare. But when Romeo hears of Juliet's death, and reacts by commanding his servant, 'Thou knowest my lodging. Get me ink and paper,/And hire posthorses. I will hence tonight' (V i 25–26), he may be setting up Lear's more violent but equally swift reaction to Goneril's disobedience: 'Darkness and devils!/Saddle my horses, call my train together!' (I iv 213–14). Was Burbage's playing of the first moment in Shakespeare's mind when he created the second? Did experienced Burbage-watchers see a link?

What stands out is the speed of attack that such moments require. They leap out of the longer, slower, more reflective passages that surround them and set them up. The actor pounces suddenly, like a cat that has been creeping up on its prey. The effect marks climactic moments like Romeo's 'Well, Juliet, I will lie with thee tonight' (V i 34)—echoed in Hamlet's sudden resolution 'I'll watch tonight' (I ii 241)—and gives little attention-getting bursts of speed to quieter scenes, as when Richard declares, 'We are not safe, Clarence; we are not safe' (I i 70). Ferdinand catches Bosola, and the audience, off guard with his sudden, abrupt, 'There's gold' (I i 246). He repeats the effect more dramatically with the Duchess, bursting into her private reverie with 'Die then, quickly!' as he hands her a poniard (III ii 71). Macbeth reacts to the ghost of Banquo with sudden outbursts of panic that take his hearers completely by surprise.

In later plays in particular this speed of attack becomes characteristic not just of the leading role, but of his dialogues with other characters—as though Shakespeare had decided it was time to make Burbage's speed part of the company's teamwork. Lear asks Kent who put him in the stocks:

```
KENT                        It is both he and she:
        Your son and daughter.
LEAR                  No.
KENT                     Yes.
LEAR                        No, I say.
KENT  I say yea.
LEAR            By Jupiter, I swear no.
KENT  By Juno, I swear ay.                    (II ii 189–92)
```

A leading boy actor gets to match his speed with Burbage's after the murder of Duncan:

```
LADY MACBETH   . . .Did not you speak?
MACBETH            When?
LADY MACBETH         Now.
MACBETH                     As I descended?
LADY MACBETH  Ay.                    (II ii 16–17)
```

There are similarly quick exchanges between Lear and the disguised Kent at their first meeting (I iv 16–27), and between Othello and Desdemona over the handkerchief (III iv 78–83). Webster picks up the effect:

```
BOSOLA      Must I see her again?
FERDINAND                Yes.
BOSOLA                      Never.
FERDINAND                        You must.   (IV i 133)
```

A sketch of 'A common player' by 'J. Cocke' includes the criticism that 'When he doth hold conference upon the stage, and should look directly into his fellow's face, he turns about his voice into the assembly for applause-sake, like a trumpeter in the fields, that shifts places to get an echo'.[15] A good actor, then, works with his fellows, and Burbage regularly had to use his talent for the swift attack in dialogue.

He was also called upon to change course abruptly; his characters can turn on what used to be called a sixpence. The Folio Hamlet goes in a moment from the cry of 'O, vengeance!' to 'Why, what an ass am I?' (II ii 559–60). He can change subjects without warning: 'Go thy ways to a nunnery. Where's your father?' (III ii 129–30). (Contriving business to show that Hamlet knows he is being spied on makes the moment less strange, and I suspect less authentic; we need to feel the strangeness.) Dealing with the news that Cornwall and Regan will not see him, Lear shifts rapidly between bursts of anger and attempts at patience, calling himself to order as Hamlet does. In his later madness he is quiet, reflective and conniving, then suddenly explodes:

> It were a delicate stratagem to shoe
> A troop of horse with felt. I'll put't in proof,
> And when I have stol'n upon these son-in-laws,
> Then kill, kill, kill, kill, kill!   (IV v 174–77)

Ferdinand takes several sharp turns. One comes after an apparent reconciliation with his sister, in which he has shown an uncharacteristic mildness:

> DUCHESS (aside)   O bless'd comfort!
>   This deadly air is purg'd.
>   Exeunt [all except FERDINAND]
> FERDINAND   Her guilt treads on
>   Hot-burning coulters:—   (III i 55–57)

He gloats over her death, then suddenly cracks: 'Cover her face: mine eyes dazzle: she died young' (IV ii 264). The sudden onset of Leontes' jealousy— 'Too hot, too hot' (I ii 110) bursting into a scene of slow, polite conversation—however it may puzzle us now, may have registered on the first audience as a Burbage moment.

Richard can change the mood of a scene with a brisk entrance line. He breaks in on Lady Anne's mourning with a sharp command, 'Stay, you that bear the corpse, and set it down' (I ii 33). Entering with Hastings, he interrupts a worried family conversation about the health of King Edward with 'They do me wrong, and I will not endure it' (I iii 42). The effect is to bring a totally different conversation, already under way, on to the stage, and the rest of the scene is a squabble. Other brisk entrances may not change the tone of a scene, but they produce a sharp rise in its energy level, like Lear's 'Let me not stay a jot for dinner. Go get it ready' (I iv 8). They can also catch us by surprise. Lear ends his curse on Goneril with 'Away, away!' (I iv 252) and a quick exit. His part in the scene has ended, on a note of high drama, almost a demand for an exit round. Then seconds later he is back: 'What, fifty of my followers at a clap?/Within a fortnight?' (257–58). Ferdinand makes a brisk, businesslike entrance after the murder of the Duchess: 'Is she dead?' Bosola's reply, 'She is what you'd have her' (IV ii 256–57), reads like an attempt to slow him down and get him thinking about what he has done, to bring his savage energy under control.

With the savage energy goes an equally savage wit. It is one of Richard's keynotes. He can make us catch our breath with his impudence, as when he expresses tender concern over his brother Edward's health: 'He cannot live, I hope, and must not die/Till George be packed with post-haste up to heaven' (I i 145–46). Richard was presumably seen in Shakespeare's time, and can still be seen, as a tragic lead; but an actor with no gift of comedy will be severely handicapped in playing it. I suggested earlier that there are unexpected touches of Richard in Burbage's later roles, and a certain dry, sardonic wit is perhaps the most important of these. Criticizing the rigid solemnity of French actors, David Garrick 'suggested that "there must be *comedy* in the perfect actor of tragedy"'.[16] Burbage, I have argued, was remembered as a tragic actor; but he was also England's Roscius, and Roscius was a comedian. Hamlet can be as grimly funny as Richard; this too is a part for a tragedian who can play comedy. If *Timon of Athens* ever got to the stage, Burbage would have had to call on similar gifts in the last two acts:

FIRST SENATOR   The senators of Athens greet thee, Timon.
TIMON   I thank them, and would send them back the plague
                               Could I but catch it for them.   (V ii 21–23)

(I recall here Paul Scofield's throwaway delivery of this line.) Even the normally humourless Othello, in a line quoted earlier, can stop a fight with a joke. And Macbeth too has at least one moment that, grim and unamusing though it is, is his form of wit. A messenger runs on stage:

MACBETH   The devil damn thee black, thou cream-faced loon!
                    Where got'st thou that goose look?
SERVANT   There is ten thousand—
MACBETH   Geese, villain?
SERVANT   Soldiers, sir.   (V iii 11–14)

In a much lighter vein, Romeo (after an initial effort) can engage in banter with Mercutio. And Hamlet's first utterance is not an impassioned soliloquy but a bit of cross-talk with his friendly uncle:

KING CLAUDIUS . . .But now, my cousin Hamlet, and my son —
HAMLET   A little more than kin and less than kind.
KING CLAUDIUS How is it that the clouds still hang on you?
HAMLET   Not so, my lord, I am too much i' th' sun.
                                                                          (I ii 64–67)

Give them each a straw hat and a cane, put them side by side, facing the audience in a spotlight, and you have part of the effect Shakespeare is aiming at.

Only part, of course. The dynamic of straight man and comic can have a touch of hostility, as it does here. With Richard, Hamlet and Macbeth the wit has an edge of danger, as it certainly does with Ferdinand. In dialogue with his sister he makes a false exit, then turns back quickly (that speed again) with a joke:

> Fare ye well: —
> And women like that part which, like the lamprey,
> Hath ne'er a bone in't.   (I i 335–37)

The danger we feel when Ferdinand is on stage is not eased but sharpened when he starts making jokes. Watching him from a distance, Pescara notes, 'Lord Ferdinand laughs' and Delio knows this is not good news: 'Like a deadly cannon/That lightens ere it smokes' (III iii 54–55).

If I had to find one word to summarize the effect I imagine in a Burbage performance, that word would be danger. It is the danger we feel whenever Ferdinand comes on to the stage: the sudden pouncing attacks, the quick mood changes, the startling entrances, the bursts of violence and (perhaps above all) the wit that does not dispel fear but heightens it. It is revealing that Burbage, as we know from the cast list printed with the 1623 Quarto, played Ferdinand. There is a strong case for saying that the leading male role is Bosola, and not just because of the length of the role. Scene after scene centres on him, he guides us through the play if anyone does, and from the half-way point the Duchess's most important relationship is with him. Her dialogues with Bosola are far more dynamic and exciting than her dialogues with Antonio; so much more is at stake. Yet Burbage played Ferdinand. This suggests we should not be too quick to assume that Burbage always played the leading male role. Bosola may be that role; but Ferdinand is a Burbage part. This leads to a speculation about *Julius Caesar*: we tend to assume that Burbage played Brutus; but Antony is the Burbage part here, and he may have been drawn to it as—all other comparisons aside—Beerbohm Tree was (to say nothing of Marlon Brando).

The keynote of the Burbage part, I argue, is danger. Hamlet is explicit:

> I prithee take thy fingers from my throat,
> For though I am not splenative and rash,
> Yet have I in me something dangerous,
> Which let thy wiseness fear.   (V i 245–48)

He tries to rein in this quality as he goes to see his mother, but in the event he so frightens her that she calls for help. Watching him with Ophelia is like

watching her in a cage with an unpredictable animal. Romeo, who seems a
nice, polite young man when we first meet him, turns on his own capacity for
danger at the throw of a switch: 'Away to heaven, respective lenity,/And fire-
eyed fury be my conduct now' (III i 117–18). From this point, each time he
fights he kills his man. Othello may be a dupe, but he is terrifying when
roused—and not just to Desdemona. There is a solid stage tradition that on
'Villain, be sure thou prove my love a whore' (III iii 364) he physically attacks
Iago, usually taking him by the throat. Iago responds with spluttering outrage,
behind which we can sense panic. The key difference between the Lear of the
old *King Leir* play and the part Shakespeare wrote for Burbage is that the first
is a mild, pathetic old man who creeps away quietly when he knows he is not
welcome, while the second alternates pathos with terrifying rage. Macbeth,
Coriolanus and the Antony of *Antony and Cleopatra* in their different ways all
bring this sense of danger on to the stage. As a tyrant, Macbeth frightens
others; in the early scenes, he frightens himself. Coriolanus has a hair-trigger
temper, and his handlers find it impossible to control him when he is roused.
It may seem safer to toy with Antony, but it is never quite safe, as Thidias
learns when the old general finds him kissing Cleopatra's hand.

One final speculation, however idle, is hard to resist. How much of this
sense of danger in Burbage's acting sprang from something in Burbage
himself? In *The Roman Actor* Paris denies that his roles have anything to do
with himself (he is dealing with the Emperor's mistress, who is infatuated with
him, and having seen him play a lover assumes he is himself one). In fact, in
the play as a whole Paris seems to have no particular personality of his own:
he is a blank space to be filled with what a scene requires; he responds to the
needs of the moment. In the Cambridge comedy *The Second Part of the Return
from Parnassus* and in Webster's Induction to *The Malcontent* Burbage comes
on stage as himself; in the latter he would have played himself. In the *Parnassus*
play he and Will Kemp audition some university students. Kemp dominates
the stage, laying down the law and generally displaying a huge actor's ego.
Burbage, when not simply acting as Kemp's feed, is quiet and businesslike.
His speeches are as notable for their brevity as Kemp's are for their length.
In the *Malcontent* Induction he is one of several company actors who appear,
some as audience members, some as themselves, and again he is businesslike.
He offers a stock defence of satire, explains the King's Men's decision to add
new material, and leaves early, presumably to dress for the leading role. The
livelier passages in the scene, indeed the scene itself, belong to the other actors.
In neither case do we have any sense of Burbage other than as a man doing a
job. Is that all he was?

These are of course dramatizations of Burbage, not direct evidence about
the man himself. We have such evidence, a glimpse of Burbage, not yet a star,
at the age of 19. The widow of John Brayne had come to the theatre to collect
a share of the take, awarded to her by a Chancery order. She was accompa-

nied by Robert Myles, his son Ralph, and Nicholas Bishop. They were met by young Burbage, who 'fell upon the said Robert Myles and beat him with a broom staff, calling him murdering knave'. When Bishop protested, Burbage, 'scornfully and disdainfully playing with [his] nose, said that if he dealt in the matter he would beat him also, and did challenge the field of him at that time'. When John Alleyn (brother of the famous actor) arrived on the scene and asked what was going on, Burbage answered 'in laughing phrase how they came for a moiety, "But," quod he (holding up the said broom staff) "I have, I think, delivered him a moiety with this, and sent them packing"'.[17] No other report like this survives of the private Burbage, who from this point figures in wills and legal documents. But as the alarming, violent, witty Richard set the tone for later performances, so in early adulthood Richard Burbage seems to have been a dangerous actor, with a laugh to beware of, on stage and off.

CHAPTER TWO

Thomas Betterton and the Art of Acting

Jane Milling

Thomas Betterton (1635–1710) was the pre-eminent actor of his generation. After Burbage and before Garrick, he was possibly the most significant performer on the London stage. He perhaps sits uneasily in the company of popular performers here. After all, Betterton was not a John Lacy, Joe Haines or William Pinkethman, a clown or player of clownish roles, with a successful sideline in fairground entertainment or entr'acte performance. Betterton, to our knowledge, never strolled with his company to 'popular' audiences in regional playing places, except the more elevated venue of Oxford, nor regularly appeared in farce or burlesque. But as actor-manager in the theatre companies he ran, he was responsible for popular innovation. In fact, as we shall see, he consistently strove to diversify the theatrical offering to please an audience. Commercial imperatives were interlaced with a desire not to 'serve' the populace but, particularly from 1695 onwards, to win a new metropolitan audience. Calls for a popular theatre in France in the early eighteenth century, a people's theatre, figured it as a place that might 'mould the morals and manners of the citizens'.[1] By the end of his life, Betterton was being hailed on exactly these terms, as the embodiment of the improving effects that stage representation might have on the citizenry of London. Commentators usually praise his acting at the expense of the less improving arts of performers in fair booths or of 'foreign' innovations, forms that Betterton had been in part responsible for introducing into an increasingly diversified bill in the London patent houses. So perhaps the best defence of Betterton's popular status lies only in the broadest sense of the word: he regularly drew a crowd of the widest sort to watch him at work. His performing body became the focus of much contemporary and posthumous attention, and the debates that surrounded his acting and management helped to transform him into a kind of hero of the middling sort.

Dubbed 'our English *Roscius*' (like Burbage before him), Betterton's rise to prominence as one of London's most popular players was in great part due to his careful control of his performances and repertoire as actor-manager of the companies with which he performed, as well as the compelling quality of his acting.[2] Most of the commentary on Betterton and his performance was produced at the very end of his life and posthumously. The picture of Betterton with which we are probably most familiar today emerged from these biographies and histories of the stage: Betterton as the model rhetorical performer and founding father of the *art* of acting in England. However, the images and examples his biographers give of Betterton's rhetorical acting, coupled with Anthony Aston's brutally frank physical portrait of him, might leave us wondering how Betterton managed to hold such continuous sway on the Restoration and early eighteenth-century stage. Aston acknowledges his acting ability, but implies this was in spite of

> an ill Figure, being clumsily made, having a great Head, a short thick Neck, stoop'd Shoulders, and fat short Arms, which he rarely lifted higher than his Stomach.—His Left Hand frequently lodg'd in his Breast, between his Coat and Waistcoat, while with his Right, he prepar'd his Speech.—His Actions were few, but just.—He had little Eyes, and a broad Face, a little Pock-fretten, a corpulent Body, and thick Legs with large Feet.—He was better to meet than to follow; for his Aspect was serious, venerable and majestic; in his late Time a little paralytic. His Voice was low and grumbling; yet he could Tune it by an artful Climax, which enforc'd universal Attention, even from the Fops and Orange-Girls. He was incapable of dancing, even in a Country-Dance.[3]

Aston is apparently not intending to denigrate Betterton here, as he hastens to assure his reader in his introduction, but he does further construct Betterton's rhetorical credentials. As Joseph Roach has pointed out, the control of the arms, in particular the lodging of the left hand in the breast and using the right hand to guide the audience through a speech, was a potent symbol of the accepted modes of rhetorical performance. This does not imply emotionless performance, of course, rather emotion controlled, in keeping with early modern understandings of the relationship between the performer's body and the power of represented passions, 'a coherent physiological system designed to regulate the great natural forces of the body for artistic and hygienic effect'.[4] But it is difficult for the modern reader of the carefully developed hagiography of Betterton as a model rhetorician to envisage the particular thrill of his acting and what it was that made him so extraordinarily successful—the image of the short, fat, immobile actor cannot be the whole story.

Like many members of the Restoration audience, Samuel Pepys was drawn back to the theatre to watch repeat performances of his favourite plays and players. Betterton's performances in early roles in *The Bondman*, *Hamlet* and *Mustapha* elicited superlatives from Pepys: 'he is called by us both the best actor in the world' Pepys notes, in one of the few diary entries that record consensus between himself and his wife.[5] That Pepys did not tire of seeing plays that had been in the repertoire some time seems to be much to do with his experience of the leading players' performances: 'after dinner Mr Creed and I to Whitefriers, where we saw *The Bondman* acted most excellently; and though I have seen it often, yet I am every time more and more pleased with Baterton's action'; and of *Hamlet*, Pepys thought 'Batterton did the Prince's part beyond imagination'.[6] Although given to hyperbole, Pepys was not an innocent observer of acting, as revealed by his comments on the first production at the Nursery, Killigrew's training theatre for young or novice actors:

> the Musique better then we looked for, and the acting not much worse, because I expected as bad as could: and I was not much mistaken, for it was so. However, I was pleased well to see it once, it being worth a man's seeing to discover the different ability and understanding of people, and the different growths of people's abilities by practice.[7]

Interestingly, Pepys chooses to comment that he was captivated by Betterton's *action*. Richard Steele too, much later in Betterton's career, praises his action as a whole: 'I have hardly a notion that any performer of antiquity could surpass the action of Mr Betterton in any of the occasions in which he has appeared'.[8] Both Pepys and Steele may be using action here in the classical rhetorical sense, where 'action' resonates with the sense of emotional, gestural and vocal matching of character to physical embodiment of the orator. However, as we shall see in looking closely at the work of Betterton on stage, action in the broader sense of physical placement on stage, speed and quality of whole body movement, and physical interaction with other performers and the audience, must also be implied here. Pepys was watching Betterton's rise to popularity in the first decade of the restored stage, and Steele, at the end of Betterton's life, echoed the sense of his dominating significance. So what was it that marked out Betterton's performance and body on stage?

Betterton's remarkable hold on the contemporary stage was due, in part, to the sheer amount of time he spent on it. Of the nearly 400 plays performed by the theatre companies he worked with and managed, the Duke's, the United and the Actors' Company, we have records of his appearance in at least 180 of them. Over the course of his 47-year career, Judith Milhous estimates that he may have played in many more of the hundred or so plays for which we have no cast list.[9] If we remember that favourite plays were often held in the repertoire for several years, but rarely played on successive nights, the number of roles Betterton undertook required if nothing else an extraordinary feat of memory. We might wonder how it was that Betterton was able to acquire so many roles under the patent system where plays were, at least initially, the property of one company alone, and where the distribution of roles within any given play remained extremely stable, only changing hands when illness, death or company reorganization required. Betterton bought a share in Davenant's Duke's Company at its formation in 1660, and by 1674 he had the largest actorly shareholding of three and a quarter shares; only Lady Davenant herself held more. Managers or non-actorly investors in the shares of theatre companies seem to have had a fairly relaxed relationship with enterprises they invested in, as evidenced by the complex re-selling and disbursement of part-shares that led to the financial ruin of Alexander Davenant. For actors, shareholding in a theatre company had a very different significance—it more or less guaranteed them a controlling influence over the range and type of roles they undertook and the stage they had invested in. Davenant's invitation to Betterton to become one of the overseers of accounts of his new troupe was both the enticement of a keen young actor with some operating capital to invest and a gamble on the potential of one of the impressive young performers in John Rhodes's company. As he became a major shareholder in the Duke's Company, Betterton's control over his own roles, the repertoire and the development of the theatre itself was unshakeable, even after the Duke's Company merged with the King's Company to form the United Company in 1682.

However, at least in the very first stage of his career with the Duke's Company, Betterton seems to have been an ensemble player. He did not always choose dominating roles or heroic leads for himself. Mr Art in Orrery's *Mr Anthony* is a tiny supporting part. Likewise, Monsieur Brisac in Porter's *The Villain* is almost a peripheral character, but one which played to Betterton's strengths as a young performer and embodied the ideology of a nostalgic courtly chivalry so popular on the early Restoration stage. A young colonel with a strong moral sense, Brisac challenges his superior officer Clairmont over his ungentlemanly conduct towards Brisac's beloved Charlot. In a thrilling moment the combatants agree to duel, and strip in preparation. 'We'll do it decently, Not like the rage that choler works men to', asserts Betterton as Brisac, before the fight in which he kills his opponent and is himself fatally wounded. This allows Brisac a touching deathbed scene in the following act, but it is by no means the end of the play, which plots on with more gory deaths, revenge and retribution courtesy of the Iago-style figure, Malignii. This brings us on to the question of the physical and sexual frisson of Betterton's presence on stage. The concern with formality and decorum that rhetorical action implies might suit the complex verse declamation of heroic tragedy, but a quite different sort of performance is called for in the dark tragi-comedies of the early Restoration period, and the demanding tragic and comedic forms that developed on the later Restoration stage. The parts that Betterton performed required a physically and mentally lithe performer.

If we look at the roles he made his own and those that were written with his skills in mind, some intriguing characteristics emerge. Betterton seems to have specialized in parts offering opportunities to transform suddenly from one believable and highly-strung emotion to another, most usually to and from towering, murderous rage or violent love. This skill was amply demonstrated in passionate roles in tragedy he chose for himself. In Aphra Behn's *Abdelazar* (1676), Betterton as the eponymous revengeful moor has a desperate encounter with the virtuous Leonora. In the space of two minutes playing time Abdelazar kneels to woo her, rises quickly in anger at her scorn, weakens and kneels once more in love to receive the death blow of rejection from her, rises as she cries and tries to leave before empathetic tears well in his own eyes, returns to ask for her love one final time and when refused immediately blazes in fury and attempts to rape her, is interrupted by one of his guards, whom he stabs in frustration and races off to fight his rival, Alonzo (V ii). Likewise the stage tension rises and falls with enormous speed when in Lee's tragedy, *Caesar Borgia* (1679), Betterton played the tormented Caesar Borgia, who marries his brother's beloved Bellmira. When Borgia finds his brother, Gandia, and Bellmira apparently making an escape, he runs at Gandia:

BORGIA	Dye then Traytor!
BELLMIRA	Hold, Borgia hold! Hear Bellmira speak.
BORGIA	Confusion! off: and play not thus with Thunder,
	Lest it should blast thee too; Hence, off, I say:
	Tho thou deserve'st a Fate as sharp and sudden,
	I will take leisure in thy death. Be gone.
BELLMIRA	Behold I grasp the Dagger. . .
BORGIA	Is this possible?
	Ha! Borgia! where! Where is thy Fury now?
	Where thy revenge? O Woman in perfection!

Within ten lines Borgia moves from towering fury to melting love (III i). Similar quicksilver emotional changes are required from the jealous Don Henrique in *The Adventures of Five Hours*, the plotting Duke in *The Duke of Guise*, Jaffeir in *Venice Preserv'd* and Crimalhaz in *The Empress of Morocco* amongst many others. For these sudden shifts of passion to have worked within the plots of the tragedies and tragi-comedies, the audience must have been persuaded by Betterton of the sincerity of his characters' differing states. Steele attested to his ability to make 'dry, incoherent and broken sentences', like those of Othello's great jealous rages, seem natural. Anyone who had 'seen Betterton act it, observes there could not be a word added; that longer speeches had been unnatural, nay impossible, in Othello's circumstances'.[10] The stage directions, the implied movement in the dialogue and the sense of the unfolding stage picture also required Betterton to embody fully these diverse passions in fairly demanding and choreographed physical activity, in relation to other performers in the stage space.

Betterton was able to use the dextrous emotional and physical technique in his comedy roles too. For example, every flash of changing emotion finds physical expression in the comedy of *Sir Salomon Single* (1669), whose tortured love for the determinedly innocent Betty is constantly tested by her infatuation with his friend, Peregrine. In one scene Salomon paces the stage from side to side, wracked by competing emotions, dogged by his trusty steward Timothy who is trying to arrange Salomon's wedding. Tormented by his shame, Salomon briefly envisages hanging himself, before addressing himself to an invisible Peregrine, vowing a bloody revenge and, overcome with frustration, kicking the bemused Timothy off-stage:

> SIR SALOMON   There's your despatch, impertinent Varlet
>   [*He kicks him off the stage*]
> TIMOTHY   Why sir! 'tis I: Who d'ee take me for?   (IV i)

The repressed passion and the potential physical threat that such an active performer as Betterton could summon was mocked in *The Female Wits* (1696), a play probably penned in part by his rival, George Powell. Powell parodies both heroic writing and the extreme twists of emotion that the stage had popularized. *The Female Wits* was a rehearsal play that poked fun at the rash of new female-authored playwriting that had appeared on the London stage in 1696. Marsilia, a female dramatist, is rehearsing her overblown tragedy, harassing and coaching the 'players' from the sidelines.[11] Powell plays himself, and is attempting to act the unbelievable Fastin in the tragedy. Fastin is given the picture of his stepmother, and immediately falls in love:

> FASTIN   What's this thou hast given me? There's more than necro-
>   mantic charms in every bewitching line. My trembling
>   nerves are in their infancy. I'm cold as ice!
> MARSILIA Ay, ay, Love comes just like an ague fit.
> FASTIN   What alteration here? Now I am all on fire! Alcides's shirt
>   sticks close. Fire, incestuous fire. I blaze! I burn! I roast! I fry!
>   Fire! Fire! [*Exit*]   (II i)

To master his heroic part Marsilia instructs comedian William Pinkethman to imitate the Betterton style, 'Fetch long Strides; walk thus; your arms strut-ting, your voice big and your Eyes terrible' (III i). For fellow actors during his lifetime, Betterton's presence on stage was an active one. By the time Cibber is writing of him, the presentation of Betterton's acting has somewhat gentri-fied his raging activity and terrible eyes. Cibber has nothing but praise for Betterton's ability to:

vary his Spirit to the different Characters he acted. Those wild impatient

Starts, that fierce flashing Fire, which he threw into Hotspur, never came from the unruffled Temper of his Brutus (for I have more than once, seen a Brutus as warm as a Hotspur) when the Betterton Brutus was provok'd, in his Dispute with Cassius, the Spirit flew only to his Eye.[12]

Cibber is not talking about performances he has seen here (indeed Betterton probably never played Hotspur) but is using Betterton to illustrate the principle of restraint in impassioned acting. In the 1740s, when Anthony Aston is discussing Betterton's great looks and terrible eyes, he has completely transformed Betterton into the restrained rhetorician. Gone is the physical threat of the wild, impatient starts of a Hotspur character, for Aston Betterton becomes a static image:

His younger Contemporary . . . *Powel*, attempted several of *Betterton's* Parts, as *Alexander*, *Jaffeir*, etc. but lost his Credit; as, in *Alexander*, he maintain'd not the Dignity of a King, but out-Heroded Herod; and in his poison'd mad Scene, out-rav'd all Probability; while *Betterton* kept his Passion under, and shew'd it most (as Fume smoaks most) when stifled.[13]

Both Cibber and Aston begin to reclaim Betterton's acting as rhetorical, describing his performance as increasingly understated. Obviously, however, repressed passion does not represent any threat unless the audience occasionally sees it burst forth in dangerous, disorderly physical action onstage.

Betterton might not have been a violent man, although he was tried and fined as part of an assault and kidnap of a messenger from the Master of the Revels, Edward Thomas, in 1662. However, he was repeatedly cast in the role of raging tyrant or frenzied lover, and he was clearly a skilled swordsman for he battled it out in comedy and tragedy alike. His rakes like Bevil in *Epsom Wells*, Belville in *The Rover*, and Don Juan fight for fun, his heroes like Brisac in Porter's *Villain*, Mercutio or Hamlet fight for honour, and his villains fight to the death. Swordplay was, of course, a crowd pleaser, as Ruffle in Southerne's *The Wives Excuse* (1692) articulates. The roguish Ruffle offers to fight anywhere in town, 'at Will's Coffee-house before the Witts, or in the Play-house, in the Pitt, before the Vizard Masks and Orange Wenches; or behind the Scenes, before the Women-Actors; or any where else, *but* upon the Stage; and you know, one wou'd not willingly be a Jest to the upper Galleries' (III i). The frequency with which swordplay is called for by all kinds of plays suggests that it was as expected a component of a night's entertainment as the dances and music. Betterton must have been able to pull off a vibrant fight, and one appropriate to the differing demands of his various roles, or the upper gallery would not have tolerated it.

Nor was it only the threat of violence or high emotion that characterized the performance style of many of Betterton's roles. He evidently exuded a considerable sexual charisma on stage, particularly necessary in his rake and tyrant parts. Among the notorious roles he made his own was Don John in Shadwell's *The Libertine* (1675). Here Betterton plays a violent, sexual predator, quite unheroic in nature. Downes says that 'the Libertine perform'd by Mr Betterton Crown'd the Play', and for the play to work, the audience must be at once thrilled and repelled by the active vice of Don John; it is a part that is absolutely dependent on sexual threat and unrelenting energy.[14] In one early scene Don John fights and runs through a rival suitor, makes love to Maria keeping up a continuous stream of banter with the audience in asides, fights and kills Maria's brother, beats off five or six servants with drawn swords and wrestles the key to the garden from the feisty servant, Flora. The unrelenting activity of the stage plot, centred on Don John, continues with his besieging by 'a battalion of [six] courageous women', all of whom think themselves married to him, who pull him about on stage before being engaged in a mock wedding dance. When one of them stabs herself rather than be raped by his friend, Don John sagely comments 'Now, see my Providence: if I had been married to none but her, I had been a widower' (II i). The play cannot work unless Don John is believably attractive to the many women in the play who devote themselves to him in the face of his brutal resistance. Nor can it work unless the audience can be seduced by the thrilling, energetic anarchy of the performer's comic timing, verbally and physically.

The promise of illicit sexual pleasure off-stage is built into many roles which end seduction scenes with him leading women off to the bedroom, as Jupiter exits with Alcmena in Dryden's *Amphitryon* or Tom Wilding with Lady Galliard in Behn's *The City Heiress*. Equally often he was pictured in illicit arms, as when the discovery scene opens in Act III of Settle's *Empress of Morocco* to reveal Betterton as Crimalhaz, asleep on a couch with the Queen Mother, or later stepping forward hand in hand with her in a state of undress from the bedchamber. Nor were the sexual exploits of his rake roles always heterosexual. The unbridled villainy of Nemours in Lee's *Princess of Cleve*, is clearly signalled from the first moment the audience sees him, lounging with his servant Bellamore, to the sound of eunuchs singing. Nemours's attentions promise much for the young Bellamore: 'By this damask Cheek I love thee; keep but this gracious form of thine in health, and I'll put thee in way of living like a man'. Nemours then dismisses Bellamour on an errand quickly, 'lest Ravishing shou'd follow thee at the heels'. In the dedication of *The Princess of Cleve* (1689) to the Lord Chamberlain, Lee seeks to excuse 'this Farce, Comedy Tragedy or meer Play. . .for when they expected the most polish'd Hero in *Nemours*, I gave 'em a Ruffian reeking from *Whetstone's Park*. . . the *Libertine*, and *Epsom-Wells*, are but Copies of his Villainy. He lays about him like a Gladiator in the Park.'[15] Whether playing the early loveable rakes, who swagger on stage full of restored, royalist triumphalism, or the later tainted rakehells, whose sexual excess has been transmogrified into socially-threatening villainy, Betterton offered a body primed for sudden violence, emotional outburst or sexual attack.

Many of the roles he played allowed him moments alone with the audience in soliloquy and asides. He was regarded as the exemplary prologue or epilogue speaker, able to command attention from a busy, talkative pit. Never a clown or a lowly servant figure, Betterton was not afraid of playing the buffoon or doting old man roles, with plenty of slapstick, as we have seen in Sir Salomon, or Colonel Jolly in *The Cutter of Coleman Street*, for example. He was never to be 'the Flower of Bartholomew-Fair, and the idol of the Rabble' as Critic and Sullen dub William Pinkethman, but he was a populist at heart, ready to thrill and please the audience with whatever novelty might serve.[16] As manager this meant spectacular innovation, entr'actes, foreign specialists and semi-opera. Betterton introduced drop scenes after the French style onto the London stage in his *The Prophetess* (1690).[17] The only mention James Wright makes of Betterton in his strange study of the theatre companies of the Restoration, *Historia Histrionica* (1699), is to note that scenes 'introduced upon the publick Stage by Sire William Davenant at the Duke's Old Theatre in Lincolns-Inn-Fields, but afterwards very much improved, with the Addition of curious Machines, by Mr. Betterton at the New Theater in Dorset-Garden, to the great Expence and continual Charge of the players'.[18] Some of the curious machines allowed spectacular lighting changes for the first time, as in Shadwell's version of *The Tempest*:

> And when the Ship is sinking, the whole House is darken'd, and a shower of Fire fall upon 'em . . . In the midst of the Shower of Fire the Scene changes . . . when the Lights return discover that Beautiful Part of the Island, which was the Habitation of Prospero . . .[19]

Betterton's propensity for spectacular winching effects, such as Juno's descent by peacock-drawn chariot through the clouds to the stage in the opening act of *Albion and Albanius*, was another of the 'Betterton' effects parodied by *The Female Wits*.

Betterton also seemed to take a delight in foreign costume, not only for his leading ladies but also for himself, particularly for Moorish, Arabic or Indian roles. Colonel Jolly in the *Cutter of Coleman Street* first appears in Indian dress for no good reason. In his early days at the Duke's Company, Betterton may almost have been said to specialize in Moorish or Arabic roles, playing three versions of Solyman in Davenant's *Siege of Rhodes* (1661), Orrery's *Mustapha* (1664) and Settle's *Ibrahim the Illustrious Bassa* (1675), the beleaguered moors in *Abdelazar* (1676) and *Othello*, Crimalhaz in *The Empress of Morocco* and Alphonso, disguised as Osmyn, in Congreve's *The Mourning Bride* (1697). It is difficult to assess the extent to which Betterton would have blacked up for these roles—Abdelazar, Othello and Osmyn all make explicit reference to their blackness—and become a symbol of the exotic otherness that the theatre could summon. More importantly almost all these characters were kings, or considerable leaders, who would have required lavish dressing in the latest imported silks and expensive fabrics. These rulers, with their fatal avaricious or sexual flaws, may have been read as comments on contemporary English monarchs at the same time as they exemplified England's burgeoning connection, through commerce, with a wider, richer world. The expensive displays of scenery and costume would have undoubtedly fed the London imagination and have glamourized Betterton himself, decked out in a fantasy of the power of English imperial trade.

In the early days of Betterton's career, Pepys tried to find out more about his favourite performers from Benier, an intimate of the theatre. He was told that Betterton was considered 'a very sober, serious man, and studious and humble, following his studies, and is rich already with what he gets and saves'.[20] In many ways Betterton embodied an archetypal middling sort, plying his trade assiduously for profit, as a shareholder with a capital investment in the theatre companies. His mercantile roots as apprentice to John Holden, the bookseller, were to be used against him as he attempted to elevate his social status in later life. Like many of the middling sort, a key part of this elevation was to come through a bold gamble on an investment in the East India Company. In 1692, when the French captured a vessel laden with his cargo, which would have netted him an enormous sum, he was ruined. Added to this, part of his disgruntlement with the United Company was his reduced income from shareholding and his move to mere salaried actor.[21] The criticism of his financially and socially modest background and his attempts to 'improve' his place in the world became most pronounced after he led the company of seceding actors out from under the 'tyranny' of Christopher Rich's management of the United Company at the end of 1694. The Actors' Company that was formed by this breakaway group was the first theatre company to hold a licence without noble patronage and to be headed by commoners. The new company went to considerable lengths to claim 'a fondness the better Sort shew'd for 'em',[22] although it is difficult to assess whether there was any social distinction in audiences between the two houses. Betterton certainly continued to mix with the literati in pursuit of material and cultural credit for this Actors' Company. As he had done with Dryden on *Don Sebastian* in 1684,[23] so John Dennis thanks him 'for the Hints I received from him, as well as for his excellent Action' in *Liberty Asserted* (1702).[24] However, although a thorough defender of the theatre, in a later essay Dennis was critical of the move towards the middling sort's control of the stage, which Betterton had begun:

> The theatre was not then as it is now in the Hands of Players, illiterate, unthinking, unjust, ungratefull and sordid . . . At the Restoration the

Theatres were in the Hands of Gentlemen, who had Done particular services to the Crown . . . They had Honour, learning, breeding, Discernment,
Integrity, Impartiality and generosity.[25]

Although Dennis was mainly talking about the Cibber, Wilks and Booth
triumvirate, the move towards more actorly control had been born with the
Actors' Company in 1695.

Satiric commentary on Betterton's managerial aspirations focused on his
body, in a variety of ways. His background was quite distinct from the aristocratic rakehells, emperors, monarchs or decayed gentry figures he mostly
portrayed. The divergence between the physical body of the 'Stage Ape'
Betterton and the idealized body of the decorous, leisured, aristocratic sort
were suddenly brought into perspective in an anonymous satire:

> For who can hold to see the Foppish Town
> Admire so bad a wretch as *Betterton*
> Is't for his legs, his Shoulders, or his face
> His formal stiffness or his awkward Grace
> A shop for him had been the fittest place
> But Brawny *Tom*: the Playhouse needs must choose
> The Villains Refuge & Hell's Rendevous.[26]

Robert Gould offers an almost identical critique of Betterton's lowly beginnings as a small tradesman, and the contrast with his current role as manager:

> Here *one* who once was, as an *Author* notes,
> A *Hawker*, sold *old Books, Gazets and Votes,*
> Is grown *prime Vizier* now, a Man of parts,
> The very load-stone that attracts all Hearts,
> In's own conceit that is, for ne'r was *Elf*
> So very much Enamour'd of himself: [27]

Such criticism was of a piece with the reforming zeal of the turn of the century,
after Jeremy Collier's high Tory invective against the stage had not only
berated every contemporary playwright for their representation of gentry
figures as less than wholly virtuous, but had begun a witch-hunt against the
performers. The socially inferior actors' presentation of themselves as aristocratic or gentry figures on stage was an upending of the social hierarchy that,
even in fictitious representation, Collier could not stomach. 'Brawny Tom'
offered a working body on stage, a labouring body, its actuality undeniable.
In key moments the body of the performer stood apart from its representational form, as when stretched on the rack as Montezuma in *The Indian*

Emperour, or sweating and breathless after a sword fight, or 'surprised . . . by those acute pains of gout' in later years.[28] As Farquhar quipped in his preface to *Love and Honour* (1702), one might watch Alexander the Great in Lee's *The Rival Queens*:

> Yet the whole Audience at the same time knows that this is Mr. Betterton, who is strutting upon the stage and tearing his Lungs for a Livelihood. And that the same Person shou'd be Mr. Betterton, and Alexander the Great, at the same time, is somewhat like an Impossibility, in my Mind. Yet you must grant this Impossibility in spight of your Teeth, if you han't Power to raise the old Heroe from the Grave to act his own Part.[29]

Farquhar's attempt to rebut Collier in the ongoing debate about the legitimacy of theatrical representation and the usefulness of the stage found expression through the body of Betterton.

There begins here to be a slippage between the stage roles and the stage persona of Betterton in the eyes of his satirists, so that his management is figured as the rule of the tyrants he played:

> . . . being chief, each playing Drab to Swive
> He takes it as his just Prerogative
> Methinks I see him mounted, hear him Roar
> And foaming Cry; God's blood you little whore
> Zounds how I fuck; I fuck like any Moor. [30]

The ideology of mercantile aspirations is here linked to sexual excess, a contrast to the previous incarnation of *aristocratic* rakishness as sexually insatiable. The link between financial and sexual rapacity and the image of the moor is repeated twice by Robert Gould in another satire, where he uses the role of Osmin to identify Betterton, for his 'Wealthy Lot' and his sexual incontinence:

> Witness Mill-Bank, where Osmin keeps his Trulls
> With what, by sharing, he exacts from Fools.[31]

The reference tries to link Betterton's successful playing of Moorish roles with one of the circulating racial stereotypes of the African and Eastern nations (with which England was happily trading, of course), that of the harem-owning lasciviousness of their rulers. After the secession of the Actors' Company, perhaps fuelled both by the reformers' anti-theatricality and the commercial pressures of competition, comments on Betterton's acting are rarely complimentary. Satiric descriptions of his performance style fall into two modes of denigration—either of his dignified formality or his excessive enthusiasm; his 'formal stiffness, or his awkward grace', or his 'strutting' and 'tearing of lungs'.[32] In part this was because of an increasing divergence between the roles he took on and his physical abilities. Before the secession, the patentees had accused him of engrossing roles to himself, that he 'had put himselfe into all great pts in most of ye Considerable plays Especially in ye Tragedy's and yet a Man at 60 is not able to doe That wch he could at 30 or 40'.[33] Betterton continued playing young lovers, like Hamlet, Osmyn in *The Mourning Bride*, Valentine in *Love for Love*, or Alexander in *The Rival Queens*, into his sixties and seventies.[34] Yet, audiences continued to flock to performances despite these discrepancies, and it is clear that the representational economy of the stage was not illusionistic naturalism. Betterton's body was allowed to stand in for much younger men because it had become in some way elided, as the satires explicitly show, with types of roles he had played for many years. Provided his delivery made sense, which even critics admit it always did, his body, through the choreography of other familiar roles on stage, and what we might now call his performance energy, was understood by an audience as standing for that type of young lover. George Powell tried to draw attention to these discrepancies in his epilogue to his own *The Fatal Discovery* (1698):

> We pluck the Vizor off from t'other house:
> And let you see their natural Grimmaces
> Affecting Youth with pale Autumnal faces.
> Wou'd it not any Ladies Anger move
> To see a Child of sixty-five make Love.
> Oh! My Statira! Oh, my angry dear [Grunting like Betterton]

But this strategy was not effective. The Actors' Company, with its older, more experienced performers, continued to be highly successful in youthful roles. Betterton's Alexander in Lee's *The Rival Queens*, a young hero's role he took on late in life, resurrected excitement and interest in an old play and it was frequently revived from 1694 onwards.

   While satirists and anti-theatrical performers attacked him, defenders of the theatre, such as Richard Steele, chose to recreate Betterton's body as an exemplary image of the theatre's potential for improvement. Through the *Tatler* and *Spectator*, Steele and Addison attempted to reconcile the genteel middling sort and urban gentry to the theatre as a site of civility and reformed manners, rather than courtly decadence. Steele was a playwright and his financial interest in the theatre was developing, so it is perhaps no surprise that he was one of Betterton's most outspoken defenders. His account of Betterton's funeral in May 1710 jumbles up the idea of Betterton's person with the roles he played. Steele mourned:

a man whom I had always very much admired, and from whose action I received more strong impressions of what is great and noble in human nature, than from the arguments of the most solid philosophers, or the descriptions of the most charming poets I had ever read . . . There is no human invention so aptly calculated for the forming of a free-born people as that of a theatre.[35]

He goes on to contrast good English playwriting and acting to the triviality of opera, conveniently forgetting Betterton's foundational influence, as a manager, in the development of opera in London and the peopling of the London stage with foreign novelties. Likewise, Charles Johnson mourns Betterton in his preface to *The Force of Friendship*, a play Betterton was rehearsing when he died. Johnson discusses the degeneracy of the theatre and the danger of commercialization in the competition between the two play-houses:

> Roscius indeed is no more, and Tragedy mourns with real Tears his Loss; that mighty Genius (let me call him so) for to become so perfect an Actor, a Man must have almost all the Qualifications of the greatest Author; he must have the most Exalted Soul, the Deepest Judgment, and the most lively Fancy; and Nature too must be liberal in her outward Endowments, She must adorn him with a Graceful Person, and an easie Utterance; to all these Accomplishments the utmost Art and Industry must be join'd: Nature had indeed been very bountiful to Mr Betterton, and yet Art and Labour had improv'd him wonderfully, and he confessed but very lately, He was yet learning to be an Actor. If then an Actor is not to be made like an Artificer, by Seven Years Apprenticeship, and hardly two good ones arise in an Age, we ought to keep those few that are so together; there is no other way to Banish Posture-Masters, Foreign Monsters, Tub Scenes, &c from the Theatre, to preserve the Reputation the Stage yet maintains with the most Learned and Polite, and to make it become, as it certainly may be, both Ornamental and Useful to the Government.[36]

By his death Betterton had come to embody solid, English mercantile endeavour, trained in the city manner through 'Art and Labour', aspiring to perfection in manners, morals and commercial success in the face of foreign monstrosity and innovation.

In the early eighteenth century Betterton's picture in mezzotint, a version of Kneller's portrait, was on sale everywhere in London, according to Cibber. Charles Gildon attempted to cash in on the Betterton phenomenon the year after his death, with his *Life of Mr Thomas Betterton*, adorning its frontispiece with this image of Betterton, bewigged and swathed in satin, with one hand 'lodged in his breast'.[37] The *Life* (the first of what was to become a lucrative tradition of performers' biographies) in fact contains very little biography of Betterton, but is a complex collection of oratorical materials from classical texts and French studies predominantly concerned with the art of the voice. Dedicated to Richard Steele, Gildon contributes to the construction of Betterton as an exemplar of English rhetorical acting, in defence of the some-what perilous state of the English stage. Gildon's desire was that he should offer, through the fitting figure of Betterton, an antidote to French studies of the art of the stage, and rather that he 'might form a System of Acting, which be a Rule to future Players, and teach them to excel not only themselves, but those who have gone before them'.[38] In the 1740s a history of the British stage emerged, apparently written by Betterton, which lent further weight to the idea of 'Betterton' as the exemplary, genteel Englishman, father of an art of acting that was static, rhetorical and declamatory. And that perhaps is how we might continue to view Betterton, were we not to return to the exacting, physical demands of the roles he played and to wonder how it was that Pepys was ravished 'beyond imagination' by Betterton's very presence on stage.[39]

CHAPTER THREE

Tom and Jerry in Russia
Popular Imagery of the *Commedia dell'arte* from Peter the Great to Catherine the Great

Laurence Senelick

A recurrent phenomenon of the modern age has been the traumatic introduction of so-called 'backward' cultures to the fruits of progress. Without the benefit of an incremental and gradual acculturation, pre-industrial peoples are plunged into the maelstrom of technology, venture capitalism and mass media. The results of such encounters are unpredictable, often surrealistic. When one sees photographs of Amazonian Indians, naked but for a headdress of feathers, entranced, holding boom-boxes to their ears, the abrupt linkage of two totally different world-views and ways of life accelerates the debate on the benefits of interculturalism.

An earlier and extreme instance of this kind of confrontation was the attempt of Tsar Peter I to impose European manners, science and governance on a closed and conservative Russian society. The performing arts and popular celebrations were part of this reform movement. Peter had a taste for jesters, so his efforts included the attempted naturalization of the Feast of Fools and April Fool's Day, but they failed to take root. A public dramatic theatre, staffed by the German troupe of Johann Christoph Kunst which had arrived in Moscow in 1702, also failed for lack of interest on the part of the public, which shared the Emperor's preference for *trionfi* and fireworks.

The only professional players in Russia were Western Europeans who had to rely on mime to appeal to an illiterate and parochial public. Towards the end of his reign, in 1720, Peter did offer an invitation to actors 'who could speak Slavonic or Czech', but it had no takers. Only a foreign circus troupe, led by the *Starke Mann* Johann Eckenberg, came through Petersburg in 1719 and 1723–24.[1] Not until the reign of Peter II in 1728/29 did a freelance *bande* of French players, Jacques Renaud and his family, confront a mixed audience in Petersburg and Moscow. For the most part, however, the same xenophobia that segregated non-Russian diplomats, merchants and artisans into the so-called 'German' quarter confined foreign actors to court circles.

Theatre historians once believed that the first *commedia dell'arte* troupe visited Russia some time between 1733 and 1735; this was deduced from a Russian translation of the scenarios of comedies and interludes played by Italian actors in St Petersburg during those years.[2] Thanks to newly uncovered documents, it is now known that an Italian ensemble of twenty-two actors arrived in Moscow from the Polish court in February 1731, headed by the composer Giovanni Alberto Ristori. His father, Tomasso, a Scaramouche, led the *commedia dell'arte* portion of the troupe and, with two assistants, served as machinist and set-designer. The company was a distinguished one, including Bertoldi as Pantalone, Belotti (just recovered from a fever) as Arlecchino, Malucellio as il Dottore, Cafanio as Brighella and Rosalia Fantaria as first *amorosa*. Barely a week after their arrival, on 6 February, they played at court before an audience of six hundred a comedy of amorous intrigues, *The Happy Cheat*, and a musical interlude, *Velasco and Tilla*. Perhaps because few in the audience, including the Empress, understood Italian, the interlude was applauded more warmly than the comedy, but as the spectators became attuned to the conventions of the genre, the entertainments increased in popularity and complexity.[3]

The next arrivals were a company of German singers and musicians headed by the conductor Johann Huebner and impresario Josef Avolio in August 1731 and another Italian troupe which came to supplement them in 1732. The names of the actors in this last company are given in their passports in a Russified form. The most important of these was Pyotr Miro, i.e. Pietro Mira, a fiddler and comic actor, whose playing of Pedrolino in comedies and interludes won him the nickname Pedrillo or Petrillo at the Russian court. Other names as they appear in the passports include the singer Aleksandra Stabilla and her mother Apollonia, Nina and Zhanna Sak, Ferdinand Colombo and his wife, Peter Pertichi, Camillo Ganzaga, Antoni Fioretti, Andreyan Sak and his mother and sister, and Antoni Sak and his wife. Antoni Sak is of course the actor called great by Carlo Goldoni: Giovanni Antonio Sacchi, known as Truffaldino (1708–88). Zhanna Sak is his sister Adrianna.[4]

In April 1735 another sizeable Italian troupe of comedians, opera singers and ballet dancers arrived in St Petersburg. It was known generically as the 'Italian Company' and, as a sponsoring body, incorporated other foreigners engaged at court including Karoline Neuber's German dramatic troupe (1740). According to a letter of General LeFort, the Empress Anna Ioannovna 'received great satisfaction from the comedies and that her satisfaction might be greater, she hopes that these comedies be translated into Russian, which are played on stage, so that one might better understand the plot and gestures, which accompany the dialogue'. This hope was in fact an order, which led to the academician Shtelin creating short librettos in German which were in turn translated into Russian by Count Vasily Levenvold-

Trediakovsky and printed in a run of a hundred copies by the Academy of Sciences.[5] The stock characters included, along with the familiar Italian gambler and opera impresario in the Canary Islands, the conventional Molièrean miser and hypochondriac.

What must be stressed is that in Russia the Italian comedy was a court theatre, not a popular one. In the first half of the eighteenth century, it was inaccessible to the populace at large, although eventually it would come to influence Russian popular entertainment and circus, both in style and content. This development arose not simply from an urge to imitate a foreign example, but rather to assimilate something novel and attractive to familiar ways of life. For instance, one of the favourite 'interludes to music' of Avolio's company was *The Gambling Husband and the Sanctimonious Wife*, commonly known as *The Gambler at Cards*. Translated, verses and all, into Russian under the title *Discord between Husband and Wife*, and performed by amateurs, the dialogue and customs of this sung two-hander became suffused with Muscovite local colour.[6] In the translation of another play, a wandering ghost impersonated by the servant-girl Smeraldina was transmogrified, in its Russian avatar, into a *kikimora*, a female domestic goblin out of Slavonic folklore.

Familiar points of contact enabled assimilation. The Italian troupe of 1731 had amongst its properties 'four little puppet theatres, made of wood, glued with grey paper',[7] and the puppets may have been based on *commedia* masks. Puppets which personified specific human actors had spread the fame of the latter throughout seventeenth-century Italy, and something similar may have occurred in Russia, where a native puppet tradition already existed. Martin Nierenbach brought a German puppet-theatre to the Northern capital in 1744, and he was quickly followed there and in Moscow by a host of others. Between 1759 and 1762 Johann Hilferding displayed 'a set of large Italian dolls two arshins in height [approximately 56 inches] who will move freely about the stage . . . so as to seem alive'.[8] As the comic repertoires of live theatres became obsolete and vanished from the flesh-and-blood stage, these German puppet-theatres preserved and perpetuated them.

Masks were also a common feature of Russian amusements, worn at the annual *Koliada* and *Maslenitsa* holidays. The fairs that accompanied these Christmas and Shrovetide festivities were, by 1750, housing comedies, interludes, farces, the whole spectrum of the *commedia dell'arte*. The native Russian performers were amateurs: tradesmen, apprentices and merchants, costumed as jesters and buffoons. They now shared space with foreign clowns, jugglers, wire-walkers and puppeteers. Professional Italian players offered diversions no less ribald and rowdy than those of indigenous merry-Andrews.

In the mind of the Russian spectator, these comic actors would be conflated with pre-existing notions of the fool. Fools were members of entourages at great houses, but their presence could be felt across all layers of society. Three varieties are distinguishable in Russian culture. First comes the *yurodivy*, the 'holy fool' or 'fool in Christ', a legacy from Byzantium, familiar to Europeans from the play and opera *Boris Godunov*: a sanctified idiot whose religious inspiration allowed him to speak unwelcome truths. Literary tradition has him serving much the same function as the Fool in *King Lear*, speaking home truths to authority figures. In actuality the *yurodivy* was a good deal less outspoken than his portrayal in literature would suggest.[9] Then there were the *skomorokhi*, counterparts to the European *Spielmänner* or minstrels, itinerant entertainers who sang, danced, led bears, juggled and generally entertained in an improvisatory manner. They too had learned to curb their tongues, which could be literally bobbed by the authorities. Since a direct assault on everyday life was dangerous, the *skomorokh*'s verbal aggression was channelled into an oblique critique, the creation of an alternative, carnival world, that of Butter Week or *Maslenitsa*. In 1648, the *skomorokhi* were banned by Peter the Great's father, Tsar Aleksey Mikhailovich, ostensibly for perpetuating pagan practices and seducing Christians from church attendance.[10]

The distinction between the holy fool and the itinerant entertainer is, in fact, religious in origin. An etymological explanation is offered by Sandra Billington: in the Hebrew Bible the root *ksl* identifies a wilfully evil person, the demonic fool, and the *tam* stands for an innocent fool.[11] St Paul adopted this dual usage, reserving *stultus* for the latter, as when he advocates becoming 'fools for Christ's sake' (1 *Corinthians* 4: 9–10). Christ, in medieval Passion plays, is often called a fool (*stultus*) by his torturers, who, in drama and pictorial imagery, wear the diabolical guise of the evil *insipiens* figure. In Russian Orthodox doctrine, the *yurodivy* may be seen as the *stultus*, with the *skomorokh* identified as the *insipiens*, a latent cause for the Tsar's prohibition.

This ban, preceding the influx of foreigners under Peter the Great, led the *skomorokh* or *Volksnarr* to be supplanted, in the mind of the literate, by the *Hofnarr*. The native entertainer, circulating among the people, dropped out of sight, while the court entertainer, often of foreign origin, replaced him in anecdotage and pictorial imagery. Peter maintained more clowns and jesters than any of his predecessors (over a hundred, with more than seventy dwarves in addition). The practice became traditional with his successors; one professional jester at Anna's court was lodged in a magnificent chamber hung with fifty portraits of his predecessors. Even Catherine the Great, patroness of the Enlightenment, kept as fool the simple-minded Matryona Danilovna.[12]

When Western stage comedians arrived on the scene, no sharp distinction in the public imagination was made between them and the pre-existing notion of the court jester. Kunst's *Komische Persone* Trazo, an earthy Hanswurst type played by the actor Bendler, was considered the high point of the comedies in which he appeared; his asides often dealt with burning issues of the day. Pedrillo's comic talents won him great favour with the Empress Anna Ioannovna, and he became something of a licensed truth-teller. The gamut of the jester repertoire under Anna was unusually wide, from the crudest physical pranks to the refined and theatricalized conceits of comic poets and musicians. According to one contemporary:

> The ways in which this sovereign was amused by these people was passing strange. Sometimes she ordered them all to stand against a wall, except for one who beat them to a pulp and well nigh forced them to fall on the ground. Often they were made to fight amongst themselves, and they pulled each other's hair and scratched each other till they bled. The sovereign and all her court, entertained by these spectacles, died laughing. Balakirev,[13] who did not care for such sports, once refrained from toppling to the floor, thinking that his apology would be accepted. The poor young man was mistaken and had to endure a beating with rods.

That's an example of the first kind of amusement.

One of Pietro Mira's stunts may serve as illustration to the second kind.

> The Duke of Courland once told Pedrillo the jester that his wife was a nanny-goat. Pedrillo replied with the deepest respect that it was true and as soon as his wife was delivered of a child, he dared ask Her Majesty and all her court to visit the mother in hopes of collecting from the guests a sum of money sufficient for the best (appropriate) education of his children. This joke was imparted to the whole Court. On the appointed day they bedded him with a goat beside him. When the curtains parted, everyone saw Pedrillo and his wife in bed. The empress, handing him a gift, personally stipulated the amount each of her courtiers was to give the mother.[14]

As encouragement to similar antics, the Empress founded a special jester's order of St Benedetto, which was awarded to Pedrillo and Jan Lacosta.[15]

The theatrical antics of such jesters were disseminated beyond the court by a book entitled *Adventures of the German-Frenchmen* (German in this case simply means foreigner). Its author, a master of practical jokes and itinerant entertainer, Johann Christian Trëmer, had been a jester at several European courts, among them Dresden. For sixteen months, from September 1734 to February 1736, he served at the court of Anna, where he practised the tomfoolery he then described in his book. The book could inform only the literate, however. A more effective means of communication was prints.

The arrival of foreign performers coincided with a more extensive dissemination of the *lubok* or popular coloured broadside.[16] Originally, the *lubok* had been a religious image, hand-drawn in pencil and tinted with tempera. Nurtured by Peter the Great's encouragement of printing and secular literacy, brightly coloured woodcut prints, later produced by copper-plates, began to pour from the presses, illustrating folkloric, legendary or satiric subjects in addition to the more time-honoured religious themes. Eventually, the adjective *lubochny* came to mean *garish,* an equivalent of the English 'tuppence-coloured' or 'chromo'; and it is interesting to note that *lubochny teatr,* a term for fairground theatricals, is pejorative whenever applied to the legitimate theatre, investing it with a taint of crude barn-storming.

The increasing appearance of fools and dwarves in *lubki* is said by some historians to indicate a growing taste for an evolving theatre based on Western models.[17] These zanies are considered to be transitional figures between the *skomorokh* and the *Hofnarr.* Duchartre, a most unreliable authority, goes so far as to state that the court jesters can be recognized by their striped jerkins and the bells on their caps, and that the names given them were supplied by the artists.[18] The matter is nowhere near so straightforward, however.

Let us take the example of one *lubok* which depicts a male and female dwarf dressed in court costume, with fashionable beauty-spots, powdered wigs, panniers and simpering manners (Figure 1). Since jesters traditionally parodied contemporary fashions, we might expect this to be a direct satire on the court, not only offering portraits of a couple of popular fools but also commenting on the Empress's penchant for things Western. However, as the art historian Wilhelm Fraenger pointed out, this is simply not the case. As

Figure 1. Dwarves. The inscriptions on the wall are Russian translations of the original German captions. The new Russian captions have the characters praising their qualities. Eighteenth-century woodcut.

with many *lubki*, there is a foreign prototype from which the image is copied, often from the copper-plates produced by Elias Beck and Joseph Friedrich Leopold of Augsburg. In this particular case, the original can be identified as two separate plates, 'Mademoiselle Jolicoeur' and the 'Marquis de Sauterelle', published in Amsterdam by Wilhelm Koning in 1716 and re-engraved by Beck with a German text (Figure 2). They were readily available in the very popular collection 'Il Calotto resuscitato oder Neueingerichtetes Zwerchen Cabinet': fifty or so copper-plate engravings on grotesque themes, many based on Callot.[19] The indiscriminate pillage of Callot's imagery is obvious in another *lubok*, which one Russian historian bizarrely identifies as 'a masquerade at the court of Anna Ioannovna'! (Figure 3).

Beck's original caricature may refer to an actual phenomenon, mocking something the artist or his audience has presumably observed: if not the dwarves themselves, then the fashions they sport. The caption's reference to an opera of 'Le Village en Provence' suggests a performance of grotesque dance in the court masque tradition. The Russian artisan, on the other hand, is copying a picture and adapting it to the conventions of his format. He adds draperies and a tile floor, and incorporates the caption into the image so that it becomes an inscription. What had been two consecutive pictures on sepa-

Figure 2. 'Mademoiselle Jolicoeur, danceante [*sic*] avec son Amant Monsieur le Marquis de Sauterelle l'Opera du Village en Provence.' Copper-engraving by Elias Beck and Joseph Friedrich Leopold (Amsterdam: Wilhelm Koning, 1716).

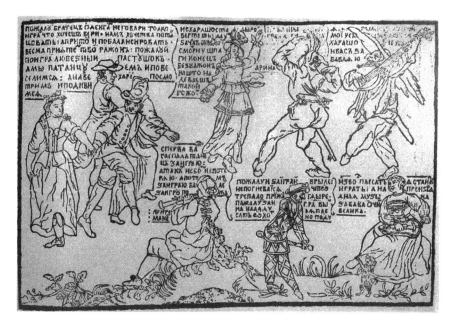

Figure 3. Untitled *lubok* based on Western originals, including Callot. The dialogue
in the balloons is rhymed. Mid-eighteenth-century woodcut.

rate pages, bound by a caption, are combined, so that they now constitute a
comic *scène galant*, a parodic love scene. The frame of curtains implies a stage.
In other words, the Russian artisan, confronted with unfamiliar matter,
probably never having heard of an *opéra comique* about 'Miss Prettyheart' and
'Marquis Grasshopper', yet cognizant of the existence of court dwarves,
provides his own theatricalization of the context. When the Tsarevna Anna
Ioannovna married the Duke of Courland in 1710, the amusements included
a parallel wedding of dwarves 'dressed in French caftans', celebrated with
pomp and circumstance.[20] The artist of the *lubok* may well have heard of or
even beheld the ceremonies, and intended his picture as a souvenir of them.
A possible actual performance of one sort is transmuted into a possible actual
performance of another sort. Guesswork is not uncommon in such cases of
cultural transference. The Dresden court conjurer and jester Joseph Froelich
was immortalized in porcelain, but when the St Petersburg porcelain manu-
facturers copied the portrait figurine they labelled it 'Falstaff'.[21]

An early eighteenth-century coloured version of the dwarf caricatures takes
us even farther away from the original sense of the picture, since in its scheme
the wigs are black, which obviates the satire of powder. If we turn to the 'List
of Colours and Patches' which appeared in the second half of the eighteenth
century, we now have a specific referent, Nikolay Kurganov's famous *Pismov-
nik* or *Epistolary Manual* (1769), a cyclopedic compendium. This print was

meant to provide a symbology of colours and an explanation of the significance of the placement of patches on the face, reminiscent of Hogarth's order of periwigs. Western manners were now sufficiently familiar to warrant commentary.

Another telling combination is the conversation between a foolish suitor and a stupid matchmaker, a theme so popular that it was reproduced well into the nineteenth century. Staging elaborate nuptials for court fools had been a regular entertainment under Peter the Great, usually at Lefort's residence, and was perpetuated by such grotesque variations as the Ice-Palace Wedding under Elizabeth.[22] A scene between a fool and a matchmaker, the latter played by an actor who had shaved off his moustache, was performed before Peter; the fool is advised to wear a mask and array himself in 'German [i.e. foreign] attire', to meet the bride (also played by a youth). After an improvised wedding ceremony, the fool turns out to be poor as a churchmouse and, knocked about by his father-in-law in a series of acrobatic tricks, ends up spitting out his teeth. Meanwhile, his bride appeals to a passing cavalier-lover to do away with her husband.[23] In this *lubok*, as well as in its epigones, the matchmaker is dressed in Russian peasant garb, but the suitor, presumably in his 'German attire', wears a costume similar to that traditionally assumed by Molière's Sganarelle and which is in turn based on Tiberio Fiorilli's Scaramouche outfit (Figure 4).[24] The foolish gallant, who offers 'smoked ice' as a treat, has been Frenchified, while the go-between who promises to bring him a nanny-goat as bride is solidly grounded in the muck of Russian village life. As we have seen, the union of a fool and a goat had already been acted out at court.

We are therefore dealing with pictures that cannot be accepted either as portraiture or as documentation: their creators adapt foreign compositions to folk themes or concoct a synthetic medley of folklore, *commedia* imagery and popular Russian performance. In particular, the added captions draw heavily on performance traditions. The pioneering collector Dmitry Rovinsky identified fourteen *lubki* as probable or likely texts for a typical fairground interlude, cross-talk between adversaries. The rhymed texts in these pictures are *rayoshnye stikhi*, a verse form which accompanied market-place peepshows called *rayki* (sing. *rayok*), and others are in the rhymed prose of the *intermedii* or comic interludes, commonly presented between the acts in eighteenth-century Russian dramatic performance.

The oldest identifiable folk clowns in the *lubki* are Foma and Yeryoma, names which translate as Tom and Jerry.[25] Yeryoma came to be a common noun, the generic term for tavernkeepers and fairground actors, on the order of Hanswurst or Tom Fool. A seventeenth-century manuscript quoted by Rovinsky tells us that Yeryoma is one-eyed, Foma has a white fleck in his eye; Yeryoma is bald, Foma has scabies; both have noses like a bung, beards like a harrow and mustaches like a knout. Both are fat-paunched and fat-witted.[26]

Figure 4. Suitor and matchmaker. An eighteenth-century woodcut showing the suitor in the costume of a Europeanized buffoon, and the matchmaker, probably a male comedian in drag, wearing Russian peasant dress. This *lubok* was reproduced well into the nineteenth century, often appending a poem by the neoclassic poet Aleksandr Sumarokov.

So they were depicted in their comic quarrels in fairground performances, and so they appear in the broadsides (Figure 5). In one, Yeryoma is wearing a fox tail, and the caption runs 'Is your wife at home?' 'No, brother.' 'You should stay home polishing spindles for your wife and your wife has only to spin thread and put it in the storeroom', a piece of dialogue whose *double entendre* sounded more scabrous to an audience acquainted with such household furniture. In another print, the two brothers have capsized into the water, for all their adventures end in disaster, and they are beaten in a fight by the quick-witted sexton Paramoshka.

Paramoshka is more usually paired with the fall-guy Savoska, as in the *lubok*: 'Paramoshka played cards with Savoska and Paramoshka won. Savoska looked in his purse and found only two kopeks. The other laughed at him, so Savoska tore out his hair' (Figure 6). By the 1760s, as another print shows (Figure 7), these indigenous clowns had taken on some of the attributes of the professional buffoon. Astride a goat, Paramoshka is playing the spoons, while Savoska accompanies him on a rebek. They have exchanged the costumes of medieval Russian *skomorokhi* for the long trousers and wide-brimmed hats of the *commedia zanni*.

Figure 5. Foma and Yeryoma. The dialogue is translated in the text. The cock may be a reference to a standard jester's attribute in Western Europe: their costumes are peasant dress bedizened with clown appurtenance. Mid-eighteenth-century woodcut.

Figure 6. The sexton Paramoshka cheating Savoska at cards. Coloured woodcut of the 1760s.

On the other hand, Gonos and Farnos seem to be exclusively of foreign origin, possibly based on Western performers. If so, they would exactly constitute a transition between the *skomorokh* and the *Hofnarr*.[27] A late eighteenth-century portrait of the jester Farnos the Red-nosed ('nos' is a play on words, since it is Russian for *nose*)[28] displays a number of suspect attributes (Figure 8): the outward appearance resembles that of Pulcinella and his hat is that of Dutch, German or Austrian peasant comics, such as Hanswurst. However, the activities of both Farnos and Gonos are generic; while decked out in festive costume, they make music, ride animals, play cards, fist-fight and generally play the fool.

Mayhem and scatology are endemic to both native and foreign comics. In a wholly Russian scenario in another *lubok*, 'the peasant Pashka after eating some porridge and drinking home-brew got on a goat and took a big knife to

Figure 7. Savoska with a rebek, and Paramoshka on a goat, saying 'I may play the spoons, but you'll get a taste of the cat o' nine-tails'. Both are in Western *commedia* costumes, though Paramoshka wears a Russian seminarian's cap. Mid-eighteenth-century woodcut.

Figure 8. Red-nosed Farnos, riding on a boar. 'I am not a rich fellow. My nose is hooked. I am very taken with my own person. My name is Red-nosed Farnos. I am puffed up three days running. I am wearing shoes for dancing. I have put on a fool's cap with feathers and have filled my pants with silent farts. Once fully dressed I went out, mounted on a wine-coloured pig. My pig grunts and snuffles out his delicacies.'
Coloured woodcut, *c.* 1760.

kill it. Meanwhile his brother Yermoshka picked up the goat's tail and it shat in his face.' Contrast this with the captions to a picture of Gonos the Fool, tricked out in theatrical garb, directly copied from a German copper-plate (Figure 9). The upper caption reads: 'The fool is astride a stick while his arse silently breaks wind. Over his shoulder he carries a crow to defend his arse.' The lower one reads: 'I spread a smell by my behind and that's how I guard against mosquitoes'.

With the commercialization of popular entertainment, the *lubki* begin to be exploited as advertisements, as with the portrait of Bernardo Gigli, the giant from Trentino, exhibited on Devichye Pole (Maidens' Field) in April 1765.

Figure 9. The jester Gonos. The caption reads, 'The fool is astride a stick, while his arse makes noiseless farts. Over his shoulder he carries a crow to defend his arse.' He is saying 'I spread a smell by my behind and that's how I guard against mosquitoes'. Woodcut.

Giving his height in arshins (8 feet, 2 inches) it relates his previous appearances throughout Europe and concludes: 'Everyone may be assured that no one has ever yet set eyes on a man of such extraordinary stature and that such a person has never yet appeared here'. The engraving was on sale at his lodgings in the 'foreign quarter'.

By the mid-nineteenth century, the *lubok* becomes somewhat self-reflexive. Broadsheets of peepshows published in Moscow in 1858 depict the common folk peering at panoramic *lubki* through the round holes (Figure 10). But what they are staring at is no longer the homely stuff of folk performance or the exotic comedians from abroad. A different kind of interculturalism is

Figure 10. *Russkiy rayok*, copper-engraving printed in N. Golovin's lithographic studio, and published by Andrey Abramov, Moscow, 1858. The *rayok* is the equivalent of the French *parade*, the diversion provided outside fairbooths to draw a crowd. Russian fairbooth entertainments. A mid-nineteenth-century broadside, with a peepshow in the foreground. The picture includes such standard features as a pickpocket, and banners advertising equestrian and funambulistic feats. The peasant weighing out berries or nuts in a balance is a more Russian detail.

apparent, for the objects of their scrutiny are crude depictions of the Crimean War, the ape-woman Julia Pastrana, and the temptations of 'Gay Paris'. Moreover, these copper-plate engravings depict the people at play in order to amuse a lower-middle-class audience which sets itself apart from the naïvely curious. The distinctions are no longer between court and common folk or between the foreign and the native; the social configurations of the spectators have grown in complexity.

SECTION TWO
The Celebrated Actor
as Cultural Icon

SECTION TWO

The Celebrated Actor as Cultural Icon

Introduction

Jane Milling

The four sets of performers studied in this section operated within the evolving theatre industries of Britain, Ireland and America, and it is their interaction with the industrial context that most concerns the writers here. These performers were not working in the most popular forms of the period, burlesque, music hall or variety in saloon or boulevard theatres. Nor were they involved in the spectacular large-scale extravaganzas, having to hold their own against breathtaking scenic effects, nor part of the intimate world of portable or touring theatres, or penny gaffs.[1] However, all of the performers here achieved widespread popular acclaim and celebrity, through the mechanisms of the industry. The same transport engineering developments that fuelled the British empire's military and trade aspirations allowed English actors to pursue regular international tours to America. Relentless touring with a successful product was the fate of many of the companies Don Wilmeth discusses, or extended runs where the recent explosion in urban population and the accessibility of suburban or provincial audiences, guaranteed a continual turnover, as Gertie Millar and the success of musical comedy at the Gaiety Theatre shows.[2] Likewise, all of the actors here were subject to the newly popular and increasingly widely-distributed theatrical review in newspaper and periodical. Debates about acting, which might once have been conducted by the educated few who saw themselves as arbiters of a cultural taste, were now the preserve of 'professional' theatre critics and reviewers of all kinds, employed by papers to talk to a wide social readership. Acting and actors were no longer exposed only to the scrutiny of sympathetic friends like a Steele or a Lessing, but rather to a myriad of voices in the provincial presses. Gertie Millar's battle to control the circulation of her own image crystallises the way in which the processes of the theatrical and other cultural industries were driven by the logic of mass production. The cultural iconography of the actors, which circulated more widely, geographically and socially, than ever before, became a key component of economic success in the theatre industries.

This cultural iconography was profoundly connected to the political and economic worlds, even to the extent of symbolizing the desires and aspirations of nationhood, as two of the essays that follow illustrate. Laurence Senelick's recent documentary study has revealed the interrelations of class and commerce in the cultural self-identity of emerging nation-states in Scandinavia, central and northern Europe:

> Nationhood was strongly endorsed by a burgeoning bourgeoisie, which substituted 'the nation, the culture and traditions of the fatherland' for the unattainable high culture of the aristocracy. Sprung from the folk, yet devotees of the ideals of enlightenment and high culture, the ambitious middle classes were anxious to establish traditions of which they themselves would be the guardians. Since the bulk of the populace was illiterate, the best way to educate it to new nationalistic ideals until such time as it learned to read was by spectacle and sound: hence the crucial importance of the theatre to nationalistic movements.[3]

Senelick contrasts this movement against the older more established cultural histories of England, France and German, whose high cultural exports operate as both exemplary models and contaminating foreign invasion. Here, Ger Fitzgibbon considers this phenomenon in relation to the Irish theatre. His chapter does not chart the familiar story of the Abbey Theatre's search for an Irish literature, but instead charts the more complex search for an Irish acting, and actors able fully to embody and articulate the burgeoning repertoire of the emerging Irish literary nation. It is no surprise that it should be the working-class theatrical brothers Willie and Frank Fay who were able to draw on pre-existing folk and local acting traditions to meld into this distinctive Irish acting. America too was undergoing cultural self-definition. Don Wilmeth explores the gradual decline in popularity of the residual colonial exports of the British theatre, and the evolution of an American actor.

The acting genealogies that these essays chart show how economic and cultural pressures intertwine. For all of these performers, acting was the family business. Despite the moral and theological dubiousness of public display, theatrical families exemplified in microcosm an idealized middle class. Successful actresses, like Siddons and the Dare sisters, exploited to the full the sentimentalizing of the redemptive power of the family, echoing the commodification of the domestic both within their repertoire and in the iconography of their celebrity. The extraordinary popular success achieved by the actors discussed here was inexorably linked to their careful manipulation of and engagement with these processes of the cultural industry.

CHAPTER FOUR

'Acting and the Austere Joys of Motherhood'[1]

Sarah Siddons Performs Maternity

Jan McDonald

In 1809, Ann Catherine Holbrook wrote in her memoirs:

> An actress can never make her children comfortable; ill or well, even when sucking at the breast, the poor infants, when the theatre calls, must be left in the care of some sour old woman who shakes and scolds them into fits; or a careless wench, out of whose clutches if they are freed without broken or dislocated bones, 'tis wonderful. The mother returning with harassed frame and agitated mind, from the various passions she has been portraying, instead of imparting healthful nourishment to her child, fills it with bile and fever, to say nothing of dragging them long journies at all seasons of the year, all hours of the night and through every inclemency of weather.[2]

At the same time as Ann Holbrook was bemoaning the lot of the travelling player, Sarah Siddons was starring in the leading theatres of London, Dublin and the provinces. While the former expressed disgust at the lack of education and manners of those she encountered in the profession, Mrs Siddons appeared regularly before the royal family, and her circle of friends included the most accomplished artists and writers of the time. Yet the maternal trials experienced by the leading and the lesser lady were not dissimilar. Throughout her long and successful career, Mrs Siddons was constantly preoccupied with her family, and her relationship with her children was in itself complex and impacted significantly on her public life.

Sarah Siddons provides a good model for an investigation into the conflicting roles of mother and actress in the late eighteenth and early nineteenth centuries, first because unlike many of the leading women performers

she had a large family, and secondly because her life and career are well documented in biographies (fictional and ostensibly factual), in the press, in her
own and in her daughters' correspondence with friends, and in the biographies of some of her famous contemporaries.[3] She was painted many times
and was the subject of poems, novels and considerable gossip. Thirdly, and
most importantly, an examination of the symbiotic relationship between her
maternal roles on stage and her performance as a mother in private life shows
a woman who was both exploited by her family and who in turn exploited
them to further her theatrical career.

This essay begins by giving a brief critique of Mrs Siddons's stage representations of motherhood which brought her much acclaim and goes on to
examine how she used her personal experience to inform the creation of such
parts. It proceeds to explore the ways in which she 'performed' herself as a
good mother before her audiences to excuse her 'unwomanly' ambition as an
actress in the public sphere, and concludes by attempting to interpret an incident in her private life when her daughters' happiness was destroyed as a result
of 'The Tragick Muse' giving a performance that is more reminiscent of
contemporary soap opera than of classical drama.

Mrs Siddons was considered particularly skilled in the representation of
maternal emotions on stage, both in Shakespearean and contemporary drama.
In Shakespearean roles, Constance in *King John,* Volumnia in *Coriolanus*,
Queen Katharine in *Henry VIII* and even, by default as it were, in the most
highly acclaimed Lady Macbeth, Siddons chose to highlight, and was seen to
be particularly effective in, the maternal aspects of the part. As Constance,
she was seen by her biographer, Thomas Campbell, as 'the embodied image
of maternal love and intrepidity', and he records from her autobiographical
notes that her 'idea of *Constance* is that of a proud and lofty spirit, associated
with the most exquisite feelings of maternal tenderness, which is, in truth, the
predominant feature of this interesting personage'.[4] In the role of Volumnia,
'the Roman mother of Mr Kemble', she abandoned the stately dignity of her
habitual stage movement to 'roll' exuberantly from side to side in the
triumphal procession, full of unconcealed motherly pride in the triumph of
her hero son. As Queen Katharine, whose 'object is to do nothing that will
compromise her *own* rights or those of her *daughter*', she was praised for
'matron dignity'.[5] In her essay *Remarks on the Character of Lady Macbeth*,
Siddons makes particular mention of the lines in which the 'fiend-like queen'
talks of dashing her suckling babe to the ground:

> The very use of such a tender allusion in the midst of her dreadful
> language, persuades one unequivocally that she really has felt the yearn-
> ings of a mother towards her babe, and that she considered this action the
> most enormous that ever required the strength of human nerves for its
> perpetration.[6]

Making reference to the same passage, clearly a 'point' in the performance, Boaden called the actress in her self-conscious rejection of the motherly impulse, 'the true and perfect image of the greatest of all natural and moral depravities'.[7]

The plays of the period abound in representations of motherhood, particularly of mothers under stress because their children have been 'lost', rendered fatherless by death, absence or neglect, or denied their birthright by the exigencies of war, feuds or intrigue. The mother is frequently portrayed as the child's only protector against a hostile male world, a situation with which Mrs Siddons was familiar in her own life as she was for many years the sole earner in the family and her husband's preoccupation with his health led to frequent and prolonged absences. With few exceptions, motherhood on stage was glorified, despite the fact that the social status of the performer representing this ideal remained problematic.

Regrettably, the standard of dramatic writing was not high. A sterile classical tragic mode was dipping into melodrama and the popular success of many of these somewhat sentimental works owed more to the brilliance and passion of the actress's reading than to the playwright's skills. She raised commonplace scripts to heart-rending performances. As Isabella in Southerne's *The Fatal Marriage* she conquered London in 1782 at Drury Lane where she had failed as Portia in Garrick's last season as manager. According to Boaden, 'time had bestowed the tender dignity of a mother on her beauty', but she had also had years more experience and had established a solid reputation in the provinces.[8] On this occasion, the stage child for whose sake Isabella is prepared to sacrifice all was played by her son, 'my own dear Beautiful boy', Henry, then 8 years old. He was apparently driven to real tears at a rehearsal on witnessing his mother's simulated distress. The painting by William Hamilton of Sarah and Henry Siddons, mother and son, off-stage and on, is a perfect iconographical representation of the actress as mother— image and reality.

Years later in 1803 when Henry had become an actor against his mother's wishes, he once again played her son, Young Norval, in Home's *Douglas*. As Lady Randolph, Siddons's performance 'kindled a flame in every maternal bosom around her'.[9] As Mrs Haller in the English version of Kotzebue's *The Stranger*, in which the errant heroine is reunited at the close with her moral, if morose husband and their two children help to effect the reconciliation, Siddons's intensity of feeling again caused distress to her own offspring, in this instance to her daughter Sally, who reported to her friend, 'My mother cries so much at it [the performance of *The Stranger*] that she is always ill when she comes home'.[10] Clearly this is evidence of the 'harassed frame and agitated mind' which Ann Holbrook regarded as detrimental to the well-being of an actress's family. Even as the penitent Jane Shore, Nicholas Rowe's eponymous heroine, a high 'point' of the performance was Siddons's representation of Jane's passionate concern for her dead lover's children: 'It was here that the part ascended to the level of Mrs Siddons's power—that her voice took a richness beyond the wailing of penitence, and her cheek a nobler glow than the blush of shame'.[11] Dodsley's *Cleone*, a truly negligible piece, enjoyed a brief revival as a result of the 'Maternal agonies' of Mrs Siddons, 'an eagle to a wren compared to the original heroine', but sank again to oblivion when she relinquished the role.[12]

A play entitled *The Regent*, written for the actress by her friend Bertie Greatheed, and provided with an epilogue for her to speak by her beloved Mrs Piozzi, turned, according to the latter, on 'Maternal tenderness towards her little son Carlos', but only the actress's deep gratitude to the Greatheed family persuaded her to play a role which she regarded as basically false.[13]

> This woman is one of those monsters (I think them) of perfection, who is an angel before her time, and is so entirely resigned to the will of heaven, that (to a mere mortal like myself) she appears to be the most provoking piece of still life one ever had the misfortune to meet.[14]

She played the part only once, saved from further performances ironically by a miscarriage, but nothing, not even friendship, would persuade her to deliver Piozzi's epilogue which began:

> Carlos is safe to soothe maternal sorrow
> Sav'd for tonight: you'll meet him here tomorrow.

Even the great portrayer of distressed maternity could not quite countenance such bathos.

Sarah Siddons was an actress of genius not only because of the classical distinction in appearance which she shared with her brother, the tragedian John Philip Kemble, nor solely as a result of her elegant deportment, her beautiful voice and her intelligent reading of parts. She was 'an original: she copies no one living or dead, but acts from nature and herself'.[15] When asked how she chose which parts she would play, her response was 'I look over it in a general way to see if it is in Nature and if it is I am sure it can be played'.[16] Her own observations and contemporary critical commentaries on her performances lead one to believe that she was a skilled exponent of what Stanislavsky over a century later was to call the technique of 'emotion memory', that is the use of the recollection of one's own deeply felt experiences in the creation of a theatrical persona.

Siddons was indeed criticized for exploiting her personal sorrows in order to further her stage portrayal of tragic scenes. Some time after the death of her daughter Maria, she received anonymous letters, charging her with insensitivity in her custom to attend, '*with unfeeling apathy, Death-Bed* scenes, in order to render the impression on her audience more strikingly shocking and affecting and that she had taken her latest lesson from that of her daughter, which scene she was said to represent with the nicest accuracy'.[17] Maria's deathbed was certainly highly theatrical and it was probably true that, consciously or otherwise, Siddons drew on her memory of its emotional and physical tensions in subsequent stage performances. It was, after all, on her own admission that she had 'never acted as well as once when her heart was heavy concerning the loss of a child'.[18]

Siddons in her correspondence admitted to going further than exploiting her personal circumstances in the creation of her stage roles. She acknowledged that she used the stage as an escape from domestic trials. The following was written in August 1798 to Mrs Pennington who was looking after the terminally ill Maria in Clifton:

> I must go dress for Mrs Beverley—my soul is well-tun'd for scenes of woe, and it is sometimes a great relief from the struggles I am continually making to wear a face of cheerfulness at home, that I can at least upon the stage give a full vent to the heart, which, in spite of my best endeavours, swells with its weight almost to bursting; and then I pour it all out upon my innocent auditors.[19]

Interestingly, she claims to be 'performing' off-stage in domestic surroundings, while presenting her personal distress to the public gaze.

Her return to the stage, barely two weeks after her daughter's death, may be seen not so much as professional duty or financial necessity but as therapy. The choice of part, Isabella in *Measure for Measure*, was judicious in that it was 'a character that affords as little as possible to open wounds which are too apt to bleed afresh', but, as was astutely pointed out by Mrs Piozzi, Siddons's return to the stage was 'a med'cine for her grief'.[20] Such a release was however not possible when, in 1815 after her retirement, her son Henry died of consumption, at 41 years old. She wrote to Mrs Fitzhugh on 7 April:

> I don't know why, unless I am older and feebler, *or that I am now without a profession, which forced me out of myself in my former afflictions*, but the loss of my poor dear Henry seems to have laid a heavier hand on my mind than any I have sustained [my italics].[21]

She confessed to Thomas Moore that she had 'got credit for the truth and feeling of her acting when she was doing nothing more than relieve her own heart of its grief'.[22] The stage icon of maternal sorrow was created from domestic reality.

As a result of her great talent, her accomplished manners and her apparently impeccable private life, Sarah Siddons suffered only rarely from the stigma that afflicted many women performers who were regarded as being socially deviant in publicly exhibiting both their persons and their emotions for money. She further removed herself from the common perception of the actress as whore by presenting herself, on-stage as well as off, as a good and caring mother who in happier circumstances would have shunned public life and relished domesticity, but whom financial constraints had forced into employment in the theatre in order to support the offspring she adored. There is a degree of truth in her repeated assertions that she had to assume the role of provider for her family. Her husband, William, was a pleasant enough man, but was long-term unemployed and 'enjoyed' indifferent health, the treatment of which occasioned his absence from the family home for long periods. 'One of his useless agitations' caused him to miss her first successful London performance. He had an ambivalent attitude towards his wife's professional success, being both glad of her substantial income and jealous of her social and theatrical prominence. In the early days of her career he antagonized the proprietors of the theatres where she was to be engaged by petty quibbling over terms. Later his unsuccessful investments of her money largely in theatrical ventures exacerbated marital strain. As the inimitable Mrs Piozzi put it, 'What a thing it is that the husband cannot at least count and keep together the money she gets for him'.[23]

There is evidence that in the early days of her marriage she enjoyed her domestic life and was a fond and doting mother. A family friend, the actress Mrs Inchbald, wrote in her *Memoirs*: 'Mrs Siddons was indefatigable in her domestic concerns for her husband and child [Henry]. She almost threw away ambition, and, buckling to her hard lot, passed many a day washing and ironing for her family.'[24] The use of the word 'almost' is significant! In letters she represented herself as inordinately proud of her offspring: 'Sally is vastly clever; Maria and George are beautiful; and Harry is a boy with very good parts, but not disposed to learning'.[25] She described the baby Cecilia to Mrs Piozzi, the child's godmother, as 'as healthful a Baby as ever the sun shone on'.[26] On the other hand, the increasing demands of her successful career took her away from home for extended periods of time, and there is no doubt that her children felt her absence: 'I count the Minutes till I return to my dear Girls whose tender reproaches for staying so long (silly children for whose sake do I encounter these fatigues and inconveniences?) almost destroy me'.[27] As her career progressed Mrs Siddons seems to have been increasingly possessed of the notion that her pursuit of theatrical celebrity was almost entirely motivated by her concern for the well-being of her family. On each occasion when adversity confronted her, she vowed that she wanted to abandon the stage but was forced to continue for the sake of her children.

After her disastrous London debut with Garrick in 1775—a disaster that was, at least in part, due to the fact that it occurred only a few weeks after Sally's birth—she was mentally and physically ill for eighteen months. Tate

Wilkinson, the manager of the York circuit, where for a time she found refuge, proclaimed himself deeply concerned about whether the fragile creature which she then was could ever get through a major part. She did appear to be 'hastening to a decline'. In her words:

> Who can conceive the size of this cruel disappointment, this dreadful reverse of all my ambitious hopes in which too was involved the subsistence of my two helpless infants. . . For the sake of my poor babies, however, I exerted myself to shake off this despondency.[28]

She indeed 'exerted' herself and achieved a place at Bath, one of the most fashionable provincial theatres, where she was 're-discovered' and returned to London in triumph, but not before she had taken a tearful farewell of her adoring Bath public, protesting that were she a free agent, she would never leave them. She had, however, as she told the audience at her last performance (in appropriately enough, *The Distress'd Mother*), 'Three Reasons'. The 'Three Reasons' were then produced on stage: Henry, Sally and Maria.

> Stand forth, ye elves, and plead your mother's cause:
> Ye little magnets, whose soft influence draws
> Me from a point where every gentle breeze
> Wafted my back to happiness and ease-
> Sends me adventurous on a larger main,
> In hopes that you may profit by my gain
> Have I been hasty?—am I then to blame?
> Answer, all ye who own a parent's name.[29]

Sarah Siddons appeared in her own person before her public, performing herself in a maternal role (with her children as extras), similar to those for which she was celebrated on stage. In fact she had received 'an offer which she could not refuse'. Here was the vindication of her summary dismissal seven years earlier, of her hard work in the provinces, of her dedication and determination.

Some years after the Drury Lane triumph, Siddons was accused of parsimony in apparently failing to support the Irish benefits of West Digges, a popular old actor, and Brereton, who had been one of her most successful stage partners. Persecuted and heckled by the audience, she was eventually forced to retire and reputedly fainted in the wings. In line with her usual strategy, of attributing to maternal duty what was hard-headed ambition, she wrote:

> I was besought by my husband, my brother and Mr. Sheridan to present myself again before that audience by whom I had been most cruelly and

unjustly degraded, and where, *but for the consideration of my children* I
would never have appeared again.[30]

Her crippling summer touring schedule was undertaken, according to her, to
furnish her family with sustenance: 'for I must go on *making*, to secure the
few comforts that I have been able to attain for myself and my family. It is
providential for us all that I can do so much'.[31] The Irish tour which she
undertook in 1802–3 was planned to earn the money for a redecoration of
the London house in Great Marlborough Street and for the 'kitting out' of
her son George, prior to his departure for India. As a result of this
absence, she was not present at Henry's wedding nor at the deaths of her
father and Sally. Sadly, while ostensibly providing for the material needs
of her brood, she was neglecting their emotional need of her. It is too
simplistic to assert that Sarah Siddons consciously exploited her family's
financial dependence on her, but it seems very much in the manner of
the time for a deeply respectable woman like Siddons to sublimate her
'unwomanly' and relentless ambition to be a 'star' into the socially acceptable,
highly desirable and respected role of a mother struggling to provide for her
young.

No doubt the actress was genuinely concerned about providing materially
for her family. She was the sole wage-earner for the majority of her married
life, although according to the matrimonial laws of the time all her earnings
automatically became her husband's property: Mr Siddons paid her a quarterly allowance. At the same time she earned a great deal, certainly after her
outstanding success at Drury Lane in 1782, when her average salary rose from
the £6–7 she had been paid at Bath to ten guineas a week in the 1782–83
season and to over double that in 1784. By 1786, when her average annual
salary was about £5,000, she was able to write to the Whalleys that she had
achieved the £10,000 savings that she needed to fulfil her dream and retire
quietly to a cottage in the country with her family. The money may have been
to hand but the will was not. Yet another strenuous summer tour netted £900
in nine weeks. Tate Wilkinson commented:

> Mrs Siddons certainly for four or five years drew more money, not only
> in London, but in many distant Theatres in England, Ireland and Scotland,
> than any actor or actress ever did, or perhaps ever will do, and at higher
> prices (Mr Garrick not excepted).[32]

Although Siddons earned substantial sums, the money was not always forthcoming because Richard Brinsley Sheridan, the Drury Lane manager,
although brilliant as a dramatist and parliamentarian, was hopelessly incom-
petent in the conduct of his fiscal affairs. Siddons complained bitterly to Mrs
Piozzi in March 1796 that she had to tour in the summer since Sheridan had

not only failed to pay her salary but had 'lost' the substantial profits from her benefit in the Drury Lane coffers.

However, by the time Siddons was working with her brother at Covent Garden, she was once again earning substantial sums, rising to £50 a night when she retired in 1812. At the time of her separation from William in 1804, he settled £20,000 on her, yielding an income of £1,000 a year, and on his death four years later, she was the sole beneficiary, gaining back the remainder of her previous earnings. In short, Mrs Siddons, despite Sheridan's malpractice, despite her husband's much-criticized investments in theatrical enterprises that came to grief, and despite her uncertain health which at times prevented her from performing, was a reasonably rich woman. Contemporary opinion, coming to much the same conclusion, repeatedly accused her of meanness. A cartoon entitled 'Lady Sarah Save-all' depicted the actress as Melpomene clutching at moneybags while under her robes were sacks stuffed with gold and silver coins. She was also the subject in 1796 of William Combe's *The Devil on Two Sticks*, a portrait of a famous actress consumed by avarice. Even the devoted Mrs Piozzi thought that her friend's appearance as Lady Macbeth in April 1794, a few weeks before Cecilia's birth, was injudicious, not from the point of view of health or decorum, but because 'People have a notion she is covetous, and this unnecessary Exertion to gain Money will confirm it'.[33]

It would seem reasonable to conclude that Siddons felt most fulfilled and comfortable when she was on stage, but had to make it appear that these hectic 'exertions' were being undertaken not for pleasure but from necessity. Her chosen biographer, Thomas Campbell, saw both sides: 'With a family chiefly of daughters she was too affectionate a mother not to be anxious for the gains that were to secure their independence: neither was she unambitious of continuing her celebrity'.[34] Demands from her family could be very trying: 'I believe one half of the world is born for the convenience of the other half—I shall never begin to live for myself I believe and perhaps I should not like it, were it in my power'.[35] The last clause is typically Siddonian backtracking into 'good-womanliness'.

The final question to be addressed is how Sarah Siddons negotiated 'the austere joys of motherhood' in the conduct of her private life. Mrs Piozzi believed that the actress was a martyr to the selfish demands of the Siddons clan. In 1788 she wrote that Sarah was 'by no means beloved by the members of her family . . . They all like to get what they can out of her; but all the affection flows from her to them, not from them to her.'[36] The situation according to the actress's confidante and champion had not improved by 1794: 'Mrs Siddons has come home, handsome, celebrated, enriched, adored. Everybody worships that admirable creature except her own family'.[37] Despite Mrs Piozzi's observations, Sarah Siddons's sons, in particular, benefited from her success. She was disappointed that her elder son chose to follow her into the theatrical profession—although she had introduced him as a child performer—but she was unstintingly supportive of his endeavours: 'I think when the crude materials of his composition are reopened by Time and Observation, he will be a fine creature'.[38] Her non-attendance at his wedding to Harriet Murray, an actress, was certainly not because of her disapproval of the match. She told Thomas Campbell that Henry was 'the most unfortunate man in his choice of his profession, but the most judicious and happy in the choice of a wife'.[39] On Henry's death, she came out of retirement to play in a benefit for his family in Edinburgh where he had become a respected manager. George Siddons gained a post in the Indian Civil Service at nineteen as a result of the patronage of the Prince of Wales, with whom his mother was acquainted. George rose to the rank of Collector of Calcutta Government Customs, married and had seven children. He never returned home. Mrs Siddons's relationship with her daughters was much more complex—as mother/daughter invariably relationships are. 'The cathexis between mother and daughter—essential distorted misused—is the great unwritten story. The materials are here for the deepest mutuality and the most painful estrangement.'[40] The Siddons family provides evidence for both, demonstrated most painfully in what might be termed 'the Lawrence affair'.

Thomas Lawrence, who was to become a portrait painter of great distinction, knighted for his contribution to painting and President of the Royal Academy, met Mrs Siddons in about 1774 when she was a young aspiring actress and recent mother, happily married to her 'Sid'. He was six years old, an infant phenomenon, whose talents were pressed into the service of his family, the proprietors of the Black Bear Inn at Devizes. He sketched her and must have remained in touch with her family, for her mother was the subject of one of his earliest oil paintings. Both talented young persons went on to conquer the capital and by 1793–94 it was natural that Lawrence should be a frequent visitor to the Siddonses' home. Here he met Sally and Maria. Both girls were considered remarkably attractive, particularly Maria, who was thought to have inherited her mother's singular beauty. It was to Sally, however, that Lawrence first paid his addresses and communicated his feelings to Mrs Siddons. She chose not to mention the matter to her husband, but, although urging patience on the young couple, did not forbid their meeting and merely advised delay on the announcement of a formal engagement. During one of Sally's many illnesses, Lawrence secretly switched his affections to Maria. She also fell ill with consumption and revealed her relationship with the painter to her father, protesting that his permission to marry Lawrence was essential to her future health. William Siddons, ignorant of any previous association with Sally and deeply concerned to preserve the failing health of his favourite daughter by every possible means, agreed to the engagement, promising to discharge the debts of his future son-in-law (with Mrs Siddons's money, of course). Maria's physical condition unfortunately did not improve with the promise of married bliss, and only a few weeks after the official announcement in the spring of 1798, Lawrence returned to his former love, Sally. She had been extremely discreet about the Maria interlude, although her letters to her friend, Sally Bird, reveal her distress. She fully reciprocated his renewed devotion.

Maria's health deteriorated further and in the summer she was taken to Clifton to be looked after by her mother's friend Sophia Pennington, who, according to the prejudices of either Siddons's or Lawrence's biographers, is regarded variously as saintly or interferingly vicious. She was certainly excessively sentimental. In the meantime, Siddons took Sally with her to an extended engagement at Birmingham, possibly for company, but more probably to remove her from Lawrence's influence. It would seem that Maria's sick mind dwelt on her lost fiancé and his subsequent involvement with her sister, and Mrs Pennington informed Mrs Siddons of the invalid's preoccupation. The mother at once became more unwilling to countenance the renewal of the Sally/Lawrence liaison and sent Sally to Clifton, supposedly to assist in the care of Maria but again probably to distance her from Lawrence, who, in the manner of the worst domestic drama, arrived in Birmingham for some stormy scenes with the mother, before chasing off to Clifton for secret meetings with Mrs Pennington and Sally. By late September, Maria's condition was critical and eventually her parents arrived to attend her. She died on 7 October 1798, but not before extracting from Sally a reluctant promise that she would never marry Lawrence. This vow was made in the presence of Mrs Pennington and the girls' mother, but not of William Siddons, who was not told of it until much later.

Sally's love for Lawrence was undiminished; she was highly suspicious of the validity of a promise given under such circumstances, but her mother besought her to uphold it. Her letters became increasingly hysterical, swearing that she would never see Lawrence again, that he was a 'tormentor' to her peace, but it hardly requires close reading of these documents to conclude that as it gradually became clear that her lover's judicious discretion in not engineering a meeting was fading into indifference, the girl came to realize that her future happiness was lost forever. At the same time, she knew very well that her mother was in constant contact with Lawrence, who regularly attended the theatre when the actress was performing and was entertained by her after the play. By the time of Sally's death from emphysema in 1803, brought about by her repeated asthma attacks, she had had no connection with Lawrence for some years. As her mother was in Ireland with Patty Wilkinson, Tate Wilkinson's daughter who had been invited to London as a companion for Sally, she died in the arms of her friend Dorothy Place. To be fair to Siddons, her delay in returning was occasioned by the fact that 'Sid' had sent foolishly optimistic accounts of Sally's health to Ireland and storm winds in the Irish Sea rendered an immediate crossing impossible. The rumour that the actress remained in Ireland because she was enjoying an affair with Galindo, a young fencing master, is as vicious as it is unfounded, although her encouragement of this man and his rapacious wife was certainly injudious.[41]

One cannot condemn outright Mrs Siddons's handling of what for any mother would be an extremely difficult situation, but there are some legitimate questions to be asked about this very sad affair. In the first place, why, if she were willing to allow the early Sally/ Lawrence affair to continue, did she not give it her official sanction? Possible reasons are that *she* had had to wait two years before her marriage, and she thought such a 'holding period' was prudent. Yet, despite the 'time to think', her own marriage had not been blissful and was by this time rapidly deteriorating. She may have been motivated by the known fact of Lawrence's money problems, in part the result of his supporting his large and financially demanding family, a predicament with which Mrs Siddons must have felt some sympathy. His long-term prospects were excellent. Surely it was not her reputed meanness that denied her daughter financial support? She was concerned about Sally's unstable health and indeed wrote about the unlikely success of marriages in which the wife is an invalid, but at this time Sally's health was not giving such grave cause for concern as Maria's was when that engagement was ratified in 1798. In any event, whenever possible, Sally accompanied her mother on tour, a rather more stressful occupation than being the wife of a fashionable painter in Greek Street, Soho, where Lawrence already had a comfortable establishment. And, why did she not tell her husband of Lawrence's attachment to Sally either then or when Maria sought ratification of her engagement?

It was only under considerable pressure from Mrs Pennington that she informed him of the whole unfortunate series of events after Maria's death, when she was becoming concerned that he would find out from other sources, her excuse being that 'he was unhappily so cold and repelling, that instead of tender sympathy, I should expect harsh words'.[42] He received the information 'with that coldness and reserve that kept him so long ignorant of it, and that want of an agreeing mind . . . that has always checked my tongue and chilled my heart at every occurrence of importance thro' our lives'.[43] Did she want to be her daughter's sole confidante to spite her husband, who might have her money but was not going to get the confidences of their children? Or did she fear that William, whose fondness for his daughters was not in doubt, would never again permit the man who had so trifled with their affections to have access to his home (or to his wife)?

And how could she condone the fatal vow that Maria extracted from her sister, when she knew perfectly well of the rekindled devotion of the two young people? Mrs Pennington, in a letter to Lawrence, sublimated Maria's last hours into the passing of a saint, attributing to the girl an almost divine transformation. A copy of this letter was sent to Mrs Siddons and she used phrases from it in her communication of the event to other friends. But Mrs Siddons was *present*. She did not need to take the interpretation of anyone, let alone the romantic and over-sentimental Mrs Pennington. While retaining a loving aspect to Maria, she could either have deflected the sick girl's demand or alternatively made it clear to Sally that such a promise was not binding in any way.

Finally, why did she continue to see Lawrence on a regular basis, omitting to tell Sally that she was in reasonably close contact with him and leaving the girl to find out from acquaintances? The text of Sally's letters to Sally Bird in January 1801 reveals the betrayal that she felt:

> I know my mother sees him often, and I know she cannot cease to look upon him with the partiality she always did, and always will I believe feel for him, yet she never mentions him to me, never tells me he has spoken of me, or desires to be remembered to me—perhaps indeed he never *does* think or speak for me.[44]

Losing her lover and her mother's support, or indeed losing her lover to her mother as it might well seem, created a coolness between the two. Sally wrote:

> I think all my energy is weakened since I have ceased to give delight to the three beings who were dearest to me on earth; one is gone for ever [Maria], the second is *as dead to me* [Lawrence] and the third no longer takes the same delight in me as she once did [her mother].[45]

It has been said that Lawrence's vacillations between the Siddonses' daughters came about because he was really in love with their mother, or perhaps with the whole Kemble dynasty, a view strengthened by his attachment in later years (a father's interest, he maintained) to the youngest scion of the line, Fanny, Mrs Siddons's niece. Of all the many portraits of Mrs Siddons, those by Lawrence have been regarded by critics as unique in representing the 'private' woman, rather than the great actress as in Reynolds's *The Tragick Muse* or the society lady depicted by Gainsborough. Mrs Siddons may have been in love with Lawrence and consciously or otherwise drew him into her sphere by using her pretty daughters as bait to tempt him, but would never allow him to commit to either for she wanted him, albeit at a distance, for herself. It does seem strange for a mother whose daughters have been hurt by a man to request that that same individual should be one of her pall bearers— the sign of an unusually forgiving nature, or of a lifelong attachment? At the time of the tragic incidents in Clifton and in London, the affair seems to have been kept very quiet. (Even Mrs Piozzi did not know.) Yet later in 1804, at the time of the separation of the Siddonses, reports appeared in the press of 'Mrs Siddons having gone off with a young man, an artist, who had courted two of her daughters in succession, both of whom had died, and now had adressed [*sic*] the mother'.[46] William Siddons intervened on his wife's behalf (or to protect the reputation of his dead daughters?) and offered publicly a reward of £1,000 for 'the discovery and conviction' of any person involved in the circulation of this rumour. That the actress was still in contact with Lawrence is in no doubt. She 'sat' for him until two o'clock in the morning in March of the same year. He was present at her farewell performance, and in his inaugural speech as president of the Royal Academy he called *The Tragick Muse* 'the finest female portrait in the world'.

One cannot, of course, attribute the bulk of the guilt for the grief and the deaths of her daughters to Sarah Siddons. Maria and Sally did not die of broken hearts or of maternal neglect: their illnesses were physical, and contemporary medical science was ill-equipped to cure them. Lawrence appears to have been a spiritual philanderer, and Maria was probably the 'conquest-maker' that she was accused of being by her friend Sally Bird. Nonetheless it is clear that in this episode, Sarah Siddons's greatest challenge in a maternal role, she acted unwisely, selfishly and somewhat dangerously for the well-being of her children. Boaden believed that 'in any signal crisis in her own life, she would be found indeed the noble creature she appeared to be on the stage'.[47] Sadly, this was not so.

Sarah Siddons began her personal reminiscences thus:

> I begin by professing that the retrospect of my Domestick life, sadly presenting little but Sickness, Sorrow and Death is too painful to any feelings to dwell upon, too sacred and delicate for communication.[48]

What thoughts she may have had in retirement in her Baker Street home regarding the relationship between the public sphere of her artistic triumphs and the private world of domestic tragedies must remain a mystery. In both spheres, she 'performed' maternity, to public acclamation and to private pain.

CHAPTER FIVE

The British Actor Invasion of the Early American Stage

Don B. Wilmeth

During the spring and summer of 2002 there was an American invasion of London theatre. Among the offerings were Tony Kushner's *Homebody/Kabul*, David Auburn's *Proof*, the world première of Neil LaBute's *The Distance From Here* at the Almeida Theatre, Richard Greenberg's *Take Me Out*, revivals of *South Pacific* and *Kiss Me, Kate,* and a London production of *The Full Monty*. This phenomenon would not have been worthy of journalistic coverage except that the trend has historically been the opposite. American theatre has experienced British invasions of productions and actors throughout its history, most recently noticeable in the 1980s and 1990s with Andrew Lloyd Webber's musicals. The reversal struck observers of theatres in both countries as unusual. Benedict Nightingale of the London *Times* observed in the *New York Times* (3 June 2002) that new American writing with 'spicy, stinging' dialogue and themes that seem to be 'subverting America's international image' were partial explanations for the popularity of these early twenty-first-century imports. However, he added that there was a simpler explanation: the presence of American stars. And indeed, this invasion, as has been the case on the American side of the Atlantic, was palpable in large measure because of the actors and entertainers, including Madonna, Gwyneth Paltrow, Matt Damon, Casey Affleck, Woody Harrelson and Summer Phoenix, along with lesser-known actors. Setting the scene for these outings on the London boards were earlier appearances by the likes of Kevin Spacey, Kathleen Turner and Nicole Kidman.[1]

This essay will focus on the more common trend of British actors on American stages and will limit its coverage primarily to the first seventy-five years of documented professional theatre in the American colonies and during the early years of the United States—that is, from the appearance of Hallam's London Company of Comedians in 1752 to the emergence of the first recognized American-born stars, Edwin Forrest and Charlotte Cushman in the

1820s and 1830s, capped by an event in 1849 of paradigmatic significance.[2] Players emigrating to the New World, or, as often was the case, simply assaying a limited tour in the hope of financial gain, were all uniquely extraordinary. Regardless of talent, the profession of actor during this formative period—a colonial British settlement, followed by the establishment of a new and diverse nation—was never easy and required considerable bravery. Indeed, most actors and companies found their existence in the colonies far more difficult than in even the remotest provincial circuit in England, and no theatre or city in the colonies could even begin to claim similarity to the larger Georgian theatre royals in major British cities and certainly not London's Drury Lane or Covent Garden.

Before I proceed, two caveats should be made in terms of my title and approach. First, until native-born American actors established their presence in a meaningful way, to call the large influx of actors from the mother country a British invasion is something of an oxymoron, for all actors in colonial America were, in fact, British, with a few isolated exceptions, such as the Placide family from France, led by Alexander, a rope dancer and pantomimist who fled the French Revolution and first appeared in the US at New York's John Street Theatre in 1792. And second, this essay is not meant to be an abbreviated history of early American theatre but rather an idiosyncratic and highly selective account of a few representative actors and, in some instances, their original and sometimes bizarre contributions to US theatrical lore.[3]

In reviewing the early history of the American theatre a number of conclusions regarding the acting profession emerge. First, virtually none of the early player pioneers in the colonies came for egalitarian, political, nor even artistic reasons. The dominant reasons were more basic. For example, the Hallam family and their company set up business, first in Virginia in 1752, because of the financial plight of William Hallam's precarious operation in London's Goodman's Fields, an illegal theatre often in trouble with the Licensing Act of 1737.[4] John Hodgkinson (called 'The provincial Garrick' and later 'the American Kemble'), a gifted actor but with a disappointing mainstream career, emigrated in 1792 to escape one wife (or partner) and regroup with a new 'Mrs. Hodgkinson'. Such a stratagem served as catalyst for more than one actor, most notably Junius Brutus Booth, who in 1821 deserted his wife in London, settled in rural Maryland with a Mary Ann Holmes, and proceeded to sire ten children (his London wife did not divorce him until 1851), including the infamous John Wilkes Booth, Lincoln's assassin, and Edwin Booth, arguably America's greatest serious actor of the nineteenth century.[5] George Frederick Cooke's historically significant US engagement (1810–12) was essentially the result of being virtually shanghied while in one of his frequent drunken stupors by actor-manager Thomas Cooper (Figure 11).[6] Even Edmund Kean, who came to the US initially with no apparent ulterior motive, nevertheless insulted his audience in Boston in May 1820 when, seeing a small group of about twenty in the playhouse for his *Richard III*, left the theatre not to return (by the curtain the house was moderately full). When he returned for a second tour in 1825, this time escaping from the disgrace and scandal caused by his affair with Charlotte Cox, the American press and audiences not only knew of this affair, which they condemned vociferously, but they also had not forgotten his behaviour in Boston. The result of the tour, despite his ultimate influence on acting style in the new Republic, was certainly not what he had hoped for. In fact, Kean's most memorable moment

Figure 11. George Frederick Cooke as Richard III painted by Thomas Sully (original at the Pennsylvania Academy of Fine Arts) during the actor's American tour.

occurred while in Canada where he was made an honorary chieftain in the Huron Indian tribe (he was named Alanienouidet).[7] His first tour had also ended with an event that partially balanced his trauma in Boston. Just before leaving for London from New York, he stopped long enough to oversee the transferral of the remains of Cooke, for whom he had great respect as an actor (though likely never witnessed on stage), from the Strangers' Vault at St Paul's Chapel to a burial plot in the churchyard with a proper monument. This monument still stands prominently where it was erected by Kean.[8]

Regardless of motivation for making this long and dangerous trip across the Atlantic, some actors were nonetheless quite courageous, carving out a permanent niche in the history of theatre in the United States. In numerous instances, they left behind major influences that rippled through the annals of American theatre for decades or longer, or, in notable instances, they established what became acting dynasties on these shores. At the other extreme was a plethora of players who quickly left the profession, deserted one company for another that might be more lucrative for them or at least allow the performer the chance to play better roles (usually parts outside of the actor's range or ability), or simply returned to England to stay. Prime examples of the latter are George Bartley and his wife Sarah Smith Bartley who came to New York in the autumn of 1818, by which time a few native-born actors of note were beginning to appear. George Bartley was a useful actor and his wife even more so, appearing in support of James William Wallack (discussed later in this essay) and in March 1820 as possibly the first transvestite Hamlet in America. In May, however, they returned to England to stay, George gaining fame as Falstaff and later as stage-manager of Covent Garden.

One result of frequent changes and desertions was the need for constant recruitment, usually in London but sometimes in Jamaica where in the eighteenth century there was a flourishing theatrical tradition.[9] Indeed, the second important company in the colonies was formed when British-born actor-manager David Douglass, active in Jamaica, married the widow of Lewis Hallam Snr there in 1758, and returned to the colonies soon thereafter as head of the now Douglass-Hallam troupe (wisely renamed in 1763 the American Company of Comedians). The early history of acting on American stages could be recounted to a great extent on the basis of these recruiting efforts. For instance, when Philadelphia's Chestnut Street Theatre planned its opening—and subsequently made this city of brotherly love New York's major theatre competitor—British immigrant and manager Thomas Wignell recruited most of his company from England, including James Fennell, Mrs John Oldmixon, William Warren Snr and Thomas A. Cooper, the last rising in the ranks to become America's first touring star, remaining active well into the 1830s.

As many have recognized, the early American theatre was not just dominated by British-born actors, albeit often third or fourth rate, but was essentially a British institution; the structure, including a sharing system, lines

of business, circuits, and even the theatre building, was a reflection of eighteenth-century British provincial theatre practice.[10] And the actors
demonstrated acting styles typified by what was also seen on the London
stage, though early American actors tended toward the more old-fashioned
rant and exaggeration of James Quin as contrasted with the more natural
approach of David Garrick. Once the profession was established, the model
shifted toward the grand style of John Philip Kemble and Sarah Siddons
(significantly neither visited America, though Charles and Fanny Kemble
did), as exemplified by such early notable actors in America as Thomas
Abthorpe Cooper, Mrs Anne Merry, John Henry, John Hodgkinson and John
Bernard. It was not until the engagement of George Frederick Cooke in 1810
(the first true visiting star in the US), followed by Edmund Kean in 1820 (and
again in 1825) and Junius Brutus Booth in 1821, that a more romantic style
was introduced on the American stage. And with the discovery in the second
decade of the nineteenth century that a starring tour could be profitable in the
US, the appearance of major stars like Cooke, Kean, James W. Wallack (in
1818) and others changed the direction of the American theatre from that of
the repertory system to stock companies dependent on visiting stars. Finally,
by the 1830s, and losing little momentum until the end of the century—despite
a diminution in the hegemony of British actors—there was a steady stream of
visiting actors, most British but some from other nations, yet all considered
stars and many with international reputations.

One final generalization: like many provincial British actors, the earliest
pioneers in the colonies faced constant challenges. And if surviving as a
provincial English actor was an arduous task, survival in the New World
during its first years of professional theatre was even more difficult, faced as
the players were with uncertainties at every turn, ranging from constant battles
with authority and moralists, fear of smallpox and frequent yellow fever
outbreaks, to financial panics and frequent debt and bankruptcies.

In fact, a dominant theme throughout the history of American theatre has
been strong anti-theatre feelings and beliefs. As the late Jonas Barish and
others have illustrated so forcefully, anti-theatrical prejudice is difficult to
eradicate.[11] A myriad of laws and attempted restrictions on theatrical production were undertaken in colonial America, especially by the Puritans in New
England but also by Quakers, Presbyterians, Lutherans and Baptists in other
parts of the colonies (only Maryland and Virginia failed to pass such laws).
Between 1700 and 1716 laws were passed against the theatre with some force
in various colonies. Yet theatre efforts proceeded with some success up to the
American Revolution.[12] The Continental Congress finally passed a resolution
in 1779 condemning all theatrical representations, as well as gambling, horse
racing and cock fighting, as sinful and intolerable. But the desire to perform
is not easy to legislate against, so during the fight for independence theatrical
events did not cease. British military officers in particular kept the theatre

alive, especially in New York and Boston, and even American troops presented a smattering of entertainments.[13]

But it has always been the position of the actor that has taken the brunt of censorship and castigation, and not just in the American colonies and the new Republic. In England actors had been long considered rogues and vagabonds, yet, although the fierce Protestantism of the English clergy 'continued to scorch the theatre with its hot breath, and to muster adherents among the pious laity when it could', well into the nineteenth century actors were allowed a tolerable measure of human decency.[14] In the US these workers in the house of the devil found it almost impossible to shake the various damnable stigmas attached to them, although surface appearance would suggest a certain degree of social acceptance. Examples are numerous but one will suffice, an event that is outside the timeframe of this essay, though the tale begins before my declared cut-off date.

In 1827 comic actor George Holland (born in London in 1791, the son of a tradesman and for some seven years an actor with a modest career on British stages), came to the United States for what became for sixteen years the nomadic life of an actor, finally locating there for the remainder of his career with several managements, including those of James Caldwell, Billy Mitchell, James W. Wallack and Augustin Daly. In time, Holland was highly valued as a 'comedian of peculiar and irrepressible drollery', and he also became the doyen of one of the noteworthy theatrical dynasties in America (four of his six children became actors). As David Rinear notes, Holland was a good family man, considered 'astoundingly shrewd, impeccably honest, and unpredictably charitable'.[15] He was one of those British actors who cast his lot with what was still a developing theatrical establishment in America; he was loved and admired by his contemporaries.

And yet despite a life that was, as Rinear suggests, 'a model of middle class respectability throughout half the nineteenth century', upon his death in December 1870 Holland was denied burial by Rev. William T. Sabine, Rector of the Church of the Atonement (where Holland's children attended Sunday School), then located at the south-east corner of Madison Avenue and Twenty-Eighth Street (later razed). It was actor Joseph Jefferson III, renowned on stage as Rip Van Winkle, along with George's son Edmund Milton Holland, then a 22-year-old actor just beginning what would become a distinguished career as a character actor, who approached Rev. Sabine. Jefferson, whose British-born grandfather came to the US in 1795 and began one of America's major theatrical dynasties, was arguably America's most respected and beloved actor. As Jefferson recounted the story, confirmed by Edmund, the clergyman demurred on learning that the funeral was for an actor, but added that there was 'a little Church around the corner where they did that kind of thing'. Jefferson responded, 'Then, if this be so, God bless "the little church around the corner"'.[16] That church was the Church of the

Transfiguration located at One East Twenty-Ninth Street. Holland's modest funeral was held on 22 December 1870, conducted by Rev. George Hendric Houghton, the founder of the parish in 1848 and its first rector. As Jefferson notes, Sabine had unwittingly performed an important christening, and his baptismal name of 'The Little Church around the Corner' survives to the present.[17]

In many ways the act of Rev. Sabine served as a gesture that reversed the plight of the actor in America. Rinear suggests that 'Holland's personal and professional life were so exemplary that the deceased comedian became a rallying point for a frontal assault on the anti-theatrical prejudice of some clergymen and the morally conservative members of the community' (170). And so it likely did. However, in one of the notable ironies of the American theatre, at least according to legend, when Jefferson tried to purchase land for a summer home on Cape Cod in the town of Sandwich, Massachusetts, he 'encountered prejudice in the form of inflated prices'.[18] So instead of Sandwich, Jefferson bought property eight miles away in Buzzard's Bay where he built a grand home called Crow's Nest. When he died in 1905, however, Jefferson's remains were buried in Sandwich's Bay View Cemetery.

During their limited visits British actors often made contributions in odd or unexpected ways. George Frederick Cooke, whose presence led to the primacy of the starring system in the US, appeared 160 times during his stay in the US at New York, Boston, Baltimore, Philadelphia and Providence; he was invariably praised by the limited number of critics writing with some perception, and the memory of his acting and the impact of his stage appearances continued to be mentioned for years after his death in 1812, especially when comparisons were made between him and Kean or J.B. Booth. Frequently it was Cooke who was praised most highly for a style that was far more 'natural' than what had been seen on these shores and as superior in many ways to Kean and Booth. Yet Cooke's contribution to American theatre lore took a bizarre turn as a result of Kean's generous and charitable act of facilitating Cooke's reburial in 1821. Details of the subsequent events are provided in my biography of Cooke, so only a summary follows, with a few added, later twists to this macabre tale.[19]

Apparently, in the process of moving Cooke's body, the skull was detached from the torso, as was a forefinger or perhaps a toe bone. In any case, Kean supposedly took the latter and brought it back with him to London as a precious relic. When he arrived home his first words to his wife Mary were, accordingly to legend, 'I have brought Charles [his son, who was one of a later wave of British actors to visit the US] a fortune. I have something that the directors of the British Museum would give ten thousand pounds for; but they sha'n't have it.' Mary held the relic, the story goes, with disgust and finally threw it out. Kean's response was, 'Mary, your son has lost a fortune'.

It is Cooke's skull, however, that has become a major part of American theatrical lore. From all evidence it appears to have first become a possession of Cooke's physician, a Dr John W. Francis, its disappearance not revealed to the general public until 1832 in Dunlap's history of the American theatre. Francis confessed in his *Old New York* (1856) that he once loaned the skull to New York's Park Theatre for the gravediggers' scene in *Hamlet*. The following day, at a dining club, Francis had the skull examined by several members, including a guest of the evening, Daniel Webster. These two happenings are likely true, but a long list of legends, most impossible to verify, followed. For example, it was claimed that visiting British stars Charles Kean (in 1830) and George Vandenhoff (in 1842) both used the skull in *Hamlet*. Other fanciful tales of the skull's wandering multiplied, yet, in fact the skull had indeed belonged to Dr John Francis, who in turn passed it down to his son, Dr Valentine Mott Francis, who then gave it to Dr George McClellan, then dean of the Jefferson Medical College in Philadelphia (now the Thomas Jefferson University Medical School). Upon McClellan's death in 1926 his widow presented the skull to Ross V. Patterson, then dean of the medical school, and in his will (Patterson died in 1931) the skull became the property of the medical school where it resides to this day. McClellan's bequest stirred new interest in Cooke's skull and more strange tales were born. There was also an effort to return the skull to Cooke's skeleton at St Paul's. Thereafter all was quiet for a decade until manager Daniel Frohman renewed efforts to replace the skull alongside the body, unsuccessfully. But again this effort gave birth to more stories, including one that in the 1880s Edwin Booth, while playing Hamlet in Philadelphia, was handed Cooke's skull to use as poor Yorick but was only told that it was Cooke's after the performance. But the actual wandering did not stop in the 1930s. As recently as November 1980 the skull was loaned to Mercer Community College in West Windsor, New Jersey, to be used in a production of *Hamlet*. Following this event, the University announced that it had decided to make the skull available on loan to responsible institutions, with a bond required of $25,000 for its safe return. It seems fitting to conclude this retelling of one of our strangest chapters of theatre legend by quoting portions of my earlier conclusion: 'As a motif of his life, one of paradox and irony, the skull is a fitting symbol. One could suggest in jest that in life Cooke frequently lost his head during moments of tempestuousness; thus as a headless actor after death, his fitful rest is appropriate' (286).

Another example of an unanticipated contribution to the American stage was the visit during 1822–23 and again in 1834 of the extraordinary British actor and mimic Charles Mathews Snr, widely known for his 'At Homes', a combination of story-telling, quick-change artistry, and the impersonation of a startlingly wide range of characters (Figure 12). After his first tour Mathews developed two new 'At Homes' based on his US tour to present back in England. Titled *A Trip to America* and *Jonathan in England* and both staged

in 1824, Mathews, though not the first to play a Yankee, became nevertheless the first major actor to exploit noticeably the stage Yankee. Once
American actors and audiences realized that Mathews's vehicles offered
good-humoured satire on American characters and mores and not the barbed
and anti-American sentiment expected, Mathews's stature would allow him
to exert an extraordinary influence on the development of Yankee specialists,
from James H. Hackett and George Handel 'Yankee' Hill (both creating
notable Yankees first in 1828) to Danforth Marble (first Yankee in 1836) and
Joshua Silsbee in 1840. Significantly, Mathews's influence was equally noticeable in England where Yankee actors were extremely popular during the
1830s and 1840s, often compared in temperament and stage persona to stage
Yorkshiremen.[20]

Throughout this essay I have alluded to the phenomenon of theatrical
dynasties in the American theatre, many begun as the result of the emigration
of British actors such as Lewis Hallam Snr, Junius Brutus Booth and Joseph
Jefferson I. Certainly theatrical families are common throughout the world,
especially during the eighteenth and nineteenth centuries. In England the
most obvious examples would include the Kembles, the Keans and the Terrys.
In reality, the history of the theatre (and not just in the US), perhaps more
than any of the arts, could be told through the biographies of generations of

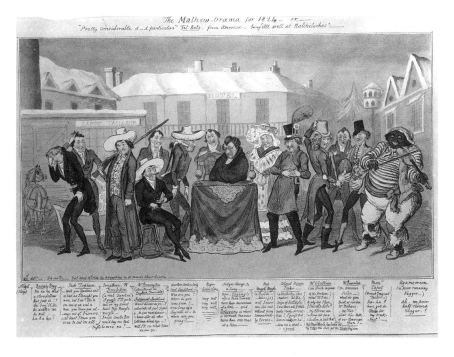

Figure 12. Charles Mathews Snr, in an 1824 engraving of his myriad characters
played in *A Trip to America*.

families who dominated the theatrical scene. In America virtually all of these began in Great Britain. In addition to those dynasties already mentioned (the Hollands, the Hallams, the Jeffersons), the great families of actors in the US have included the Wallacks, the Hacketts, the Powers, the Drakes and the Chapmans, the Davenports, the Seymours, the Drew-Barrymore clan, the Sotherns, and dozen of other theatrical families. Of those specific families enumerated, all but the Hacketts had their roots in the United Kingdom, yet James H. Hackett, interestingly, was the first American to appear in London as a star. With limited space, only a few examples of these families will be outlined here, but each family tree has similarities to all the others.

One variation on the evolution of theatrical dynasties—and a definite enrichment of stage history—is the amalgamation of two or more theatre families. I noted earlier the marriage of David Douglass to the widow of Lewis Hallam Snr in 1758. Perhaps the most striking illustration of the combination of talents in the early American theatre would be that of the British actress Mrs Anne Merry (daughter of the actor-manager John Brunton), who came to the US as a result of one the many recruitment efforts of the time, in this case in 1796 by actor-manager Thomas Wignell of Philadelphia's Chestnut Street Theatre.[21] And as with so many British actors, her motivation was not for fame or glory. Indeed, in 1792 she had retired a position at Covent Garden after her marriage to minor poet Robert Merry, who shortly afterwards lost virtually all of his money. His wife's return to the stage—and in America where she became an artistic pacesetter—was an effort to ease their financial burden. In 1798 Robert Merry died; in 1803 Anne married Wignell, and when he died only seven weeks later, she first took over the management of the Chestnut and then in 1806 married fellow actor, British-born William Warren Snr, who subsequently became co-manager of the Chestnut Street Theatre with an actor born in Canada of British parents, William B. Wood. Mrs Merry died in 1808. Warren, who later took a third wife, was the father of William Warren Jnr, one of the great comic actors of the nineteenth-century American stage.

A later, and even more prominent amalgamation leading to a dominant American dynasty is the Drew-Barrymore family, which claims to reach back to strolling players in Elizabethan England and can, with some certainty, be dated from at least 1752.[22] The maternal grandmother of the most famous members of the family—Lionel, Ethel and John Barrymore—came to America in 1825. Louisa Lane had been a provincial child actor in England before emigrating to Philadelphia with her singer/comedienne mother; she made her American debut in 1829. After marriages to two actors (Henry Blaine Hunt and George Mossop), Louisa married her third actor husband, John Drew (whose father was a theatre manager), in 1850. From this union came two important theatre progenies, and Mrs Drew on her own (John died in 1861) became an extraordinarily important actress-manager at Philadelphia's Arch Street Theatre. Her son John Drew had an illustrious career as 'First

Gentleman of the American Stage' and her daughter, Georgiana a popular comedienne, married in 1876 Maurice Barrymore, the son of a British district commissioner in India born in 1847. Maurice died of paresis in 1905 and never fulfilled his great promise, yet he and Georgie left the entertainment world the legacy of three extraordinary children, Lionel (1878–1954), Ethel (1879–1959) and John (1882–1942). The family tree is a rich and complex one, reaching to the present in the person of the actress Drew Barrymore, the daughter of John's son.

Perhaps most influential in terms of the development of early theatre in New York over a half-century were the Wallacks. Actor Henry John Wallack (1790–1870), the eldest son of Mr and Mrs William Wallack, popular performers at London's Astley Amphitheatre, came to the US with his dancer wife Fanny Jones in 1819. Although a versatile and accomplished actor, Henry John failed to receive the acclaim of other members of the family. For example, his younger brother James William had his American debut at New York's Park Theatre in 1818 and for the next thirty-three years shuttled back and forth between the US and England, finally settling in New York in 1851, opening his own theatre the following year. For the next thirty-five years Wallack's was the major stock company in America. James William Wallack, despite his name, was Henry's son, whose American debut was at the age of 4 in 1822. It was this Wallack who spread the name throughout the US as a result of extensive tours. And finally, John Johnstone Lester Wallack, son of James William—and the only American-born Wallack in this dynasty, although his apprenticeship was served in England and Ireland—had his US debut in 1847 and became an honored leading man and later manager of Wallack's Theatre (he retired in 1887 having played nearly 300 roles).[23]

Irish-born (1797) Tyrone Power, the first of that name, made several trips to the US, drowning on a return trip in 1841 when the SS *President* sank. One son, Maurice, became an actor, and another, Harold, married an actress who gave birth to actor Tyrone Edmond Power. The granddaughter of Tyrone I was the mother of Irish-born director Tyrone Guthrie. Tyrone II's career as a leading man was almost exclusively in the US; his son (also Tyrone), who died in 1958, became a major star of the American cinema; and his son, Tyrone Jnr, has had a modest acting career.

As stated at the outset of this essay, the dominance of British actors on the American stage came to an end—at least symbolically—with the rise of native-born actors with international reputations in the 1820s and 1830s. One of these, Edwin Forrest, was also a key figure, albeit unintentionally, in a specific event often suggested as a paradigmatic turning point in American theatre—the Astor Place Opera House riot on 10 May 1849 during appearances there by British star William Charles Macready, considered by some jingoistic Americans to be an effete, elitist, aristocratic and snobbish performer. This historical moment can be considered the capstone event altering and affecting the emergence of the American actor 'as the avatar of authenticity in the culture of performance', as Joseph Roach declares.[24] The salient details are as follows: for years there had been a long-smouldering feud between Macready and the American star Forrest. As Roach reports it:

> In advance of the Astor Place Riot, the forces aligned with both Macready and Forrest carried on an inflammatory campaign in the newspapers to promote the causes of the rival stars. Muscularly built with a penetrating voice, a magnetic presence, and something of a superpatriot, Forrest was heralded as the exemplar of Native American virtue, an honor he never deprecated or minimized . . . (362)

The climax of this feud—the riot—was a complex event, representing, as Simon Williams illustrates, 'nativist versus anti-European rhetoric that fuelled the riot [and] masked broader class tensions that were developing in New York City and the industrial Northeast as a whole' (328). The result: after a mob gathered outside the Opera House during Macready's performance of Macbeth and began to get out of hand, the militia was called. Confronted by cascades of paving stones from the anti-British crowd, they fired point blank into the crowd, killing at least twenty-two and wounding one hundred and forty-four. More than symbolically now, the primacy of British actors on the American stage was over, even though the extreme fondness of Americans for actors from the mother country would continue to the present.

Indeed, visiting stars from England continued to appear in notable visits throughout the nineteenth century, from Lydia Thompson and her British Blondes in 1868, giving rise to the leg show and ultimately American burlesque; to Charles Fechter in 1869; Adelaide Neilson in 1872 and again in 1880; Lily Langtry in 1882, enhanced by the notoriety that preceded her; Johnston Forbes-Robertson in 1885 and in 1915; and even Herbert Beerbohm Tree in 1895 and 1916, among many others. None of the later British stars had as great an impact in the US as did Henry Irving and Ellen Terry, and the Lyceum Theatre company. Between 1883 and 1905 the Lyceum company toured eight times, playing most major US cities and demonstrating to fellow artists in America their careful use of historical accuracy in scenery and costuming, a revolutionary artistic use of lighting (albeit gas), and a masterful coordination of all production elements. Like the earliest of British acting pioneers in this New World, Irving came not for fame or to enlighten the American audience, but, as had so often been the case, to sell his product in order to save his London operation at the Lyceum. Unlike so many of the early pioneers who actually ended up bankrupt or in dire financial straits, Irving learned much from American business practices, which by the late nineteenth century were among the most adept in the world, and after each tour he left the US financially replenished.

CHAPTER SIX

The Brothers Fay

The Role of the Actors in the Early Abbey Theatre

Ger Fitzgibbon

Standard versions of the founding and early development of the Irish National Theatre are usually based around a narrative which begins and ends with W.B. Yeats.[1] In these versions of the story the project traces its point of origin to the Irish Literary Theatre (ILT), an organization founded in 1898 by Yeats, Augusta Gregory and Edward Martyn (a West-of-Ireland Catholic landowner) 'to build up a Celtic and Irish school of dramatic literature', a project they hoped would be 'outside all the political questions that divide us'.[2] They went on to present several seasons of plays by the founders and their friends. When Martyn left, Yeats enlisted the young John Millington Synge to take his place. In or about 1902 they recruited a group of amateur players who had been working locally and formed the Irish National Theatre Society (INTS), and as a result of the success of the INTS in Dublin and London, Yeats's admirer Annie Horniman offered to buy and refurbish a small theatre which could be the Society's home, rent-free. Thus the Abbey Theatre was born. Within a year it had become a Limited Company with Yeats, Synge and Gregory as directors and with professional players. A few years later it was world famous and a new theatre movement was declared to be under way.

There are major and minor anomalies and omissions in this account. Far from being 'outside all the political questions that divide us' the ILT would find its project at the heart of them. In the second place, the prime movers knew little about theatre practice and had to enlist the help of George Moore the novelist and playwright. George Moore caustically remarked that giving a literary theatre to Dublin was like giving a mule a holiday; he assisted the enterprise in its early days and then became its enemy. The founders' insistence that a new subject matter demanded a new style and a new language meant they felt they must avoid the contaminating influence of English-influenced theatre professionals. This left the project of inventing an indigenous national dramatic literature working in a theatrical vacuum, with no company of Irish actors, no Irish 'producers' (directors) and no venue in which to play. These deficiencies were made good, however, when Annie Horniman gave Yeats a theatre and underwrote the cost of going professional.

However, if we regard the Abbey Theatre as a company of players rather than a building or a group of authors, an entirely different narrative emerges. In this narrative the point of origin is the Ormonde Dramatic Society, an amateur company founded in the 1890s by two Dublin brothers, Frank and Willie Fay, whose ambition was to forge a new, indigenous Irish theatre movement with its own structure and style. As the company developed it drew the interest of writers and activists—first George Russell, then Yeats, Maud Gonne and Douglas Hyde. Faced with gathering a large cast for Russell's first play, *Deirdre*, and feeling they were on the verge of great things, Willie Fay 'formed a new society *ad hoc*, called W.G. Fay's Irish National Dramatic Company' with members drawn largely from Maud Gonne's group (The Daughters of Erin) and the Fays' original company.[3] Although the Fays were the originators of the project, they felt they needed a figurehead who would bring prestige to the enterprise. George Russell—who had become something of a guru for the group—was proposed as President. He declined and the members elected Yeats instead, with Russell, Gonne and Hyde as Vice-Presidents. A year later this organization mutated into the Irish National Theatre Society. The work of the INTS in Dublin and London drew critical interest and attracted the support of Annie Horniman, a wealthy heiress already interested in Yeats's work. As Willie Fay puts it, she told him that if her Hudson Bay shares made enough she would 'have enough money to buy the society a little theatre in Dublin'.[4] As good as her word, Horniman bought a small theatre, appointed Willie as overseer and Joseph Holloway as architect, and funded its refurbishment. The Abbey Theatre opened in December 1904. Within a year the INTS was being run on more businesslike lines: it was a limited company with power concentrated in the hands of the three directors (Yeats, Gregory and Synge); Frank and Willie were salaried employees; Horniman was a ghost presence in the wings dictating policy. Just over three years later, by early 1908, Russell, Gonne, Hyde, the Fays and most of the founder members of the original INTS had left the Abbey. Little remained apart from Yeats, the building and the name. Like George Washington's axe, it was all still completely intact apart from three new handles and two new heads.

There are several questions here. How did the Fays first create this company in which Yeats became involved and how did they lose control of their company so completely? What distinguished the Fays as performers, directors or teachers? What exactly did they contribute to the particular theatrical style which distinguished the INTS and the early Abbey?

Willie Fay's autobiographical memoir, *The Fays of the Abbey Theatre*, describes how he and his older brother Frank began their theatre activities as

children, fitting up stages in their own back parlour and presenting dramas
for family and friends, how he taught himself scenic construction and began
to get work from amateur companies, how he attended music-halls with 'the
lost and the lapsed' and how, having left school in his mid-teens, he left home
and joined a touring company as an advance agent. Willie's account radiates
a hunger to learn every aspect of the theatre, from publicity to set-construction, from lighting to acting and directing. Over a period of about nine years
he built a haphazard professional stage career working with touring theatres
around the small towns of Britain and Ireland.[5] Frank had already left school
in his mid-teens and become clerk to a firm of accountants, but by the time
Willie returned to Dublin and took up work as an electrician, his brother had
established himself as an elocutionist, voice coach, self-taught theatre historian and part-time critic and had developed the amateur company they had
founded together. The combination of knowledge, skills and experience the
two brothers were able to offer this amateur group already distinguished it.
More exceptional still was the radical vision they shared of fostering a national
theatre movement whose indigenous character would be modelled on the
work of Olë Bull in Norway and whose style would draw on the work of the
Théâtre Libre in Paris. Grandiose as this sounds, their vision was very much
in tune with the politico-cultural moment in Dublin. With a combination of
artistic vision and nationalistic zeal, they developed a rigorous training
programme and demanded a professional level of commitment from their
amateur troupe. As Frank Fay complained, not all the actors were up to this
level of dedication but they refused to lower the target. By 1902, then, Frank
and Willie Fay had a theatre company they had developed themselves from
scratch, and they had a small ramshackle hall of their own. Despite the disparities in terms of skills and experience, the company was run on democratic
lines, with all members having an equal say on policy and all members having
a vote on what plays should be done. A number of the company were emerging
as talented, serious and committed players with the potential, and perhaps the
desire, to become professional.

The one major problem facing the Fays' company was a paucity of new,
challenging Irish plays on which to hone their skills. Three sets of events were
set to remedy this deficiency. The first was contact with George Russell (who
wrote as Æ), who agreed to let them stage his *Deirdre*, a poetic verse drama
drawing on Irish myth. Russell brought connections to an extended literary
circle and a radical, democratic political vision that articulated the company's
instinctive procedures: everyone who shared in the work should also share in
the decisions. At around the same time Willie and Frank were asked to assist
in a production by a group called The Daughters of Erin—the consciousness-
raising, nationalist organization which occasionally presented plays and
pageants about Ireland's heroic past, downtrodden present and revolutionary
future. This group was run by the activist Maud Gonne, the love of Yeats's

life. Contact with Maud Gonne's group further extended the awareness of the Fays' work and gave them the opportunity to recruit new members. The third contact was through Frank's journalistic work. Prompted by a puff piece from Yeats, Frank wrote an article in *The United Irishman* about the success of Yeats's play *The Land of Heart's Desire* in America. This led to a correspondence between the two regarding the challenge of speaking verse drama. As Gerard Fay puts it, 'this passionate interest in the spoken word was the strongest link between Frank Fay and Yeats'.[6] Discovering that the Fays were producing Russell's *Deirdre*, Yeats offered his own *Kathleen Ni Houlihan* as a curtain-raiser with, amazingly, Maud Gonne herself agreeing to play the leading role. It is hardly surprising that the Fays jumped at this opportunity.

While the Fays undoubtedly felt honoured by such august company, Yeats and the moribund Irish Literary Theatre also stood to benefit significantly. In their search for a company to present their work, the ILT had overlooked local, indigenous talent and had recruited English actors and producers to play short seasons in Dublin and London. Unconsciously the ILT had re-enacted rather than countered the condition of cultural colonization: opposing the English stage, proclaiming the uniqueness of Irish identity as expressed through art, they seemed desperate to win critical acceptance in London. The ILT production of *Diarmuid and Grainne* by Moore and Yeats, with members of Frank Benson's Shakespeare company in the lead roles, proved a watershed for one critic: 'At last the Irish Literary Theatre has succeeded in its objectives. It has produced a work in which English actors are *intolerable*' (my emphasis).[7] Parochial as it sounds, this article put its finger on the central anomaly of the ILT. The writer was Frank Fay. As he saw in performance, and his brother Willie had noted while observing rehearsals of the play, the actors simply could not manage the Gaelic phonics of character names such as Caoilte and Grainne or the cadences of Irish speech. Willie later wrote: 'I came away from rehearsals more convinced than ever that these plays, if they were to be successful, must be played by Irish actors'.[8] Even the tone-deaf Yeats must have realized the problem, for shortly after this he began his overtures to the Fays.

The production of Russell's *Deirdre* and Yeats's (or, more correctly, Gregory's and Yeats's) *Kathleen Ni Houlihan* has long been identified as a landmark in the evolution of the Irish theatre—the first (and last) time the literary movement, the theatre movement and nationalist politics were united to everyone's complete satisfaction. In the case of *Kathleen Ni Houlihan* the attractions of this marriage are easy to see. For the Fays there was the distinction of premièring new works by the most famous Irish poet of the day, with all the concomitant press and public interest; for the nationalists there was a platform for revolutionary views; for Yeats it was a chance to engage Maud Gonne with his theatrical interests and, perhaps, woo her with a starring role. Maud Gonne, after some hesitation, had decided this deviation into theatricals was made worthwhile by the political potency of the fable—a view possibly validated by the comment of an audience member that one should not put on plays like that unless one wanted people to go out and shoot or get shot. Everyone, it appeared, got what they wanted and the occasion was deemed a triumph by all concerned. But underneath that triumph could be seen tensions and contradictions that had the potential to fragment the whole theatre movement.

Willie Fay was 'stage-managing' the production, but from the outset he did not have much control over Maud Gonne. The lack of a stage door in the venue meant the only way in for the cast was through the auditorium and Willie was seriously vexed by the unprofessional behaviour of Maud Gonne, who arrived late, in costume, and walked in through the gathering audience. This may have served to reinforce the notion that Maud Gonne was, in certain respects, playing herself. Maire Nic Shiubhlaigh's account of the occasion captures perfectly that blurring of distinction between the role and the actor as she describes Maud Gonne as Kathleen as 'the most beautiful woman in Ireland, the inspiration of the whole revolutionary movement . . . the very personification of the figure she portrayed on the stage'.[9] And yet, the occasion also came dangerously close to disaster and bathos. For one thing, the play itself opens in a country kitchen with two semi-comic peasant characters discussing the money that will come to the house from their son's impending advantageous marriage. Even with the arrival of Kathleen Ni Houlihan herself, the dialogue continues in a semi-comic vein of prosaic misunderstanding. For another, Willie Fay's gift for comedy asserted itself, subverting Yeats's high seriousness, and many of the audience responded appropriately with laughter. The play's tone changes, however, when the betrothed son of the house becomes entranced by Kathleen Ni Houlihan, abandons his young sweetheart and goes out to die in the revolutionary rising of 1798. This is a startling turnabout from several points of view. A character who starts out as a comically bewildered old woman makes her exit as the embodiment of Ireland 'with the walk of a queen'; the young lover becomes a heroic patriot; mundane self-interest is replaced by heroic self-sacrifice; kitchen comedy turns into political propaganda; realism is revealed as allegory. Most significant of all, perhaps, is the transformation in the audience's reading of the work of the theatre movement. Having taught the audience to mistrust the apparent simplicities of a mock folk-play and to decode it as political symbolism, the INTS would have to deal with the consequences. When subsequent audiences insisted on repeating that decoding exercise on plays of an entirely different complexion, there was dissension and strife. We might also note, with hindsight, that the play's plot turned out to be curiously prophetic: this promised marriage of art, personal passion and nationalism would never take place. Ideology would have its day and nationalists who supported this production would soon be attacking the theatre movement itself.

The fall-out was immediate. By attracting the interest of such heavyweights as Yeats, Maud Gonne and Douglas Hyde, the theatre movement was already in the process of being taken over. Strains quickly began to show: accusations of political timidity influencing play choice; arguments over whether artistic criteria should outweigh political ones; an invitation for the company go to America that proved too tempting for some members. Willie Fay later wrote: 'I lost the three players I could least spare . . . the first break in the original team'.[10] Such tensions between individual and collective ambition are a commonplace, but, given the company's ensemble style and relative inexperience, there were particular difficulties for Frank and Willie, who had to recast the repertoire and accelerate the training of younger actors. Over the next four years, the Fays' control of the theatre company they had started was eroded step by step.

The first step was Yeats's assumption of the Presidency of the INTS. Although this was conceived as a figurehead role, Yeats transformed it into the captaincy of the Society, making policy decisions and pronouncements and engaging in crucial negotiations on the Society's future. The second was Annie Horniman's offer of a theatre which brought with it a change in structure. The INTS members became shareholders but the majority of shares were now vested in three people—Yeats, Gregory (in whose name the patent was granted) and Synge—who could overrule the members at any point. As Adrian Frazier has argued, 'in buying the INTS the Abbey, it may also be said [Horniman] bought the Abbey the INTS'.[11] Once the theatre was up and running other changes became more or less inevitable. Shortly after the INTS became a limited company in late 1905 the decision was made to become a professional company on the basis of a revenue guarantee from Horniman. At the fateful meeting Yeats, with Horniman's offer in one hand and a directorial majority shareholding in the other, forced the decision through against the wishes of two-thirds of the members. More players, including Maire Nic Shiubhlaigh, left.

Had Frank and Willie left at that point, there would have been no company. The three outstanding acting talents in the company at the time were Frank, Willie and Maire Nic Shiubhlaigh. She owed her entire training to Frank and Willie and had indicated she would leave. Had the Fays gone, the rest would have followed and Yeats, Gregory and Synge would have once again been a group of playwrights with no company capable of doing their work. In the event, it was a safe enough bet that Frank and Willie would vote to accept the subsidy and have a professional company. Willie had been a professional before and was already on the payroll; Frank had been awaiting the day. They would have guaranteed wages, a theatre to work in and a paid band of actors. What had previously been the authority of skill and experience would now be the authority of management. There were misgivings. The pace of change was not being dictated by the members or by the level of public support but

by the sudden access to financial backing from someone with a very specific
artistic agenda and a political outlook profoundly at odds with the majority of
the members. At each stage the company had lost original members, and now
only a few remained. But at least Willie and Frank were still in charge.

What followed over the next three years was the painful erosion of Willie's
authority as company manager and main stage director. Gradually the Board
became more and more involved in the day-to-day running of the company;
decisions on casting, touring and play choice were made with little reference
to the Fays; Annie Horniman—for a complex mixture of reasons—began to
behave as if she had a pathological hatred of Willie Fay and sent a constant
stream of correspondence to the directors about what she saw as falling standards on-stage and off.[12] Through correspondence with Yeats and the other
directors she attempted to monitor and control every aspect of the company's
work, and Yeats in turn used what was seen as his close relationship with the
company's benefactor as a way of getting what he wanted.

As company manager Willie Fay's responsibilities could include wages and
discipline, supervising set-construction and lighting, production management
on tour, directing realist work as well as acting comic lead roles. In theory he
was also responsible for casting, but with a board consisting of three playwrights, it would always be difficult to draw a line between reasonable
authorial concern and inappropriate Board interference. As their confidence
in him was being steadily undermined, the difficulties became intolerable.
Rows were frequent, relations among the actors and even between Willie and
Frank were strained.[13] In 1906 Yeats insisted on bringing in an English guest
star (Florence Darragh, a friend of Horniman's) to play the lead in his own
Deirdre. Willie, writing to Yeats while on tour with the company, offers a
nightmarish image of a manager left with all the responsibility but little power,
trying to clear up the mess left by the interference and indecision of the directorate.

> Dear Mr Yeats,
> I am sorry my bad composition made my letter difficult to understand but
> I will try again. You asked me in Longford to get Miss Allgood to let Miss
> Darragh have Dectora. Act 2. Lady Gregory wrote to me in Enniscorthy
> that you wished Miss Allgood to have her choice of Deirdre or Dectora[.]
> Act III You write this morning and say Miss Darragh must have Deirdre[.]
> Now what am I to make of it. I don't care a red cent . . . I've got to keep
> down rows here but I can't if we change about week by week.[14]

The situation in which he had now been put was clearly impossible. Apart
altogether from questions of discipline and morale, to Willie's eyes the impact
of such an imposition on a carefully constructed ensemble-based house style
was seriously disruptive, like putting 'a Rolls Royce to run in a race with a lot

of hill ponies up the Mountains of Mourne, bogs and all'.[15] He does not disparage Miss Darragh's undoubted ability, but merely points out that she was completely out of step with the established style of playing. As a result, 'Miss Darragh made our company look young and simple, and . . . their youth and simplicity made her look as if she were over-acting'.[16]

These difficulties eventually led to the imposition of a new temporary manager, Ben Iden Payne, a young English director appointed at Annie Horniman's behest. For Willie this was more or less the last straw, but as Payne's appointment was temporary and Willie would resume as manager after Payne, he reluctantly agreed to stay. Payne found the company ill-disciplined and difficult, and failed to develop any relationship with them. He left at the earliest possible moment and Willie decided it was time to clear the air. He wrote to the directors demanding appropriate terms—casting authority, disciplinary authority and a clear chain of command. When the directors delayed for almost two months and then refused, he resigned, taking his wife Brigit, his brother and another actor with him. The Fays and their original company were virtually no more; the directorate and their sponsor were in sole control of the building and the enterprise.

But what had the Fays brought to the Abbey apart from enthusiasm and commitment? When he emerged as an actor with the newly formed Irish National Theatre Society, it was Frank Fay's distinctive qualities of voice that immediately drew the attention of Yeats as his reverence for text and his mode of delivery seemed to correspond with what Yeats wanted. Yeats's theories of 'cantillating', as he called it, were, according to Shaw, a nonsense. Shaw maintained that 'cantillating' could be heard from the pulpit of any Church in England every Sunday. Either way, Frank Fay offered Yeats a vocal technique and style he appreciated and which served well the rhythm and line of his plays. In due course, Yeats would dedicate his play *The King's Threshold* to Frank Fay 'for his beautiful speaking of the part of Seanchan' (the poet who is also the pivotal character in the drama).

According to his brother's account, it was Frank's determination to overcome a poor physique and a weak voice that drove him to master voice production.[17] To further inform his practice he studied the history of acting and acting styles, so that by the time the brothers formed the National Dramatic Company he was regarded as something of an expert on matters of theatre history and the history of acting. With his own work and training received from Maud Randford, he had become voice coach and elocution teacher for the company and spent hours developing the vocal range (and taming the accents) of his young working-class actors. Writing of Frank's own accent at this time, Willie pointed out that he had retrained his own voice to the point where it was impossible to say whether he was Irish, English or Scots. A Dublin actor who worked with Frank some years later observed that 'my unfortunate teacher had to spend most of his time grappling with my pronounced Dublin accent which he was determined to eradicate at all costs'.[18] To modern ears, this sounds dangerously like an elocutionist's obsession with Received Pronunciation, and certainly Frank's coaching emphasized clarity and audibility, though it is clear from other accounts that the actors by no means suppressed the Irish tones of their speech. Whatever its origins, voice production and acting techniques associated with the vocal demands of verse drama became a long-term obsession for Frank and it was his training which allowed the young amateurs of the Ormonde Dramatic Society to attempt the high poetic drama of Æ, Yeats and others.

As the new society established itself and built its repertoire, Frank Fay became the regular choice for parts requiring a particularly stylized and elevated mode of delivery. Though not often given to unbridled enthusiasm, Joseph Holloway becomes quite lyrical in describing Frank Fay's performances. In Frank's portrayal of the Saint in Synge's astringent comedy *The Well of the Saints*—a play Holloway hated intensely—he was 'dignified' and even 'thrilling'.[19] The skinny and unimposing Frank was hardly designed by nature to play heroic warriors, yet clearly as Cuchulainn in Yeats's *On Baile's Strand* his vocal powers supplied the necessary stage presence: 'What could be finer than Frank J. Fay's beautiful delivery of the poetic lines put into the mouth of Cuchulainn . . . Their melody fell as sweetly on the ear as though brought into existance [*sic*] by a master-musician from an instrument.'[20] And on seeing a revival of *The King's Threshold*, Holloway felt that 'Mr F.J. Fay's Seanchan remains his finest poetic study and the words ever fall from his lips in melodious musical tones'. Uncharacteristically, he does find that 'perhaps his final speech was chanted in too deliberate, long-drawn notes'—the influence of Yeats perhaps.[21] Certainly, everything that is said of Frank Fay identifies him as a harbinger of the Gielgud rather than the Olivier school of vocal performance.

Frank is also largely responsible for the cult of stillness in Abbey productions, for he felt that language is the core ingredient in drama and that nothing which distracts from the beauty of language should be tolerated on the stage. Early reviews of the INTS and the Abbey repeatedly mention the stillness and ensemble focus of the company's work and the avoidance of obvious stage business. Yet there is a paradox here. The emphasis on beauty of diction and musicality of delivery that is so recurrent in accounts of Frank Fay's work seems at odds with the equal insistence on an apparently artless, simple, hyper-realist form of playing. As Holloway noted on 3 October 1905, the players are often described in these early days as presenting the audience with a 'reality we thought before us so genuine and unaffected was the mimicry'.[22] One young player, playing the part of an aged man, 'had completely vanished in the wretched, worldly old miser . . . Here was nature itself and nature unadorned.'[23] Even Frank at times subscribed to this house style. In April 1905, in the realist piece *The Building Fund*, his work was marked by a 'quiet easy real method of "living" the character'.[24] In October the same year, in another realist piece, *The Land*, Holloway admires the way 'the timid shuffling-gaited, gentle old Master of F.J. Fay became a reality before us'.[25] Perhaps the meeting point is in the phrase Holloway quotes as the motto the players swear by: 'Nature pure and simple and art pure and simple'.[26]

The apparent contradiction here may be illuminated by the commentary of Gabriel Fallon, who was coached by Frank in 1920. According to Fallon, Frank made a clear distinction between the technique and the art of acting, the connecting point between them being found in the theory and practice of Constant-Benoit Coquelin, who was 'Frank's idol in acting'.[27] For Frank, the key element of Coquelin's theory was that the actor occupied two conditions simultaneously as the actor had to be both the detached, controlling artist and the character being created. This offered Frank a way of balancing the technical demands of the 'player' with the empathic immersion demanded by Antoine-style hyper-realism.[28] Fallon goes on to illustrate the point with reference to the work of Sarah Allgood, whom Frank had trained. And yet this sits oddly with Frank's assertion to Holloway, when asked about his awareness of the audience during a performance, that 'one who is acting never knows how the play is going'.[29]

The contradiction here is more apparent than real, for the actors' work oscillated between dialect-based, faux-peasant plays of rural life and high poetic drama drawing its material largely from the Irish heroic sagas. Frank's vocal technique became the basis for the company's work in one direction, just as his brother's strength in realist comedy was the basis for the other. Everyone in the company had to make such stylistic transitions, but not all did so equally well. It is also clear that, despite his coaching, not all the actors could produce Frank's impressive verse delivery. Even with four years work behind them, as late as 1907 Willie was firmly of the opinion that, while they had built up a strong international reputation for their realist work, it would be ten years or so before they would be capable of anything similar in verse drama.

Given his critical writing, breadth of reading and intellect, and his dedication to a high art theatre, Frank Fay would have seemed the obvious candidate for theatrical leadership of the group. Yet as a teacher Frank could be moody and unbending and as an actor he could be something of a prima donna. Holloway notes on 25 October 1905 that at a rehearsal of Lady Gregory's *The White Cockade*, when the author showed him 'with great clarity and dramatic effectiveness . . . how she would like a certain passage . . . given, he turned crusty and sulked at it, saying he was out of mood with the role, adding that if he wished to make Sarsfield [an eighteenth-century Irish national hero] a comedy part he would play it as such!'[30] By contrast, in terms of practical and theatrical experience, directorial skill and temperament Willie was the natural leader. Every account of him in the early days of the amateur company and the INTS period emphasizes the cheerful, humorous practicality of his personality.[31] And this impression is reinforced by James Cousins's account of the contrasting approaches of the two brothers:

> more than once it [a production] nearly didn't happen through the appalling earnestness that Frank Fay put into his work of rehearsing us . . . But it was Willie who showed us stage-magic. He was fed up with Digges' inability to fall dead properly. So he did it himself as a model of dramatic departure . . . he became the nerve-soother when the word went round 'Frank is very nosey tonight' and we girt up our loins to resist our own tempers.[32]

Not that Willie took the work less seriously. Cousins's account makes it clear that rehearsals were solemn, that lightmindedness was frowned upon and that the order of the day involved 'constant drubbings'. But they were also inspirational: 'the company was in due time infected with a portentous feeling that it was continuing Irish theatre history, if not actually making it. We talked of "the movement", discussed dramatic theory and . . . walked home with shining eyes and heightened colour to dream dreams of great plays.'[33]

A combination of personality, skill in character comedy and cultivated contrast with his brother seems to have led many to assume that Willie was solely a 'get-on-with-the-job' pragmatist. Yet from his account of the period, from his subsequent work as director, producer, actor and teacher, and from the numerous articles he wrote and talks he gave on the question of a national theatre it is clear that he had a very strong sense of his vision and purpose in his work. Willie's touring experience had taught him both to respect his audience and to read them, and unlike Frank, Yeats, Gregory and Horniman, he believed in a theatre that came from and served the ordinary people. His own memoir radiates a desire for the liveliness and hunger of a working-class audience and his consistent line in relation to a national theatre is that it must spring upwards from the work of ordinary people, not be handed down from on high. As far as the Abbey was concerned, however, he was an invaluable jack-of-all-trades, excellent at adjusting a set or inventing comic 'business' but not sufficiently serious to be trusted with high art.

That said, as an actor and director Willie made a major contribution to the theatre's development. If Frank focused on individual voice production, it was Willie who instilled the sense of ensemble discipline in the company. It is clear from his remarks on Miss Darragh that he had an astute and informed sense of theatre style. And as an actor of certain comic roles he was outstanding. In October 1905 Holloway noted that Willie acted in the 'quiet, natural, effective way that recalls the best methods of the French stage'.[34] On the 1904 English tour, William Archer described him as 'that born comedian', and in *Vanity Fair* PC described him as 'the admirable stage manager of the society, and certainly its ablest actor'.[35] A subtler note is also heard in accounts of this time. The *Daily Chronicle* critic described his playing of one part as having 'humourous [sic] pathos that recalled Coquelin's Cyrano de Bergerac' and *The Times* praised his sense of 'mingled sadness and fun'.[36] The following January *The Daily News* considered him 'a comedian of genius' who can rise to 'great heights of tragic power'.[37] Within a month of their departure from the Abbey, Holloway was noting the degeneration: 'the acting was more individual and less artistic than under Fay's management. Individual actors shone at the expense of the ensemble, and some of the actors occasionally were out of the picture.'[38]

Naturally, a great deal of gossip and speculation surrounded the departure of the Fays from the Abbey, but press comment was not exactly strident or uproarious. If the full significance of their departure was not apparent at the time, it was progressively borne in upon the directors as one disastrous replacement followed another. The illness of Synge, the loss of important players, the disastrous row with Horniman which led to the withdrawal of her financial support, and most significantly the loss of people who could train young actors in the methods that had become the 'house style' gradually began to enervate the company's work. Even eight years later, some were still hankering for the lost leaders. St John Ervine wrote to Lady Gregory suggesting a drastic plan to reconstruct the company: 'I think if we can get together a new Company with Miss O'Neill, Miss Allgood, Miss Magee, Willie Fay, and his brother, Frank, to train new players, we shall do very much better'.[39]

At the time of the departures, Yeats had tried to keep matters under control by implying that Willie had left to take up more lucrative offers abroad. There was a fragment of truth in this. Through an influential London agent, Willie had succeeded in setting up a small American tour with Brigit and Frank. The tour—marketed as if they were the Abbey players—was a modest success only and they returned to England and the hard grind of finding professional work. Frank's almost obsessive focus on vocal technique and his desire to concentrate on verse drama and on Shakespeare led him into the Shakespeare touring circuit, where he worked with Alexander Marsh's company for a period. On these tours he tended to play one of the book-end authority figures doubled with character or minor villain roles: the Duke and Old Gobbo in *The Merchant of Venice*; the First Player and the Priest in *Hamlet*; Duke Frederick and Corin in *As You Like It*.[40] In an undated letter to Joseph Holloway he speaks of his admiration for William Poel's mode of production but he despairs of English audiences ('imagination is dead here') and fantasizes about a return to Dublin and setting up a company, 'rehearsing a play for a couple of months, perhaps eventually making it notable for Shakespeare performances as we made the Abbey Theatre for Irish performances'.[41]

In 1915 Frank had the sour satisfaction of noting the Abbey players touring 'one of the Manchester Music Halls next week. "Oh what a fall was there, my countrymen!" The Apostles of High Art are on their knees before the great god Mammon *like the rest of us*, "but oh the Pity of it"' (my italics).[42] That phrase 'like the rest of us' is probably more revealing than the lofty tone, for clearly at this point Frank felt he had lost his chance to do something great and unique. The knowledge that the grand enterprise itself may well have perished as well is no great comfort. A couple of years later he returned to the Abbey to play a number of minor roles and give voice coaching to some of the new generation of players but it was an unhappy experience. Dublin, he found, was full of amateurs. Even Holloway, his former admirer, noted that Frank's acting seemed strained, his articulation mannered and excessive.[43] The following year a letter to Dudley Digges comments bitterly that 'None of the crowd ever write to me. They've feathered their nests nicely out of what I put into them, but I never hear from them.'[44]

In terms of temperament, experience and skills, Willie Fay was better equipped to survive the challenges of such change. His story includes some very lean periods of desperate searching for work, but he was always busy: he played numerous theatre roles, in which he continued to distinguish himself by his authenticity of style; he ran theatre courses for impassioned amateurs; he wrote articles on the idea of a Scottish national theatre and ran seasons of plays in Glasgow; he produced, wrote books of instruction on theatre matters, including a glossary of theatre terms and instructions on how to build sets and small stages; he co-wrote a mischievous one-act comedy in which he and Brigit starred;[45] he wrote a book of instructions on acting, *Merely Players*, as well as his autobiographical memoir *The Fays of the Abbey Theatre*.[46] The initial period after leaving the Abbey seems difficult, but his records show strong income from the 1920s on and his latter years brought him a steady stream of film work, both scriptwriting and acting. In the 1930s his income varied considerably, dropping to £144 in 1937–38 but the previous year had brought in over £900—certainly enough to ensure comfort.[47] His critical success in film was slower, but eventually came when he worked with director Carole Reid.

The story of the Fays, Annie Horniman and the Abbey Theatre is laden with ironies. Yeats (with Horniman's aid) set out to create a 'high art' poetic theatre and succeeded in founding a predominantly realist one which, as his own writing developed, could no longer satisfactorily stage his own work. In the process he lost the one actor-director who seemed to have a real sympathy with his aims and work. Annie Horniman, whose sole focus was the creation of an a-political theatre of high art as a platform for Yeats's emergence as a dramatist, accidentally founded a deeply political national theatre; far from forwarding her personal relationship with Yeats, the venture generated intensifying acrimony between them. The ironies surrounding the Fays are perhaps bitterest of all, for having founded the National Dramatic Company they found themselves, within a few years, being effectively ousted from the enterprise to which they had given its distinctive style. Instead of being at the core of an indigenous national theatre movement, they had to seek haphazard theatrical careers in America and Britain. Willie, against whom Annie Horniman seemed to wage war for a time, made much of his living out of the repertory theatre movement she had virtually founded. Years later, when she was honoured for her services to British theatre, Willie Fay was the only one of the original company to write and congratulate her.

CHAPTER SEVEN

Gertie Millar and the 'Rules for Actresses and Vicars' Wives'[1]

Viv Gardner

28 and 29 January, 1907. The King's Bench Division: before Mr Justice Darling and a Common Jury.

Mrs Monckton got her living as an actress, and was constantly before the public. She allowed people to photograph her and she took money for it. She also allowed her photograph to appear in fancy costumes. It might well be that if you wished to take a person who lived retired from the world and published a photograph of her in fancy costume, it might be libellous. Supposing, for instance you were to publish a photograph of the vicar's wife as La Source. She would have reason to be annoyed. But that is not quite the same as publishing the picture of a lady, who had often been photographed in fancy costumes, in another fancy costume. It might be a libel, it might be . . . In conclusion, His Lordship said that the jury must act impartially in the matter and must not be affected by the fact that on one side they had got a commonplace man carrying on business and on the other a lady of exceptional charm, exceptional ability and exceptional attractiveness.[2]

That 'lady of exceptional charm, exceptional ability and exceptional attractiveness' was the musical comedy actress Gertie Millar. The 'commonplace' businessman was one Ralph Dunn, a manufacturer of picture postcards, whom she was suing for libel. Ralph Dunn admitted having superimposed Gertie Millar's head onto other women's bodies on three postcards. The case itself is a revealing one, and not just for what it tells us about the attitude of the judiciary towards performers, particularly the female actors of the period, but also for its insights into the 'industries' surrounding and linking celebrity, the popular stage and the ubiquitous Edwardian 'glamour' postcard. The case reveals precisely how important the dissemination of the 'celebrity' image was, not just to the performer herself, but also to the theatre which 'owned' her, her photographer and the postcard company which held the monopoly on her 'image'.

Much has now been written about 'stars', but largely in the context of Hollywood and film. As early as 1962 Francesco Alberoni had written an academic essay on the 'powerless elite . . . the phenomenon of stars', an interesting description given the decision in the Millar case.[3] But as Richard Dyer has pointed out in his own first work on the star phenomenon, there is a mistaken belief that the deliberate manufacture and manipulation of the star phenomenon first occurred with Carl Laemmle's planting of a story in the *St Louis Post-Despatch* in March 1910, to the effect that Florence Lawrence, the original Biograph Girl, had been killed by a trolley bus. This has been seen as 'the first occasion that a film actor's name had become known to the public', the 'first example of the deliberate manufacture of a star's image'.[4] Of course such 'history' ignores the prehistory of *stage* stardom.[5] The Millar case raises questions about how far the court case, whichever way the decision was destined to go, served, and may even have been set up to serve, the interests of the 'star industry' surrounding the Gaiety Theatre and its 'girls', and how central the picture postcard was to that industry in the days *before* the film star and the mass production of film fanzines, posters and all the other commercial paraphernalia of 'fandom'.

It can be argued that in the early part of the twentieth century, the picture postcard, rather than the performance in the case of the popular stage, represented the site where the 'point of intersection of public demand (the star as a phenomenon of consumption) and the producer initiative (the star as a phenomenon of production)' met.[6]

The Millar Case

The Millar case was reported in almost all the contemporary newspapers, including *The Times* and *The Era,* at some length and in some detail. In *The Times* it was dealt with 'respectably' under its court reports. Other newspapers are perhaps more revealing of the 'performance' detail of the case—detail which has more to do with the outfits and decorum of the plaintiff than the legal niceties of the case. The *Daily Mirror*, for example, felt that:

> had she [Millar] remained [in the court after the summing up] the ['ungallant'] jury would have found itself unable to disappoint her, for she was looking at her very best . . . Miss Millar's costume for her second appearance was even more entrancing than her first. It was a happy combination of dark velvet and ermine. Her ermine-trimmed toque made every woman in the court envious.

This question of dress was not, in the *Daily Mirror*'s view, irrelevant, as the 'staidest lawyer could be pardoned for paying close attention to the fair plaintiff's toilet for it was on the question of dress that the issue of the case turned'. And the 'counsel for the defence had frequently called attention to the disadvantage accruing to him who fought against such a fascinating lady'.[7] Much attention was paid throughout the case, as one can see below, to what Millar had worn or might wear on stage as a 'Gaiety Girl'.

The postcards concerned in the case had been produced by Messrs Dunn and Co., a postcard company too small to feature in the directories of postcard producers of the period. The first card showed Millar in a nightgown with a candle in her hand. The second 'was taken from a well-known picture called La Source [in which] the figure was draped in a peculiar way'. Some indication of just how 'peculiar' this was might be deduced from the defence counsel's question to the jury as to whether 'the attraction of the picture did not consist in the insufficiency and apparent insecurity of the costume'. The third picture was described as merely 'vulgar and ridiculous' and showed Miss Millar crawling out of an eggshell.[8] Millar's attention had been drawn to this piracy when an admirer sent her a postcard to autograph in March 1906, and 'after talking the matter over with her husband she consulted her solicitor'.[9] Ralph Dunn admitted the piracy, and that the original heads had been taken from old photographs of Millar and the nightgown picture from an advertisement for a candle manufacturer.

In court Millar was accompanied not only by her husband, the composer Lionel Monckton, but also by Mr Foulsham, her photographer and a director of the company with which she worked most frequently, the Rotary Photographic Company, and by the owner and manager of the Gaiety Theatre, George Edwardes, who is recorded as 'smiling genially' throughout much of the proceedings. Rotary was one of the largest producers of Edwardian postcards and interestingly, according to the *Times*'s account, 'before taking action, she [Millar] consulted Mr Foulsham [and he] introduced her to her present solicitor. They were both directors of the Rotary Photographic Company.'[10] She went on to sue for libel on the grounds that the postcards were calculated to bring her into 'disparagement and contempt'.[11]

The court case, as reported by all the papers, appears to have been conducted in a consistently arch manner on the part of the judge, Mr Justice Darling (a musical comedy name if there ever was one), who frequently interrupted the defence to support Millar, and the whole affair was repeatedly punctuated by 'loud laughter' from the body of the court. Gertie Millar's demeanour is more difficult to determine. The *Daily Mirror* describes her as having 'favoured the Court with her most charming smile', sweeping 'gracefully . . . into the witness-box', and how 'her eyes brightened with indignation as counsel called her attention to the pictures'. Later she 'blushingly' hastens to enlarge on a misunderstanding on her part, or makes a 'smiling admission' that she had indeed cross-dressed on stage as a Dutchman. How much this is a projection and conflation of Millar's stage and court appearances is hard to say. She is certainly cast as the 'heroine', one who treats the defence counsel's questions 'in the manner with which she addresses stage villains . . . with a contemptuous curl of her fair lip'. Counsel, on this occasion, has need to 'muster up courage' to respond to her before 'getting bolder' and going on to admit that 'it was [his] misfortune never to have seen [her] at the Gaiety'. At which point the indignant heroine transforms into the flirt as a 'roughish smile [comes] over Miss Millar's face, "You have missed a treat," she [says]', and the counsel gives out 'a sigh over lost opportunities'.[12] Other accounts are more circumspect, though the editing process of the *Manchester Guardian* and *Daily Express* clearly emphasize the comedic nature of the exchanges and record the laughter provoked.

During the court case Gertie Millar was cross-examined closely about her own costumes and those worn by other women at the Gaiety. Much is made of the fact that in the production she is currently appearing in, *The New Aladdin*, one of her fellow female performers comes on in 'a French bathing costume' and that she herself wears 'knee breeches and high boots'. In partic-ular the defence focused on the theatre in general's 'use' of nightgowns. Asked whether she would agree to appear in a nightdress if a part required it, Millar replied, 'I have to earn my living, of course, so I probably should'. She went on to agree with Mr Justice Darling that she would, however, object to being *photographed* in a nightdress.

The exchanges then became somewhat absurd, with Mr Powell, the defence counsel, ostensibly quizzing Millar on the parts she would be willing to play in a nightgown, for example Desdemona or Juliet. To the latter Millar replied that she didn't think that she *could* play Juliet, presumably because it was unlikely to form part of the Gaiety Theatre repertoire and she only ever appeared with that company. Justice Darling helpfully intervened to suggest that anyway, Juliet's night attire would most likely be 'a nightdress as worn in Verona' and that he understood 'that no one in Verona wore anything but the richest brocade day and night'. Mr Powell then took Millar through a list of actresses who had appeared on stage in night attire, and a list of operas like *La Somnambula* that demanded heroines in nightgowns and examples of clas-sical art—including H.T. Wells's 'Vivat Regina' which featured the young Queen Victoria in her nightclothes. One likes to imagine the tone of voice in which Millar dismissed Powell's question as to whether she knew the 'beau-tiful statue of Paulina Borghese' in Rome, with 'I have been to Rome once, but it rained all the time, and I did not see much'. Powell's penultimate dig was the observation that he did 'not suppose you [Millar] have ever thought of playing Lady Macbeth—it is not quite your style'.[13] The jury returned a verdict for the defendant, Dunn & Co., after only ten minutes, and judge-ment was given accordingly with costs.[14]

Seemingly, only the specialist magazine the *Picture Postcard and Collectors'*
Chronicle took seriously the issues of 'ownership' of both one's own image and
one's reputation. In its editorial for February 1907, it deeply regretted the
failure of the action and argued that:

> in law this was no doubt correct: but in practice we maintain that the prin-
> cipal of allowing publishers to make deceptive portraits of public
> characters for their own benefit is doubly wrong. For, obviously, if the
> pictures bring in money, part of it should go to the person whose likeness
> has been used to sell the pictures; and secondly, reputation may be lost by
> such untrue and indelicate photographs. Further, the publication of a
> misleading portrait of a person which is not really a portrait must be
> lowering to the whole tone of public morality.[15]

The Theatre, Musical Comedy and the Picture Postcard

What further might one elicit from this case? Any discussion must inevitably
link the evolution of the 'Gaiety Girl' and the growth of the postcard collection industry. The creation of the musical comedy 'girl' coincided almost
exactly with the rapid expansion of the postcard industry in Britain as well as
Europe and the United States. And of all the many millions of postcards
printed, posted and collected between 1893 and 1914, amongst the biggest
sellers were those of the Gaiety stars: Gertie Millar, Marie Studholme (the
most photographed), Gabrielle Ray, Gladys Cooper, Phyllis and Zena Dare,
Evie Green, Marie Tempest, Lily Elsie—the list is almost endless. The
exploitation of the image of the Gaiety Girl and the consumption of those
images are part of the commodification of the actress, and particularly, but
not exclusively, the performer from the popular stage, that characterizes the
late nineteenth and early twentieth centuries. Peter Bailey likens the production process (in both senses of the word) at George Edwardes' Gaiety Theatre
to 'the more intensified and routinized production regimes of the late
Victorian factory'.[16] The interrelationship between the publicity machine at
the Gaiety and the postcard industry is part of the late Victorian theatre's entry
into the aggressive commercial and industrial world of the *fin de siècle*. The
one exploits the other.

The first 'musical comedy', though it did not yet use that descriptor, is
usually taken to be *In Town*, produced by George Edwardes at the Prince of
Wales Theatre in October 1892. As with all subsequent musical comedies,
the 'comedy' was more important than the music, which was 'undistinguished
and hardly memorable'.[17] Dancing in the early Gaiety shows tended to be
'modest' in both senses, largely due to the contemporary fashionable dresses
the 'chorus' of girls wore, though by 1900 a more risqué edge was introduced

into some dancing by individual performers like Marie Dainton. *In Town* was 'a curious medley of song, dance and nonsense, with occasional didactic glimmers, sentimental intrusions and the vaguest attempts at satirizing the modern "masher"', opined the *Sunday Times*.[18] With its blend of contemporary setting, frequent 'rags to riches' story lines (showgirl/typist/ milliner/shop girl marries aristocrat or turns out to be an heiress; impoverished doctor/lawyer/ gardener/naval officer turns out to be an aristocrat and thus can marry same), fashionably dressed chorus of Gaiety Girls and comic interpolations, the musical comedy proved immensely popular. For many women the Gaiety Girls became 'style-setters', so that the emphasis on Millar's 'costume' in the court acquires a dual significance. On the stage of the Gaiety, as off, she is a 'fashion icon' dressed by the best couturiers of the age. When she, on the stage of the King's Bench, objects to the depiction of herself coming out of an egg ('ridiculous') wearing 'a cotton blouse with a diamond necklace' ('vulgar'), it 'pains' her, as she would never wear such a combination.[19]

Many of the musical comedies were indistinguishable from each other with their:

> Sweetly skipping,
> Truly tripping,
> Quaintly quipping
> Here we are.
> Pertly prancing,
> Ditto dancing
> Gaily glancing,
> Tra la la la!
> Sweetly singing
> Roses ringing
> Flowers flinging
> Near and far . . . [20]

music and lyrics. It is not altogether surprising, then, that a performer like Millar, brought up in the Gaiety tradition, was unable to answer the defence's loaded questions on *Romeo and Juliet* and *La Somnambula*.

The class 'positioning' of the postcard itself is important too. At the simplest level theatrical postcards were used to advertise a theatre or a production with an overprinted reverse to the card; at their most complex, they represent a matrix of commercial and cultural exchange that has relatively little to do with performance. The most significant dates in relation to the theatrical postcard are those that enabled the mass production of cheap images for mass distribution. Thus, the process of production and exchange of performers' photographic images—that arguably began with Disdéri's 'invention' of the *carte de visite* in 1854 which dominated the market until about 1880—was enhanced a thousandfold when these relatively expensive *carte de visite* and cabinet photographs of actors were superseded by the postcard. The introduction of the rotary press and the half-tone engraving process in 1894 enabled photographs to be produced on an industrial scale, and hence photographic postcards began to enter the market. Various changes in Post Office regulations accelerated the popularity and accessibility of the postcard. In 1894 privately printed postcards could be posted at a halfpenny rather than the 1d letter rate for the first time (the Post Office's own postcards had been posted at halfpenny for years). In 1897 in Great Britain messages were permitted on the back/address side of the card, thus enabling the whole of the front to be taken up by a picture. This did not prevent correspondents using the front of cards well into the next century, as any collector of Edwardian cards will know. And in 1899 postcard size was standardized in the UK to 3¼ × 5¼ inches, making mass production easier of cards, display stands and albums.

Social attitudes to postcard correspondence changed too in the last decade of the nineteenth century. Whereas in 1890 the anonymous author of *Don't: A Manual of Mistakes and Improprieties* advised his or her readers not to 'conduct correspondence on postal cards. [As] it is questionable whether a note on a postal card is entitled to the courtesy of a response', by 1900 the use of the postcard had changed correspondence habits as well as generating a mania for collecting.[21] The postcard was used for briefer and less formal exchanges of greetings and news than had been the norm amongst Victorian letter writers. The lowering of the postage on postcards and the advent of mass production also brought the photographic image, whether of a favourite performer or a seaside view, within the reach of the pocket of a much wider cross-section of the population. Additionally, it was a population with an increasing amount of surplus or disposable income: in 1850 an average family had 10¾d left for sundries, by 1914 they had 8s 10½d.

One of the points of dispute in the Millar case was the price at which Dunn was selling the pirated cards, and the judge, spotting a hidden economic agenda, had reason to observe that 'I have been thinking for some time whether this was not Mr Foulsham's action and not this lady's'. Mr Powell expressed the belief that the case had really been brought to 'boycott' his client, while Gertie Millar herself asserted her ignorance of any 'combination among the publishers of 2d postcards to prevent the publishers of penny cards getting photos from the photographers'.[22] A Millar card by Rotary, Tuck, Philco or Valentine cost 2d, 3d coloured. Dunn was selling his at 1d. The monopoly that the larger companies had on the more popular images was being undermined by these cheaper cards, often printed on thinner, inferior card, but ones which even the poorest could afford.

Cards were also now being sold through a greater number of outlets. No longer was the photographer's studio the main retailing point. Postcards were sold through newsagents, stationers and tobacconists, at railway stations and seaside kiosks, and probably through the theatres themselves.[23] One of Millar's objections to the Dunn postcards was the display of her 'degraded image' in shop windows. Photographic images were no longer localized but produced and distributed on a national scale. There developed an inevitable fissure between performance and the sale of the image. You could live in Barrow-in-Furness, never go to the theatre, and yet still collect pictures of Gertie Millar.

The industrialized process for producing cards was not complete until the introduction of multi-colour rotary press printing made colour printing economically viable in 1907. Before then, though colour printing was possible using chromo-lithography by machine press, most cards used only a few tints and were coloured by hand using stencils. In 1905 we find 'a Scottish publisher, Messrs Cynicus, [stating] that the colourists were "mostly girls or young people whose delicate constitutions have unfitted them for hard labour", who were seated round the table each applying one colour'.[24] However, a visit by the author of 'Trade Notes' in the *Picture Postcard and Collectors' Chronicle* to the premises of the Red Lion Art Company, which produced the colouring and 'jewelling' for many postcards, takes a different view when he finds:

> that the picture postcard trade has a mysterious way of attracting to its ranks a larger proportion of young ladies with good looks than any other business in the world. In fact it is a pity [he goes on] that someone does not bring out a series of cartophilic portraits of these real 'postcard girls'.[25]

Jewelling and 'tinselling' of postcards had been introduced in 1904 by the Philco Publishing Company specifically to 'embellish' its actress cards.[26] This was followed very quickly by other forms of novelty decoration as part of the cut-throat competition that grew up between postcard companies. In 1907, the year of the Millar case, Rotary introduced its 'plate-sunk' cards with much publicity.[27] In addition, it is clear from advertisements in the collectors' magazines and surviving cards that coloured paints and gels, 'Nine Brilliant Colours in a Box. Price 1s.' that 'penetrate the glaze without injury', sparkling powders, luminous pearls, frost and spangles were available for home use. Postcards could be 'individualized'.

The extension of the 'production line process' to the performer identified by Peter Bailey can be confirmed in two *Punch* sketches from 1907 which also reaffirm the symbiotic relationship between photographer and performer. The first is an outline of the Dare sisters' day:

> The Misses Zena and Phyllis Dare plead guilty to excessive strenuosity.
> Their trivial round runs thus:—
> 6.0 a.m. Rise.

6.30   First sitting for the photographer alone.

7.0   Family group.

8.0   Breakfast.

9.0   Photographed for the *Tetch*.

9.30   Photographed for the *Skatler*.

10.0   Photographed for the *Shysitter*.

10.30   Family group all standing on gates.

11.0   Shadow exercises (with photographs).

11.30   Photographed for picture post-cards.

12.0   Rehearse new parts in *The Camera Girl*

1.0 pm   Photographed at lunch.

2.0   Photographed in a motor car.

2.30   Sign autographs for undergraduates.

3.30   Photographed with father.

4.0   Photographed with mother.

4.30   Photographed with brother.

Light getting bad.

5.0   Tea interval.

5.30   Answer letters from undergraduates and crowned heads.

7.0   Dress for dinner.

8.0   Photographed at dinner by magnesium light.

9.30   Family prayers (with cinematograph).

10.0   Photographed saying Good night to father, mother and brother, all standing on the pillars of the pergola in the lime-light.[28]

The truth of this satirical account can be found by looking through any extant stack of Dare cards, which are dominated by images of domestic harmony and the family group—to which is added in 1908 a fiancé for Phyllis, Mr Stanley Brett.

A second *Punch* cartoon shows six postcards of 'Miss ——, the versatile and charming actress in some of her favourite roles'; each picture is of an identical pose and smile for each role (Figure 13). One of the pictures is of 'Miss Gladys in the Girls of Rottenberg', an obvious reference to *The Girls of Gottenberg* in which Millar starred in May 1907. The last picture of 'Anyone in Anything' is uncannily like the description of Gertie Millar at the Dunn trial.[29] What this last cartoon also points to is the standardization in the representation of the performer by the mid–1900s, as can be verified by a glance through surviving Edwardian postcards where pose after pose, whether theatrical or portrait, is the same for different actors.

Theatrical postcards fall into a number of categories. Some depict 'a moment in the performance' and some go so far as to identify a point in the performance with lines. Whether these photographs are taken on the stage or

Figure 13. Punch cartoon showing six postcards of 'Miss ——, the versatile and charming actress in some of her favourite roles', *Punch*, 20 November 1907.

in a 'mock up' of the set in the photographer's studio is impossible to tell, but they are in no real sense a record of performance beyond costume and, perhaps, a performance attitude. If, however, surviving postcards in my own collection are anything to go by, the most popular and common representations of actresses to be found are those not in role—insofar as it is possible to identify a role—but studio portraits.[30] The Millar trial and the *Punch* sketch on the Dare sisters confirm the extended relationship between the popular actor and the photographer. Gertie Millar's barrister told the jury that 'the right of photographing actresses was one for which photographers were willing to make contracts and pay for the privilege of taking the photographs', and Millar herself said that she had never sat without a fee.[31]

There are also postcards which are heirs to the type of erotic portrait photograph that Laurence Senelick has discussed in relation to early theatrical portraits where the 'incursion of thespians and courtesans—the two often came from the same world—radically challenged [the] iconic practice . . . [and brought] a dynamic of spontaneity and topicality' into the respectable world of mid-nineteenth-century photographic portraiture.[32] There were several prosecutions in the period for breaches in Post Office regulations relating to the sending of indecent material through the mail. Some theatrical postcards began to cross the boundary between the sexualized and glamorized, and the semi-erotic postcard. In my collection, on a card of the 'Butterfly' dancer Miss St Cyr in one of Tuck and Sons 'Stage Favourites' series, the outline of her body is very clearly to be seen under the muslin costume. In another, Marie Dainton, the musical comedy dancer and singer, shows plenty of shoulder, bosom and leg and a bold, direct look that is in keeping with her role in George Dance's slightly risqué *The Chinese Honeymoon* in which she starred in 1901. Other cards show female actors in classically draped costumes that owe little to historical reconstruction and more to the display of leg that it affords, or women closely 'bound' in what appear to be winding sheets that are obviously neither costumes nor funeral wrappings.[33]

Finally, there is a group of anonymous fantasy postcards—still not transgressive enough to offend Post Office regulations on indecency, but erotic, and in their very anonymity reifications of female sexuality—entitled 'Types of Beauty' and other similar names. Some come close to the type of semi-erotic photograph Gertie Millar was objecting to having herself associated with. Often drawing upon 'fine art', they depict photographs of lightly clad female figures in painted settings of classical design. Many, like 'La Source', refer to actual paintings. Ralph Dunn in his defence said that he had 'called the picture La Source because he had seen a living picture on the stage representing the scene'.[34] The *poses plastiques* were regularly under attack for indecency but defended themselves, as Dunn had done, by referring critics to the classical origins of the original. The judge seemed to have supported Dunn's view that depicting lightly clad females in water, as in 'La Source', was legitimate in giving 'expression to the common idea that every river and spring had some tutelary deity presiding over it'. He asked whether 'it was fair to say that that [La Source] was a lascivious picture when it was painted'. The image of sexualized women as part of nature, particularly water, may not have been as innocent as Justice Darling would have had his all-male jury believe, as Bram Djikstra's study of fantasies of feminine evil in *fin-de-siècle* culture has shown. It is not simply the effect of water on clothing that lends the erotic nuance to these pictures, but the association of water nymphs and their like with unbridled sexuality.[35]

Gertie Millar and the Picture Postcard

Musical comedy was sometimes saucy but never lewd, yet it traded on the physical attributes of its stars. In 1896, a writer for the *Daily Sketch* describes the scene backstage at the Gaiety:

> From the front several of the dresses . . . looked somewhat daring, but [back]stage they appeared quiet enough . . . a Sunday school meeting or a prize distribution at a girls' school could not have been more free from offence.[36]

Just as the productions offered 'girls' to be looked at, so too did the postcards of the girls, but also glamorous and free from offence. The representation of femininity in the studio portraits of Gaiety stars overtly distances itself from the erotica of some popular performance portraiture. Whilst photographic portraiture was no longer the province only of the relatively well-off middle classes, and advances in photographic technique had released the subject from the formality of pose and facial expression imposed by the head clamps and back braces necessary to keep them still, the theatrical portrait postcards have more in common with the staid projection of middle-class mores and culture than any of Senelick's 'dynamic of spontaneity and topicality'. Postcards of Gertie Millar are in many ways typical. Just as the Dare sisters 'traded' on their youth—they were only in their teens when they made their London debuts—and family-centred image, so Millar trades as a reputable, fashionable, cultured, and above all domestic woman, who also happens to be stunningly beautiful. She is shown variously as 'interrupted' reading a book 'at home', with her dog, cutting hay, playing the lute and numerous other instruments. When shown playing these or the piano, she very clearly projects Edwardian middle-class femininity as wealthy, leisured and accomplished and it is significant that the playing in each instance is a solitary activity, not a performance. She is very much Mr Justice Darling's 'person who live[s] retired from the world . . . [perhaps] the vicar's wife' in these pictures. Nowhere in these portraits is there a sense of her attested comedic and singing talent.

There is an interesting congruence between the role Millar often played in musical comedy, the rags-to-riches romantic lead, and her 'life' off stage and thus she had herself a vested interest in the promotion of this image. She had been born the daughter of a mill-worker in Bradford in 1879, and made her debut aged 13 as the Girl Babe in pantomime in Manchester. She was 'discovered' by Lionel Monckton, himself the eldest son of Sir John Monckton and the well-known actress Lady Monckton. Millar and Monckton married in 1903, when she was 24 and he sixteen years her senior. She finally retired from the stage in 1918 and married the 2nd Earl of Dudley on Monckton's death in 1924, thus ending her life as Lady Dudley. These postcard images and the court case suggest she was not without a degree of complicity, if not control in the creation and maintenance of the idealised, gendered and class-driven role for which she had trained herself.[37]

Millar's most popular role was probably the Hon. Violet Anstruster in *The Orchid* that opened George Edwardes' new Gaiety Theatre in 1903 in the presence of King Edward and Queen Alexandra, and subsequently ran for 559 performances. From this production there are a number of cards. Of these I have an ordinary uncoloured one, and a coloured and glittered card of her in the role of Lady Violet admonishing a spider (Figure 14). (I am not quite sure where the spider fits into this botanical romance, but this was an immensely popular card.) Intriguingly, I also have another card with a similar picture but a different object being admonished. The spider has become a 'Piccaninny' (Figure 15). It was the Dunn/Millar court case which revealed the 'mystery' of these three cards and much more about the complex relationships that existed between the subject of the picture (Millar), the photographers with whom she worked (Messrs Bassano in this instance) and the publishers of picture postcards. The original card with the spider was

Figure 14. Gertie Millar as Lady Violet, in *The Orchid*, admonishing a spider.

Figure 15. Gertie Millar as Lady Violet admonishing a 'Piccaninny'.

published by Philco using a photograph by Bassano. Subsequently a copy had been bought by Messrs Garbutt & Co.—none other than Ralph Dunn trading under a different name. Garbutt & Co. had substituted a 'dear little black boy' for the spider, wearing what was described by the judge as 'the ordinary costume of a Negro'.[38] When Garbutt & Co. sent a copy for approval to Miss Millar, she intervened with the photographer to gain permission for the 'faked' card to be published having showed it to her friends because she liked it. In this instance of an 'inoffensive' faking, Millar was happy to use her power to promote the card.[39] Ironically, it is the Dunn card that is clearly labelled 'Copyright' on the front and 'This is a real photograph' on the back.

The Collectors

By 1900 collecting postcards had become a mania. There were journals for postcard collectors, and albums, fancy display stands and every form of inducement to collect more. Competitions were run; new series were brought out regularly. In September 1907 the *Picture Postcard and Collectors' Chronicle* recorded that in the past year 831,400,000 postcards had been posted in the United Kingdom alone. That total did not include cards bought for collection without posting. One woman from Norwich had collected over twenty thousand Raphael Tuck cards alone to win one of their competitions.[40] When Ralph Dunn pirated his three Gertie Millar cards, he printed 21 gross each of the 'egg' and 'La Source' cards and 34 gross of the 'nightdress' one. He had sold more of the nightdress picture than the others'—at 22 gross.[41] Figure 16 shows the bedroom of a fanatical 'Gertie Millar collector' in which every available surface is decorated with cards of Millar. The urge to collect is a strangely common one. Walter Benjamin wrote that 'ownership is the most intimate relationship one can have to objects' and that 'the phenomenon of collecting loses its meaning as it loses its personal owner'.[42] But the nature of that 'ownership' when it comes to picture postcards is complex. Perhaps Roland Barthes goes some way to explain the attraction of portrait postcards in his essay on photography when he says:

> One day . . . I happened on a photograph of Napoleon's youngest brother, Jerome, taken in 1852. And I realised then, with an amazement I have not been able to lessen since: 'I am looking at eyes that looked at the Emperor'.[43]

For him, 'photography is a kind of primitive theatre, a kind of *Tableau Vivant*. A figuration of the made-up and motionless face beneath which we see the dead.'[44] A 'living picture' of a motionless face. And as Benjamin wrote, the photograph 'enables the original to meet the beholder half way . . . in his [*sic*]

Figure 16. The Gertie Millar collector.

own particular situation, it reactivates the object reproduced'.[45] So the collector of Gertie Millar's image on a postcard is able to connect with and to 'possess' the original through the eye of the camera in a way that, as Benjamin argues, is not possible through a painting. And I would argue that that relationship is intensified by the personalizing of the cards that home tinselling or colouring effects, and the creation of 'special' collections in albums and decorative stands.

The object reproduced in these Edwardian theatrical cards is not usually the performance itself. The card is not an *aide memoire*. Of the hundred and odd cards I have only one refers to performance, and then it is not to a specific performance event. The card is from 'Bertie' at Marlborough to 'JM Alington Esquire' at Cambridge. The front reads: 'This will do rather well for your book. I couldn't get a card of Delia [Moody] so I thought you'd like Hilda.' The back reads:

> Tell Auntie to write soon and I'll answer. I thought you'd like this more than a letter til there is more news. Don't write too much about plays in your letter as I am going to work fearfully hard this term. Missed you awfully Tuesday night with no one to talk to and to hear the Miller's Daughter! Hope you are enjoying yourself and getting ready for a good term. Write soon. . .

Interestingly this card is one of the very few I have from a man to a man. There are some between men and women, but the majority are pictures of women sent by women to women. There is not space in this essay to explore the question of desire and consumption by women of these female images, but much of the writing on Hollywood stars has centred on the preponderance of same-sex relationships between stars and their fans, and observers of the Gaiety performances in the early part of the twentieth century commented on the appeal of the Gaiety phenomenon to women. Fashion was one area of attraction, as was the centrality of the Cinderella myth for many 'ordinary' women. Whilst one can see that the 'idealized notion of femininity' pictured in the Gertie Millar postcard perpetuates an image constructed by a patriarchal hegemony, there must also have been for the women exchanging these cards a level of celebration of the Bradford mill-girl-made-star whom the postcard 'enables the beholder [to meet] half way'. It is a celebration of a world of the imagination, a fantasy made up of idealized scenarios and wish fulfilment as opposed to the so-called world of 'reality'.[46]

A Summing Up

The actual techniques of 'faking' photographs were well known in the trade, and photomontage had been in use for almost as many years as the postcard had been in existence. But as the *Picture Postcard and Collectors' Chronicle* argued in relation to the Millar case:

> Until recently it was believed that 'photography cannot lie', and even today it is probable that more than half the world would take a photograph to be a faithful representation . . . and when the features of an alleged likeness are those of a person whose name appears under the picture there are also few people who would not take it for granted that the body was also his or hers.[47]

That Millar was 'faking it' in real life—she was no aristocrat born nor a vicar's wife living a life secluded from the world—we do know. That she may have been 'faking it' in court we cannot know, but it is clear that in some way this defence of her 'image' and reputation was an important fight for her to engage in. In the end the court case may have genuinely disappointed Millar—we do not know, she left no autobiography or reminiscences—but it did allow her a stage on which to play out another scene in her own dramatic and visual montage that reaffirmed her ascendancy in the aristocracy of the stage. And the 'collectors' of Millar had a few more cuttings to add to their collection.

SECTION THREE
Extraordinary Acting for Popular Audiences

SECTION THREE

Extraordinary Acting for Popular Audiences

Introduction

Christopher McCullough

The patterns of twentieth-century culture in the 'West' are notoriously more difficult to pin down to a clearly defined narrative than many other periods in history. This group of essays focusing on the twentieth century serves as an exemplar of that seemingly random narrative complexity. At first glance this seems a disparate collection of thoughts on an equally disparate group of 'popular' performers: Lena Ashwell, George Formby, Leo Fuchs, Peter Lorre, Morecambe and Wise, Maggie Steed and Mark Rylance. This is the order in which they appear, but, apart from a vague sense of historical chronology, there seems to be no particular reason why they should be in this order.

Then there is the subject matter that leaps like Superman (who could easily find himself a place here) the tallest buildings with a single bound: the Northern sublime, two become one (think of the Spice Girls), Northern (again) television comedians, a North American Yiddish comedian, a cross-dressing player of Shakespeare, an Austro-Hungarian actor who became a spoof horror cartoon figure, a left-wing actress of the heyday of British political theatre, an early-to-mid-century actress and director who operated in every sense on London's cultural margins. I have changed the order of listing merely on the grounds that there doesn't seem to be much of a reason not to.

Despite appearances to the contrary this is not an attempt at weak wit, nor is it flippant. The twentieth century is difficult to define as a single and clearly defined narrative and the apparent disparity in the range and style of these essays does seem to be particularly apposite to a discourse on popular and extraordinary performers of that period. We cannot, nor should we, hope for such single clarity in the period represented by these essays. We may be certain that the authors, all of whom had a free rein in their choice of subject, chose to write about a performer who was, to them, extraordinary. However, while the extraordinariness is clear, at least to the authors, we are less certain in our definition of their claim to be popular. John McGrath's well-known distinction between 'popular' and 'populist' in *A Good Night Out* does not serve our purpose in this context, for while many of the performers represented are quite clearly working within a commercially driven system of cultural dissemination, they are motivated by many other factors.[1] Herein lie a series of internal contradictions—the performer striving to perform what is important (to her or him) often through a medium or economic structure in tension with the subject—that, in the teasing out that is accomplished in these essays, reveal ever more contradictions, or, like Peer Gynt's onion, maybe nothing. King Lear's often-quoted 'Nothing will come of nothing' became a mantra for mid-twentieth-century existential theatrical readings, which saw a number of efforts to absorb popular performers (Max Wall being the obvious example) into the realms of high art. Was this 'extraordinary conflation' an attempt to highlight contradictions, or was it to suggest that underlying seeming difference there was a seamless whole (narrative) to culture?

The passion that represents Leo Fuchs or Morecambe and Wise demonstrates clearly a far more complex system of motives than profit margins (although we cannot discount that factor as an element). Even where the original work is founded in experimentation of a radical leftist nature, such as is demonstrated in the essay on Peter Lorre and the conversation with Maggie Steed, commercial imperatives, intrinsically embedded, are a deciding factor in the continuation in its original form, or not.

'The centre cannot hold, mere anarchy is loosed upon the world' (W.B. Yeats, 'The Second Coming'). Cultural centres, clearly defined single narratives, could not hold in the twentieth century, no more than they can in the twenty-first century. I am not convinced about anarchy, mere or otherwise, in any shape or form, as my sense is that anarchy has its roots in an earlier European form of individualism and the reified self. However, Peter Thomson has often expressed the view that he would like to be able to move centres to margins and, by implication, margins to centres. I have always understood him to mean, by aspiring to this state of cultural affairs, a form of cultural de-centralization. In contemporary Britain we are familiar with the concept of de-centralization in the form of political debating chambers. In the Western world (which to a large extent forms the 'binding' subject of this collection of essays) we are familiar with centralized cultures and the attempt to move centres to margins. On the large scale, do we accept Paris, Berlin, New York or London as the place where the centre is to be found; or could it be Montpellier, Hamburg, Seattle or Newcastle? Of course, this is a rather crude model based on cities. What may be of much greater concern is a sense of the value of margins in ways of thinking or acting. Anyone who knows London will support the view that the centre, if there be one, is rather small in the overall scale of the conurbation; and there is no guarantee that it will always be in the same place.

Having no guarantee that the centre will always be in the same place means that we may consider that the shift of culture from margins (edges) to centres, and vice versa, extends beyond a geographical location (although that notion is in itself enough to engage the intellectual curiosity) to the complex shifting sands of ideology. A margin (including self- marginalizing and concepts of constructed otherness) holds no mystical primacy or ontological acceptance of priority over a centre. However, what is of interest, in the shifting, is the changing of meaning and the challenge to the idea that the meaning never shifts from one position to another, but necessarily possesses all the qualities of quicksand. The remaining begged question is, 'does quicksand have a stable bottom'? By whichever means we engage with the fragmented vision of the twentieth century and after, we do not seek a narrative but narratives. We cannot employ certainty, but record uncertainty in the certain knowledge that lurking behind all of this is a narrative in the early twenty-first century that is too appalling to contemplate. If that is read as a contradiction, be assured that is exactly what it is meant to be.

The following essays reveal Dymkowski's Ashwell pursuing 'an ambition greater for her audiences than for herself'; Kershaw's spectres of a collapsed sublimity; Schechter's paradigm of two cultures (and yet neither?) at once; McCullough's putative Hamlet engorged by the 'swamp'; Boon's two as one construction/deconstruction; Chambers/Steed's subtle conflation of the actress and character needing to be full of life because that's what's needed; White and Rylance's informing the past by the present. This disparate selection of essays, to say nothing of a disparate collection of ideologies in writing, fails to sum it all up, and that is just as it should be. Extraordinary, don't you think?

CHAPTER EIGHT

Lena Ashwell and her Players

Popular Performers on Extraordinary Stages

Christine Dymkowski

If the movers and shakers of English theatre in the first half of the twentieth century were to assemble, improbably but hierarchically, in some celestial playhouse, Lena Ashwell could justly claim a seat in the front row. Yet her accomplishments are nearly unsung. Although feminist theatre historians have been documenting her varied theatrical activities for some time,[1] she gets scant or no mention in conventional histories of the period.[2] In this essay, I will very briefly survey her rich theatre career before focusing on her work for the Lena Ashwell Players, with special reference to the Players' 1925 production of St John Ervine's *The Ship*.[3]

Ashwell (1869–1957) began her professional acting career in 1891, finally making her name in the title role of Henry Arthur Jones's *Mrs Dane's Defence* in 1900.[4] Her ambition as an actor soon led her into management as well: as she explains in her memoirs, although she was herself a big draw, with audiences demanding their money back when she was unable to play, 'the actor-manager [prevalent in the period] needed to keep the attention of the public on himself as the centre of attraction'.[5] However, Ashwell's entry into management was inspired by more than self-interest, as she was equally concerned to 'produce serious works, and prove that there is as big a public for them, when they are of the right sort and properly presented, as for the lighter and more frivolous productions that have ruled so long'.[6] After a couple of false starts,[7] she obtained a 99-year lease on Penley's Theatre, gutted the interior and rearranged the seating, installed the latest electric lighting, and renamed the newly decorated building the Kingsway.[8] She committed her enterprise to the production of serious plays as well as comedies, to the establishment of an ensemble company and a repertory system, to the nurturing of new playwrights, and to the improvement of the standard of entr'acte music.[9] In these ways, Ashwell emulated many of the ideals of the Vedrenne-Barker management of the Court, which, having failed to survive its transfer to the Savoy, was nearing its end; in fact, many contemporary reviewers saw her venture as a possible replacement for it.[10]

The first production, *Irene Wycherley*, by the unknown Anthony P. Wharton, opened in October 1907, a critical and commercial success followed by the even more successful *Diana of Dobson's*, by Cicely Hamilton. Despite this strong start, however, the venture soon ran into trouble, with subsequent plays proving less popular and promised financial support from Ashwell's backers never materializing.[11] As a result, Ashwell was hard-pressed even to complete her second and final season at the Kingsway: it was saved only by Otho Stuart's agreement to produce James B. Fagan's *The Earth* on a 'sharing terms' basis.[12] Whatever disappointment she felt at the time, Ashwell later remarked that the failure of the enterprise left her free to organize 'Concerts at the Front' some years later, out of which the Lena Ashwell Players eventually grew.[13]

In November 1914, under the auspices of the Women's Auxiliary Committee of the YMCA, Ashwell began organizing entertainment for troops overseas, sending her first concert party to Le Havre the following January; eventually plays were also performed, with repertory companies established at Le Havre, Rouen, Dieppe, Etaples, Abbeville and Paris. By the time of the Armistice, Ashwell had 'twenty-five parties in France alone giving fifty entertainments a day, fourteen hundred a month'; even after it, the 'Lenas' carried on their work throughout the devastated and occupied territories of Europe, as well as in the Middle East.[14] Some years later, Ashwell explained that 'The experiences of those four years forced me to change my attitude towards the Theatre, and transformed me from being very ambitious for myself into being still more ambitious for a cause'.[15]

At the end of the war, the sum of £3,000 was left from the £100,000 Ashwell had raised to support the enterprise, and she now sought to put it to the service of a dual peacetime cause. On the one hand, 'some sort of demobilisation plan [was needed] which would enable some of the artists to pick up the threads of their professional life', and on the other, her wartime audiences' experiences

> made me believe that there were thousands of people who could be made
> happier if our work continued in time of peace as a relief from ugly and
> sordid conditions in town life, for the education of the soul, . . . the awak-
> ening of broader interest in the life of other nations and of other times. For
> the understanding of other people's difficulties, for the stimulating of all
> that is highest, best, and most adventurous in the human spirit there is no
> more powerful agent than the theatre.[16]

Consequently, Ashwell used the funds to give concerts in hospitals and to rent the Baths at Bethnal Green, a working-class area in London's East End, in order to present a short season of plays in repertory; when the building was turned into a cinema, she moved to a small hall at Hanwell, where her work came to the attention of the local mayor, Clement Attlee, who was also chairman of the Labour mayors.[17] He arranged a meeting between Ashwell and the other London Labour mayors, at which it was agreed that she would

> find a company of players who would play in their town halls, or, in the public baths; that the season should be the autumn and winter months; that I should meet the expenses, the company, authors' fees, music, trans-port, office, [advertising,] etc.; that we should have the halls at a nominal charge, that we should play at each of them one night in the week, that they should circulate our printed bills [with the rates demands]; that after the season we should show our books; paying a percentage of the profit.[18]

Thus were born The Lena Ashwell Once-a-Week Players, who in 1923 changed their name to The Lena Ashwell Players in order 'to relate [their] enterprise with the War work' the 'Lenas' had done.[19] Not surprisingly, given their hectic schedule, Ashwell herself referred to them as 'The Roundabouts'.[20]

The Players began as a single company, growing to two and then three and eventually having their own London theatre base. Ashwell's Appendix to *Myself a Player* reproduces the venues and charts the growth of the players, but the information there does not always accord with that printed in programmes contemporaneous with events: for instance, the Appendix for the 1920–21 season lists regular performances once a week in four different venues,[21] whereas a programme for *Candida* in the same season shows eleven regular performances a week, all at different venues.[22] As Ashwell explains in her memoirs, occasionally 'a hall or baths had to be abandoned because the audience could not hear the actors, so bad were the acoustics';[23] in addition, 'with a change of party, some of our halls were taken from us as it was not possible to meet the higher rents offered for the purpose of dancing', while 'some authorities arranged dances so near the hall that the music distracted the attention of our audiences'.[24] In such cases, 'Ashwell had to cut her losses and move on quickly', perhaps leading to her later confusion about what venues the company played in when.[25] What is not in doubt, however, is the prodigious work undertaken in the ten years of the Players' existence, from 1919 to 1929:

> Performances were given in thirty-five venues in London and surrounding districts. Some of these were one-off visits; others involved weekly performances between late September and mid April every year. In addi-tion, Ashwell tried out and used nine theatres throughout the country for summer tours between May and August . . .[26]

The routine was gruelling, but Ashwell's solution was to expand rather than to retrench:

> Playing in a different hall, a different part of London every night, involved long journeys. Added to this, a different play every week, over a period of six months, together with the long rehearsals, proved too exhausting for the sound production of all the plays in the repertory . . . Our first rehearsals had been conducted on the roof of a building. Later, the office work, the cars for transport of the 'fit-up', and the rehearsals of two companies and the wardrobe had all been accommodated in a garage; and the strain on all the workers became too great. We needed larger premises, and secured the Century Theatre.[27]

This small theatre, in Archer Street, Notting Hill, originally known as the Bijou and then as the Victoria Hall, was built in the late eighteenth century; one of the five original patent houses, it had become a cinema by 1908.[28] As it had 'space enough for the carpenter's shop, property room, wardrobe, office, and rehearsal room for three companies',[29] Ashwell acquired it for the Players in 1924 and renamed it the Century. Since the Players had 'no money for such a capital expenditure', she launched an appeal for the £1,500 necessary to bring the building up to the standards demanded by the London County Council.[30] Acquisition of the Century made the Players' schedule less exhausting: as Ashwell explains, performing plays there 'gave the actors a week of rest from the "fit-up" and the long journeys, and also the hope that their work might be seen—might lead, as it often did, to more profitable engagements'.[31] At first, one of the companies played at the Century only on Thursday, Friday and Saturday evenings,[32] but eventually the number of performances was stepped up: an undated programme for *Lilies of the Field* notes that the Players' three companies alternated between the 'A' circuit, the 'B' circuit, and the Century, with performances at the theatre and on both circuits every evening from Monday to Saturday, as well as a Saturday matinée at the theatre.[33]

Ashwell's interest in accessibility meant that tickets were easy to obtain and inexpensive. Seats at venues in the outlying boroughs were bookable at 'Town Halls, Public Libraries, and all Booking Centres', while those at the Century could be reserved not only at the box office but also at 'the usual Libraries'.[34] The cost of seats at the touring venues ranged from 6d to 2s excluding tax, or from 8d to 2s 4d including it, while charges at the Century were more widely varied and set slightly higher at 1s 2d, 2s 4d, 3s 6d and 5s 9d, including tax.[35] In today's terms, that means the cheapest seat at a town hall or bath was about 69 pence without and 92 pence with tax, while the most expensive was about £2.77 without and £3.23 with tax; at the Century, the tax inclusive prices ran from the cheapest at about £1.62 to the most expensive at £7.97.[36]

However, a programme for the 1921–22 season notes that 'a reduction on even these prices is obtainable by taking advantage of [the] system of season tickets';[37] as Ashwell was keen to encourage regular attendance and to build a steady audience, a subscription scheme was also available at the Century. The announcement of the spring 1929 programme indicates that playgoers could subscribe to see twelve plays for either 35s or 25s (£48.51 and £34.65 in today's money). The same announcement also suggests that the most expensive prices had been abolished: reserved stalls and balcony stalls seats cost 3s 6d, reserved seats in the pit 2s 4d if booked in advance, and unreserved seats in the pit 1s 2d.

The repertoire Ashwell presented to her audiences was unusually diverse, prompting critic and playwright St John Ervine to comment that 'I know of no other theatre in London where there is such a varied selection of plays'.[38] His remark came half-way through the Century's 1925 autumn programme, during which the Players presented twelve plays in the course of as many weeks, between 28 September and 14 December: Arnold Bennett's *The Great Adventure*, Alfred Sutro's *The Laughing Lady*, A.A. Milne's *The Dover Road*, James Barrie's *What Every Woman Knows*, Allan Monkhouse's *The Education of Mr Surrage*, Shakespeare's *The Tempest*, Ibsen's *An Enemy of the People*, Shakespeare's *Julius Caesar*, H.M. Walbrook's *John Drayton, Millionaire*, Noël Coward's *The Young Idea*, St John Hankin's *The Charity that began at Home* and Shaw's *Misalliance*.[39] Ashwell's truly eclectic repertoire, embracing Shakespeare and other classics, popular contemporary plays, new works and foreign drama, provided her many audiences with a varied and affordable diet of theatre not easily available elsewhere. Other non-commercial repertory theatres like the Everyman (est. 1920), Gate (est. 1925) and Arts (est. 1927) offered similar fare but were more exclusive ventures, either being run as private clubs or located in areas like Hampstead, where the 'leaven of authors, painters, actors, lawyers and other professionals and progressives . . . provide[d] the regular nucleus of an audience'.[40]

Ashwell's aim to give her diverse audiences productions of Shakespeare, 'all the great moderns and the leading foreign dramatists'[41] was rooted in her passionate belief in the value of theatre to transform lives and attitudes, by its power to challenge set ideas, stimulate imagination, and provoke thought: 'What do the people gain? A glimpse into the lives of all classes of the community which naturally gives them understanding sympathy with human life as a whole, and so breaks down class barriers.'[42] The reception of the Players' productions proved her point:

> At a time of the most extreme class antagonism we have played *The Skin Game*, by Galsworthy to enthusiastic audiences; and Ibsen's *Enemy of the People* was received with breathless interest, and this in districts where we could not play the National Anthem.[43]

The Players were performing Galsworthy's piece in January 1924, just as the first Labour government took office for a brief nine months, before falling victim to anti-Communist hysteria, both within and without the party.[44] Ibsen's play was performed in early November 1925, just six months before the General Strike, a time of growing discontent and further controversy about the role of Communists within the trade union movement, Labour Party, and England itself.[45] Some of the controversy was particularly focused on Battersea, one of the Players' main strongholds, with a Communist MP in the north of the borough and a Conservative one in the south:[46] this is probably one of the districts to which Ashwell's comment applies.

It is clear the Players' choice of repertory was not timid in the face of current events. Nor was it imposed on its audiences: Ashwell, intent on 'secur[ing] full co-operation between the Players and the Public[,] . . . to this end' formed 'The Friends of the Players' in 1923, with membership costing a minimum of 1s (about £1.39 today).[47] Margaret Leask notes that 'members had the opportunity to make repertoire suggestions which Ashwell tried to incorporate into the company's schedule'.[48]

Ashwell's commitment to Shakespeare as well as to modern and foreign drama was extensive, with the Players presenting thirteen of his plays, often tying productions to those being studied and examined in schools.[49] Ashwell herself directed *The Merchant of Venice* in 1920–21 (revived 1922–23); *As You Like It* in January 1923 (revived February 1926); *Othello* in February 1924; *King John* in March 1925; and, with Paget Bowman, *The Taming of the Shrew* in 1921–22 (revived October 1923).[50] On his own, Bowman produced *Twelfth Night* in January 1921 (revived November 1923) and *Much Ado About Nothing* in 1921–22 (revived 1922–23). Nancy Price directed *The Merry Wives of Windsor* in December 1923, while Beatrice Wilson was responsible for *Macbeth* in October 1924, *Hamlet* in November 1924, *The Winter's Tale* in January 1925, and *The Tempest* and *Julius Caesar* both in November 1925. As this list makes clear, the Lena Ashwell Players afforded considerable opportunities to women directors, who went on to make further contributions to British theatre: for example, Nancy Price founded the People's National Theatre in 1930, which provided 'an extensive programme of non-commercial drama, ranging from Euripides to Pirandello', until its building was destroyed in 1941,[51] while Beatrice Wilson continued to direct as well as to teach at the Royal Academy of Dramatic Art (RADA) and the Old Vic.[52]

Because the Players' Shakespeare revivals seem not to have been reviewed, little can be gleaned about production methods and values, apart from scant information contained in the programmes themselves. Ashwell, commenting generally about the Players' productions, records that they 'could use nothing but curtains for scenery',[53] although some evidence suggests that occasional productions were more than minimal in this regard. Ashwell also notes that the demands on a small group 'to rehearse all day, play at night, and study the new parts for a weekly change of programme' meant that

> At first the plays were not very well rehearsed. Thus, in the last act of 'The Merchant of Venice', a delightful young actor forgot his lines and, in the middle of the scene, could not remember the cue for the general exit at the end. He had to do his best: 'Come on. Let's hop it!'

Such textual infidelity was not, however, characteristic: the *Twelfth Night* programme (17 January 1921) notes that the play was 'given in its entirety, with one interval of ten minutes', while that for *The Merchant of Venice* similarly records the playing of the entire text with just one interval of twelve minutes. Some programmes note two short intervals,[54] which suggests that settings more substantial than curtains were used, and indeed the programme for the 1926 revival of *As You Like It* records 'settings designed by F. Napier Jones', who also acted the part of Le Beau.

Perhaps with a school audience in mind or perhaps simply to make Shakespeare more accessible to a general one, the programme for the 1921 *Much Ado* includes a useful glossary explaining terms and phrases like 'Signor Montanto', 'No young squarer', 'We'll fit the kid-fox', 'Daff'd all other respects', and 'We rack the value'. However, this provision should not imply that the productions were early twentieth-century versions of the blandest kind of BBC Schools Shakespeare. Following Granville Barker's lead, Wilson decided not to dress her 1925 *Winter's Tale* 'in any definite period, owing to anachronisms in the text';[55] her *Tempest*, staged later that year, was positively innovative in playing the entire opening scene with the loss of only half a line and in casting Godfrey Kenton as the first male Ariel to appear on a London stage since 1745.[56] Ariel was also given 'hair and robes of silver', a metallic depiction of the spirit that subsequently gained wide currency.[57]

While Ashwell good-humouredly acknowledged the occasional lapse in her over-worked actors' memories, other discerning critics found much to praise in their performances. In his preface to 'Sonnets of Good Cheer to the Lena Ashwell Players', John Masefield describes himself as

> deeply astonished and delighted when I found them playing with a spirit and grace which I had not seen before in any English company . . . Having seen them in a prose play, nothing would have kept me from going to hear them in poetry . . . As it happened, I saw them do *Twelfth Night*, which I have seen more frequently than any English play. I have perhaps seen every important production of *Twelfth Night* in the last twenty-eight years. I have seen some individual performances that were better, one or two scenes which stay more clearly in my memory and, of course, many settings which were far more elaborate and taking to the eye, but, I think, I have never seen or heard anything more poetical throughout. The play was the thing

with them; the bare boards and the poet's passion were all that they needed for their effects.[58]

Although reviews of the Players' productions are sparse, being reserved for premières and especially noteworthy revivals, those that exist confirm Masefield's high opinion of their standard of acting. *The Times* (23 November 1926), reviewing the revival of St John Ervine's *Jane Clegg*, comments that 'The acting is, as a whole, worthy of the play', with Esmé Church as Jane displaying 'a dignity and a subtle power that mark her as a tragic actress of high distinction'.[59] Ervine, reviewing the première of Masefield's 1927 *Tristan and Isolt*, praises Wilson's production as well as the acting, some of which was 'excellent'.[60] An unidentified review of Alfred Noyes's *Robin Hood* notes that 'the acting even of the lesser parts is more than adequate' and acclaims the 'distinguished work' of the three principals.[61]

The same review further remarks that although the production was given 'care', the stage was too small, a complaint that resurfaces in other notices, such as that for Masefield's *Good Friday*, performed in April 1925: 'having regard to the smallness of the stage, the performance is remarkable'.[62] In this case, Wilson turned potential disadvantage to good effect, incorporating the whole theatre into the performance space. The programme note asks

> the audience [to] imagine that the stage is the Gabbatha or paved court, outside the Roman citadel; that the doors at the back of the stage lead into the Roman Barracks, the main gate of which is down below; and that all other exits lead down by steep paths into the city of Jerusalem.[63]

One critic praises as 'striking' the 'distribution of the crowd entering from the auditorium and clambering up upon the stage'; another admires its 'vigour and swiftness of collective emotion very rare in the mechanical mobs of the theatre', adding that each of the amateurs comprising the crowd 'remain[s] continually aware of their parts'.[64] Both reviewers also praise the professional principals, with the first particularly admiring the way two of the company delivered the rhymed verse.

The Observer review of the Players' February 1925 revival of Lennox Robinson's *The Lost Leader*, a 'fine play'[65] about Charles Stewart Parnell, vividly illustrates the company's commitment to well-acted drama that was political in the widest sense—that is, of engaging the minds of its audiences, of crediting them with an interest in social values and structures. Originally produced at the Abbey Theatre, Dublin, in February 1919,[66] Robinson's had been

> The first play clearly and obviously of the first class to be produced in London after the period of the war and the armistice . . . and was the first

important break in the revue, musical-comedy, song-and-dance-show
mania that theatrical authority in general had decided was the stuff to give
the troops. . . Miss Ashwell's players tackled it boldly, blessed in having
Mr. Frederick Leister to give a really notable performance in the great
Parnell part, and fortunate in Mr. Harold Payton, Mr. Clive Woods, Mr.
J. Hubert Leslie, and Miss Esmé Church among the other characters. A
play of the quality of 'The Lost Leader' is easy to act, bringing so much
with it from its own content before ever the personalities of the actors have
told on the audience. But this is not to say it could not have been acted
badly. The company handled it, instead, in a way that added to their prestige.[67]

Random surviving notices such as those quoted above attest to the Players'
ad hoc fulfilment of their stated goals, but a fuller picture of the company's
achievements can emerge only from a range of reviews of the same production, and for this reason it is time to examine one of them in detail.

The production that best lends itself to such a consideration is the Players'
revival of St John Ervine's *The Ship*, first produced at the Liverpool Playhouse
on 24 November 1922.[68] Its revival by the Lena Ashwell Players in January
1925 at the Century Theatre[69] attracted wide notice in the national press not
only because it marked the play's London première, but also because it occasioned the return of Lena Ashwell herself to the stage after an absence of nine
or ten years.[70] Ashwell explains she undertook the role because 'There was
some stupid idea that the companies were composed of amateurs, so I determined to act in all the boroughs myself as no one could accuse me of being
anything but a professional'.[71] Audiences and critics enthusiastically
welcomed Ashwell's re-emergence as an actor, but as her remark makes clear,
her return was motivated by a desire to establish once and for all the Players'
professional credentials rather than by her own hankering to perform again.
The run of *The Ship* proved to be the last in which she participated.[72]

A brief plot-summary will help the reader to make sense of critical response
to the production. Ervine's three-act play opens in the Thurlow home, inhab-
ited by Mrs Thurlow, her son John, his wife Janet, and their children Jack and
Hester.[73] The audience quickly discovers that John owns the largest shipyard
in the world and that Jack no longer wants any part of it: the three weeks he
has just spent in France have consolidated his feeling that 'Machines defile
people' (p. 19), and he intends to turn to farming. His father refuses to fund
his proposed venture, but his grandmother comes to the rescue despite his
'rather silly' ideas, believing that 'no one can make you realize how silly they
are so well as you can' (p. 35).

The next act takes place five months later on Jack's farm, which he runs
with his business partner, Captain Cornelius, a hard-drinking and disillusioned war veteran who does not share Jack's enthusiasm for bucolic life.

When the Thurlows come to visit, John, still hoping to entice Jack back to the shipyard, offers Cornelius £1,000 to make the farm fail or £500 simply to leave Jack on his own; Jack overhears the attempted bribe, and Cornelius openly, rather than underhandedly, accepts the second offer in his presence. Despite his anger, Jack colludes with John in keeping the latter's worst machinations hidden from Old Mrs Thurlow: she learns about John's £500 offer to help Cornelius leave but not his attempted £1,000 bribe, and, as a result, cannot understand Jack's 'uncharitable' attitude to his father (p. 60).

Act III, returning the action three months later to the Thurlow house, begins ominously with Old Mrs Thurlow reading aloud Arthur Waller's poem 'On the picture of a fair youth, taken after he was dead'. John is ill and tells Jack, who has made a success of his farm, that he wants him to take his place on the maiden voyage of his revolutionary new ship, the *Magnificent*. When Jack refuses, John determines to go himself, even though his doctors have warned him that such a trip might prove fatal; Jack therefore relents. The act's second scene, five days later, opens in the garden with John anxiously awaiting word about the ship's progress, as its first three days at sea have broken all records. News this morning is late, and as the ship was emphatically proclaimed to be 'unsinkable' early in the play (p. 27), the audience is well prepared for the bad news that soon arrives. The final scene occurs that night, with John preparing to shoot himself when his mother enters; he hides the gun and expresses his guilt about forcing Jack to his death. When she realises, '*horrified*', what he was about to do, she reminds him that Jack's death appears to have been avoidable: he refused to leave the boat, saying ' "My father built this ship, and if he were here, he'd go down with her. I've taken his place, and I must do what he would wish" ' (p. 77). Old Mrs Thurlow explains that although John was 'wrong about Jack . . . he was wrong about you' (p. 78), finally persuading him that he owes it to his son to continue his own work. The play ends with her alone on stage, venting her own grief, before contemplating the moonlit garden, turning out the light, and leaving the room to its empty silence.

This necessarily reductive synopsis unfortunately emphasizes the play's more formulaic aspects. It reads much more engagingly than I have managed to convey, and, as a contemporary critic noted, 'It acts much better than it reads, as is the habit of Mr. Ervine's plays'.[74] Despite being categorized by some London critics obviously used to lighter fare as 'a play of the Manchester repertory gloom-and-realism type',[75] it actually has 'as much good comedy in it as the majority of plays that set out for nothing but comedy'.[76]

Reviews overwhelmingly endorse Ashwell's decision to stage the play and use it as an occasion to castigate usual West End fare.[77] No less a critic than J.T. Grein, founder of the Independent Theatre, commented that

there is something rotten in the state of Denmark when such a good play

> as this cannot find a theatre within the magic circle which has Shaftesbury
> Avenue for its centre . . . there are few plays that one can enthuse unre-
> servedly about, and 'The Ship' is one of them.[78]

Nor is his opinion unrepresentative. *Observer* critic Hubert Griffith remarked
that

> the year at its end will need to have been a very remarkably good year
> indeed if, among all the plays produced during its twelve months, 'The
> Ship' does not still keep rank as one of its three or four finest . . . its intro-
> duction [adds] one more to the long list of services that we owe Miss
> Ashwell . . . When I think of the play as a whole, and of 75 per cent. of
> the plays that during the last eighteen months have been produced as alter-
> natives to it, I do not know whether it is the theatre managers who are
> Bedlamite, or whether it is that they hold that opinion of the public they
> serve.[79]

The *Evening Standard* complained that '[only the West End managers of some
very recent productions could tell us] why one should have to go to Notting
Hill to see a fine actress and a new play that does not insult the intelligence'.[80]
Many reviewers confidently predicted that a West End management would
soon snap up the play,[81] while Herbert Farjeon anticipated that the Century
Theatre would do 'for Notting Hill what the Everyman has done for
Hampstead. It is another step in the direction of decentralisation, another
active protest against the hegemony of the West End . . .'[82]

Critical praise was not confined simply to Ervine's play but also lavished
on the standard of acting: not only was *The Ship* 'more worth while than nine-
tenths of the plays produced in West End theatres, [but] . . . the acting of
Lena Ashwell and her company is certainly far above the average of stage
work'.[83] The *Daily Telegraph* noted that while 'cynical people are apt to tell
you sometimes that if you want to see the best acting in London you must go
away from the centre of things', this production 'brilliantly proved' the point,
as 'much of its acting is nothing short of brilliant. Every part that is of any
importance is made to tell at its full value.' Grein thought 'the performance
all round . . . worthy of unstinted praise', adding that 'the whole balance of
the company is admirable, and their playing is so satisfying that all who love
a good play well acted should make the pilgrimage to Notting Hill'. Griffith
found the acting 'so admirable that I only wished Mr Ervine might have been
in England to take a look at his own play. Knowing the standard that authors
expect—and rarely get—I can hardly say more.'

While most reviews focus particularly on the performances of Lena Ashwell
as Old Mrs Thurlow, Frederick Leister as her son John, and Philip Reeves as
Captain Cornelius,[84] the number that praise virtually each of the actors indi-

vidually is striking testimony to the real ensemble work of the Players. The *Daily Telegraph*, for example, notes that Daphne Heard was 'good as Hester— much better than most of the young actresses one encounters in West-end plays', and that Katie Johnson 'score[d] as John Thurlow's wool-witted and inconsequent wife'; the *Morning Post* similarly comments that Johnson 'made a good thing of a well trained wife', and the *Daily News* reports that she made her 'commonplace view of life seem natural and unforced'.[85]

Ashwell's own performance in a part seen by some critics as not particularly 'strenuous'[86] was praised particularly for its vocal quality. Though Edith Shackleton supposed not 'one grandmother in every 10,000 can hope for so rich and tender a voice as hers', Grein urged 'younger actresses to go and listen to her speak', with E.A.B. seconding his opinion: 'they would learn . . . how a trained elocutionist . . . can give just the right inflexion of meaning to a word, so that everything the author intended is expressed dramatically and naturally'. The latter reviewer added that 'they would also learn the value of acting': he had seen the original Liverpool production, and Ashwell's performance made the part gain 'in meaning and in poignancy of emotion'.[87] The *Daily Telegraph* similarly found her Old Mrs Thurlow 'a most moving figure' who 'sets the whole tone of the play, and does it with a quiet distinction and a restrained but powerful emotion which are alone enough to make this stand out as a production out of the ordinary'.[88] It is worth pointing out that Ashwell had made her name playing a very different kind of role: as Mr Gossip noted, her 'gentle charm' here made 'her Leah Kleschna and Katusha in "The Resurrection" seem a long way off'.[89]

It is also worth examining the way in which the play hit a couple of contemporary nerves. Some reviewers, like the *Evening Standard's* E.S.H., found Jack 'the least convincing of the characters. He talks as though "News from Nowhere" has just been published, though his sister is so much of the moment that she can tell her father he "swears like a flapper".'[90] However, in a much more considered review, Cicely Hamilton argues that the play, in dealing 'with the conflict between the older and younger generation', is

> acutely modern, in its treatment of an everlasting problem. His father and son are of to-day, of our post-war world; where a youth that hardly remembers the old order is out of touch with a maturity whose ideas the old order moulded . . . Ten years ago young Thurlow would have been merely a crank—a belated adherent of Ruskin and Butler, an impossible subject for a play; today he is a type recognisable, the mouthpiece of a widespread distrust.[91]

Cornelius rather than Jack, however, hit the rawest post-war nerve, with reviewers sharply divided about the relationship of this 'unconventional wartype' to actual veterans.[92] For one, he 'propounds the common idea that after what he has done in the war he deserves an easy time as compensation', while another complains that Ervine's 'ex-officers do not speak like ex-officers in real life. They prate too much of their hardships before a mixed company. That is a thing that "isn't done".'[93] E.A.B. demurs that 'Cornelius's expression of a soldier's disillusion . . . is not really part of the drama itself' and therefore 'throws the play out of gear', while Griffith remonstrates that this 'extremely acute, penetrating, and brilliant study' of a disillusioned veteran who senses 'the hopelessness of life', although 'a true' portrait, is also a 'minority' one that needs to be answered by another play showing the opposite type.[94] Unsurprisingly, critical judgement of the character veers between damning and sympathetic: for some reviewers, Cornelius is a 'degenerate', 'disillusioned and unscrupulous', 'selfish self-appointed war hero', 'a nasty drunken fellow' who provides the actor with a 'distasteful role'.[95] For others, he is an 'unnerved victim of the war', 'war-shattered' and 'nerve-wrecked', taking his cue from the 'I'm all right, Jack' attitude displayed all too often on the battlefield.[96] The *Daily Herald*, hailing 'a brilliant study of a disillusioned ex-Army officer, up against an ungrateful society and cynically only out for a good time', thought that 'as showing the mental effect of war on a large class of young men, this sketch is admirable peace propaganda'.[97]

Critical reaction to the actors, particularly to Philip Reeves who played Cornelius, demonstrates the lack of overlap between the Players' West End and suburban critics and audiences. Reviewers on local papers mention Reeves 'was as usual very clever' and 'acted with his usual power', while Frederick Leister as John 'acted with his usual skill and clever restraint'.[98] For London and national critics, however, these players, whose acting was 'admirable', were 'quite unknown to the regular theatre-goer'.[99] Reeves was hailed as 'the "find" of the production . . . an actor of whom the sooner the West-end managers hear the better . . . Nothing so impressive has been done by an unknown actor since Mr. Frederick Cooper's achievement at the first appearance of "Outward Bound".'[100] Another reviewer claimed 'most of the superlatives in the language' would be used to describe Reeves's performance,[101] while a third declared that

> The pretended callousness with which he hides his hurt, the little outbreak in which he tells how he heard a lark singing at the front, his hardness, his weakness, his whole air of having fallen loose, are given . . . with a judgment and restraint that almost reconciles us in his case to applause that interrupts the action of a play.[102]

While the acting clearly proved a triumph for the Players' production of *The Ship*, setting—or lack of an adequate one—proved its one failure:

> The players had to struggle against that least satisfactory of stage settings,

a compromise between curtains and painted scenery, which made the
shipbuilder's massive home seem only a little less squalid than his reac-
tionary son's farm quarters.[103]

The production also simplified Ervine's settings for the three scenes of Act
III, which the text places respectively in a room of the Thurlow house, a corner
of the garden, and the same room of the house, confining all the action to the
room. Shackleton, acknowledging that 'many West-end plays are damaged
by the costliness of their settings', nevertheless felt that *The Ship* 'suffers from
its economical jumble of curtains'.[104] However, as the very positive critical
response to the production overall demonstrates, Hamilton was right in
claiming that 'the play held all through—on its merits, with the minimum of
scenery'.[105]

The Ship proved so successful that it was revived, uncharacteristically, on
27 April for a straight three-week run at the Century Theatre, which was then
extended 'for another few weeks'.[106] Most of the cast, including Ashwell,
returned to play their original parts, but there was some change of personnel:
as Jack, Robert Glennie replaced Clive Woods, who had first produced the
play, while Frederick Leister now directed as well as continued to play John.[107]
Ashwell noted in her memoirs that the production 'was very successful, financially as well as artistically', with the money—always a problem for the
Players—helping 'considerably towards the opening of the 1925–26
season'.[108]

Sadly, the Players were to have only three more seasons after that. Ashwell
complains in her memoirs that 'without the Entertainment Tax we certainly
should have survived'.[109] This tax, a wartime measure that was to have a debil-
itating effect on the theatre for the following three decades, was 'based on
gross box-office receipts rather than profit', 'which meant that the government could make money from the run of a play, even if the production lost
money for the management'.[110] Ashwell notes that in 1926–27, 'for entertaining 174,000 people, we were taxed £3,683 6. 8.' (£102,102 in today's
terms), and that 'every year [the tax] defeated our hopes of financial
stability'.[111] Ashwell's deputation to Winston Churchill, then Chancellor of
the Exchequer, 'imploring the treasury to remit the Entertainment Tax', came
to nothing, as did the public appeal signed by Stanley Baldwin, Lloyd George,
John Galsworthy, Johnston Forbes-Robertson and Sybil Thorndike, among
others.[112] When Ashwell finally discovered, 'at the end of the tenth year' of
the Players' existence, that her husband had lost £17,000 subsidizing their
activities, she 'took [her] courage in both hands and cancelled everything'.[113]
By this time, 'over fifty artists were employed in the three companies; and the
audiences had increased to 184,000 on the season'.[114]

Despite such a setback, Ashwell never lost her passion for theatre or her
belief in it as a force for change, continuing to act—in the wider sense of the

word—in many theatrical arenas until her death in 1957. Among other activities, she carried on her work with the British Drama League, campaigned for a National Theatre, advised ENSA (Entertainments National Service Association), and even produced plays for Moral Re-Armament until a few months before her death.[115] Her obituaries and posthumous appraisals recount her many firsts, but not surprisingly *The Times* had some years earlier surmised she might 'be best remembered for her pioneer work in taking a company of players to bring plays of merit to poor districts of London'.[116] Even if she had had no other accomplishments, her pursuit of an ambition greater for her audiences than for herself marks Ashwell out as an extraordinary actor indeed.

CHAPTER NINE

George Formby
and the Northern Sublime

Baz Kershaw

The Spirit is a Bone—Extremes Meet

> It is only when the music stops that I start raising provisos like a palisade
> around my liking for him. I cannot laugh when he fidgets, gapes and fusses
> flat-footed across the stage . . . and I am unable to accept the theory that
> a banality or catchphrase acquires wit or philosophy when delivered in a
> North Country accent. Simplicity and unaffectedness can be carried to
> extremes. Mr Formby works with what Henry James called 'great economy
> of means and—oh—effect'.[1]

Kenneth Tynan, fresh and no doubt cock-a-hoop from being First Player to
Alec Guinness's Hamlet, was 23 when he delivered this verdict in 1951.
George Formby was 47, turning portly, looking older than his years after bouts
of illness, yet still the audiences were raised to a pitch of near-ecstasy as he
plucked his banjulele in the musical *Zip Goes a Million*.[2] There were other
distances between the rising critic and the fading star. Tynan earned a pittance
as a junior reviewer on the London *Evening Standard*; Formby's weekly fee
was £1,500, plus profit-sharing from the box-office sell-out. Tynan was just
'down' from Oxford; Formby remembered leaving school aged 7 in 1911, to
muck-out in racing stables and train as a jockey. Hardly surprising, then, that
the review refracts a sundering of sensibilities in the traditional two-way snob-
beries between a 'common' North and a 'sophisticated' South, still strong in
this age of post-war austerity.[3] Note, too, the aesthetic abyss opened up by
Tynan's appeal to high art—through that awfully aloof Henry James—against
the populist dream-weaving of a West End show revelling in the vulgarity of
an enforced spending spree. Yet still, in this moment of teetering condemnation there is a paradoxical suturing of artist and critic that suggests a profound
vitality in the nature of extraordinary performance.

The paradox of the meeting of these particular extremes seems to turn on Tynan's oddly archaic image of the palisade. The provisos aim to enforce a conventional separation between music and acting, which rests in the Western philosophical traditions on yet more crucial cleavages between mind and body, spirit and bone. Against this I want to risk proposing a *complex singularity* in extraordinary performance, taking Formby's practice as a paradigm that denies all such binaries—for example, *only* Formby, flat feet and all, could produce the effects of that denial in precisely the way he did. From this perspective, the defensive violence of Tynan's metaphor is self-directed, because it aims to split his pleasure in Formby's performance from his horror at the signs that make it possible, in effect between his desire and rejection of the same 'thing'. The futility in this project of raising the stakes in the drama of love and loathing is suggested by where he locates it, in the moment of silence 'when the music stops'. For the pleasure and pain—however determined, say, by the critic's 'discrimination' or the artist's 'uneven skills'—cannot be separated in the silence through which they are joined. If anything, the empty silence insists that music and acting, mind and body, spirit and bone are one and the same thing. So there can be no denying, ultimately, that Formby's art, his whole extraordinary performance issued through arthritic toes, dodgy lungs and a dicky heart.[4] The paradox of such extremes meeting celebrates one of the common conjunctions in which the sublime can appear.

On the Sublime—Notes on Method

George Formby was a phenomenally successful Northern English popular entertainer in the mid-decades of the twentieth century. His records are still available on CD and his films on video. Even now, over forty years after his death, there are active websites for a fan-club as well as a George Formby Society, which meets annually in the Lancashire seaside town of Blackpool.[5] The first full biography, by David Bret, was published in 2001. Sub-titled *A Troubled Genius*, its main theme is the contrast between fabulous public success and a miserable private life. So this particular archive, appropriately dispersed across the media, is alive and gradually growing. The ghost of the Northern star still twinkles, as memories of him settle nicely into the nostalgic patina of the heritage industry.[6] Even from beyond the grave Formby's catch-phrase echoes: 'It's turned out nice again!'

So in comes I, wanting to trouble memories of the troubled genius. And why should I want to do that? Well, justification could be provided through the usual historiographic conventions used to single out the exceptional subject: he was a high-point representative of a long line of novelty popular entertainers, he made a terrifically successful transition from live music-hall to mass cinema popularity, he created a unique kind of music that influenced *even* the Beatles, he occupied a singular cultural space in the transition between the mechanical (modernist) and the electronic (postmodernist) eras, and so on; and, oh yes, he was possibly almost as popular as Stalin and definitely more popular than Churchill, etcetera. All grist to the mill of a deconstruction aimed at understanding his attraction through specifying his historical trajectory. And of course, that mill must turn in some of what follows. But also I want to disturb the record more playfully, to mess about with the webs of memory that interlace archives like snail-trails on a gravestone, to fly a frail kite of theory in the gaps between documents where perhaps the past truly moves, like eddies of air in the branches of dead trees.

But what might I make of 'extraordinary actors' that could properly complement the wisdom of the company kept here, because in this department, as the playwright Sacha Guitry said: 'The little I know, I owe to my ignorance.'[7] Fool that I am, perhaps the right task is in honestly trying to grasp something that seems to me forever beyond reach? For the extraordinary actor as such must surely, somehow, have been extraordinary in *live performance*, even if it was done for recording. But what kind of method, patently invoking an inevitable failure, might be appropriate to making such an attempt on the ephemeral? Fever for the archive in such an engagement—amassing material to provide a 'definitive account', sorting and ordering documents to 'confirm' a causality—is probably a pathology of certain critical doom. For in troubling the archive to *reveal* an extraordinary act, the uniqueness of which is inseparable from a past forever gone, we are bound to stretch all marks beyond breaking. As Derrida says of trying to identify the uniqueness of a footprint in ash:

> The possibility of the archiving trace, this simple *possibility*, can only divide the uniqueness. Separating the impression from the imprint. Because this uniqueness is not even a past present. It would have been possible, one can dream it after the fact, only insofar as its iterability, its immanent divisibility, the possibility of its fission, haunted it from the origin. The faithful memory of such a singularity can only be given over to the specter.[8]

Well, then, the exercise that follows must constitute one of unfaithful memorializing in search of a spectre, a disgraceful intrusion into the realms of the fabulous. This is why I feel compelled to evoke the sublime in my title. It will allow, I hope, for a critical strategy that may be as slippery as the question it is trying to answer, but one that might rightly take for its motto the words of another great devotee of silence, John Cage: 'I'm saying nothing and I'm saying it'.[9]

Because the sublime, according to Slavoj Žižek's interpretation of Hegel, appears in the collapse of contradiction—apparent absolute difference, say between impression and imprint, desire and disgust—into paradox.[10] Hence my subheadings invoke the weird sites of the sublime as identified by Hegel as re-read by Žižek: spirit is a bone, wealth is the self, state is monarch, God is Christ. If these appear merely as passing ciphers in my argument, it is perhaps because that is their proper place so far as the archive goes. I can make no apology for this displaced double ghost-writing, as it constitutes a necessary guying of the phantasmal specifics of the task I have unwisely set myself, of trying to resuscitate extraordinary acting. But maybe, just maybe, in this especially spectral territory for which we are heading, as a specialist in ghostly trading once said, through indirection might we find direction out. Or as George Formby put it in the song 'Believe it or Not' (1934):

> That night at 12 o'clock, just as the light she turned out,
> 'Who's that in my room,' she cried, and started to shout.
> I whispered, 'Shut-up, I'm the ghost I told you about.
> Perhaps you'll believe it now.'

Wealth is the Self—Scenes from a Life

> The Sublime [for Kant] is therefore the paradox of an object which, in the very field of representation, provides a view, in a negative way, of the dimension of what is unrepresentable . . . Hegel's position is, in contrast, that there is *nothing* beyond phenomenality, beyond the field of representation . . . the sublime is an object whose positive body is just an embodiment of Nothing. In Kant, the feeling of the Sublime is invoked by some boundless, terrifying imposing phenomenon (raging nature, and so on), while in Hegel we are dealing with a miserable 'little piece of the Real'—the Spirit *is* the inert, dead skull; the subject's Self *is* this small piece of metal that I am holding in my hand . . .[11]

Paradoxical moments of extremes meeting such as that between Formby and Tynan in 1951 can surely seem to, as the sayings go, come out of the blue, emerge from nowhere, materialize out of nothing. Perhaps this is so for most of us. But if the sublime results from a conjunction of wholly contradictory impulses provided for us by an object especially inscribed with radical negativity, then might some be able to manifest themselves as such an object? And if so, what gestures and grimaces of the body, what languages of desire or domination might produce such a radical effect? These questions beg a search for the contradictions and paradoxes that make of the subject, in the traces of the archive, a disappearing act. Now you see it, now you don't.

So, listen, George Formby's creative career was riddled with contrasts,

contradictions and paradoxes. Just take a few facts from his life as an indefatigable ENSA entertainer and film star during the Second World War. The
arthritic toes, plus a minor chest ailment, in 1940 caused an army examining
board to reject him for military service. Yet the social survey Mass
Observation found that he was the greatest single morale booster of the war,
ahead of the extremely popular weekly radio programme *ITMA* and Winston
Churchill.[12] His public persona was proudly heterosexual: his lifelong business manager, who jealously insisted always on being in the wings of the
theatre or on set when he was filming, was his wife Beryl, and his boats were
always called Lady Beryl and his houses Beryldene. Yet his 1943 film *Bell
Bottom George* had a cast that was almost exclusively, unashamedly gay and
was peppered with homoerotic scenes—just watch him singing 'It Serves You
Right' surrounded by posing, well-proportioned matelots, and imagine his
large following of closet queens swooning in secret raptures. Queer to think
that such slippery gestures and grimaces of the body should be part of a
production of power that was, in its way, greater than Churchill's.

These types of illogicality in the life-traces might be seen simply as evidence
of the kinds of excess that come with stardom, yet they contrast starkly with
the way his public persona was created through 'down to earth' social and
geographical reference. In the archive he is represented as always carrying his
past with him in an especially dense and inescapable manner, like a shark
trailing an old net full of many skeleton fish, and much of the detritus is especially marked by the forces of region and class. Referring to himself frequently
as 'an ordinary Lancashire lad', he aimed to be completely identified with the
industrial North of England. But this apparent stability of identity was, of
course, deceptive.

For example, all the Beryldenes (bar one which the Formbys hardly used)
were within sixty miles of his birthplace, the industrial town of Wigan in
Lancashire, and in a singular respect he was apparently tethered to this town
for life through the invention, by his father George Formby Snr, of 'Wigan
Pier'. Formby Jnr was fond of referring to this famous feature and it became
a corny fixture in his deliberately dire patter: 'Ah'm just an ordinary
Lancashire Lad. Ah suppose you'd call me a pup of Wigan Pier.'[13] In 1937
George Orwell helped to ensure its continuing fame through *The Road to
Wigan Pier*, though the great writer, having 'set his heart on seeing' it,
confesses that 'Wigan Pier had been demolished, and even the spot where it
used to stand is no longer certain'.[14] Indeed, not even what it physically *was*
is certain, though it appears not to have been anything like a pier, as it was
possibly either an elevated tramway or a 'small iron frame used to tip up coal
trucks to empty them into barges on the Liverpool-Leeds canal'.[15] The most
iconically powerful mark, passing from father to son, that anchored Formby's
identity to locality and class thus evaporates into nothing as the traces in the
archive shimmer with absolute uncertainly. And if *that* impression is untrust-

worthy in confirming a positive identity of the subject, then all the rest may be as well.

Moreover, the 'ties' to the north and its working-class poor also had an especially complex, perhaps phantasmal, generation through Formby's personal-professional relationship to his father. James Lawler Booth adopted the stage name George Formby around 1897 and developed his on-stage alter-ego, John Willie, in the first two decades of the twentieth century (Figure 17). A semi-destitute childhood had endowed this first Formby with a classic symptom of Northern working-class industrial life—pulmonary tuberculosis—which provided John Willie's trademark hacking cough and catchphrase: 'I'm coughing better tonight'. For many years one of the highest paid music-hall and pantomime acts in England, Formby Snr refused to let

Figure 17. 'The father whom he never saw perform.' Formby Snr as John Willie, *c.* 1915.

his son see him perform, right up until his death from a haemorrhage caused by a coughing fit in the wings of the Newcastle-upon-Tyne Empire Theatre in 1921. What uncanny forces, mostly disguised as good showbusiness sense, were at play in the next couple of years as Formby Jnr's mother, Eliza, quickly transmuted the shy stable lad into the very image of his dad? The songs, the make-up, the actual costume, and even on occasion the cough, were adopted for this strange resurrection—but not the name. For two years the second George Formby was billed under his mother's maiden name of Hoy, though usually with the sub-billing 'son of George Formby', or sometimes 'A Chip off the Old Block'.

But then the decisive transformation came in 1923, when George Hoy, still in his father's garb and more by accident than design, acquired a banjulele and almost immediate, extraordinary success with the punters. In a double shuffling of identities he jettisoned his father's appearance (except for his last pair of stage shoes, which Jnr kept as a mascot throughout his life) but finally embraced his stage name. George Formby Jnr was thus immaculately conceived through a shape-shifting of the boundaries between body and word, flesh and spirit in a ghostly passing across generations. As the name was taken, the body of the father was transformed into insubstantial stuff, an absent presence. But where, if anywhere, was George Hoy Booth in this weird trading between subjects?

George Formby Snr's photograph had hung over the main mantlepiece in the various Beryldenes. In his final public appearance on BBC television in 1960 Formby Jnr said of his father (the shift of tense seems to call up *his* spectre), 'he was certainly a great star. I don't think I'll ever be as good as him.'[16] By then, Beryl was dying and for many years he had been estranged from his mother and the rest of his family, seeing them as 'nothing but a load of money-grabbers',[17] yet he had specified in his will that he should be buried next to his father in the family grave. As the funeral cortège slowly trawled through the streets of Warrington on 10 March 1961, with Eliza in the limousine immediately following the hearse, 150,000 people lined the route, paying homage. These and many more had also paid coins in exchange for the pleasures provided by the dead man's extraordinary performances. But who—or more exactly, what—had he been? If the dense social and geographical grounding of the past as figured in the archive cannot provide adequate terms for an answer, perhaps this is because the subject had become a pathology that psychically, socially, economically, and otherwise, as it were *emptied* the life of its past, confounding expectations even as they appeared to be confirmed by incessant reiteration. The more we know, the less we think we know.

The State is Monarch—the Film Real

> Where can the subject who is thus 'emptied' find his objective correlative? The Hegelian answer is: in Wealth, in money obtained in exchange for flattery . . . The paradox, the patent nonsense of money—this inert, external, passive object that we can hold in our hands and manipulate— serving as the immediate embodiment of Self, is no more difficult to accept than the proposition that the skull embodies the immediate effectivity of the Spirit . . . if we start from language reduced to 'gestures and grimaces of the body', the objective counterpart to the subject is . . . the skullbone; but if we conceive language as the medium of social relations of domina- tion, its objective counterpart is of course wealth as the embodiment, as the materialisation of social power.[18]

The second George Formby was prolific. At the peak of his career in the 1930s and 1940s he produced records at the rate of about one a month, building to a list that eventually included almost 200 songs. Between 1934 and 1946 he made twenty-one full-length films, mainly with the Ealing, then Columbia, studios. For six years from 1938 he topped the touchstone Motion Picture Herald Poll as Britain's leading cinema box-office attraction, receiving 90,000 fan letters a year and with an official fanclub of 21,000. In a 1951 interview he claimed he had earned about £84,000 a year after tax, plus another £20,000 a year for charity; his five-year contract with Columbia alone was worth £500,000.[19] At his death in 1961 his estate was worth around £212,000. Yet he spent much of the war entertaining the troops at the stan- dard ENSA rate of £10 per week, and several of his post-war tours were indeed undertaken for charity. This ambivalence in the financial record was reflected in the purpose of the tours to Australia, New Zealand, Canada, South Africa and Scandinavia in the 1940s and 1950s, designed partly to compensate for his flagging popularity in Britain. But the pattern of his inter- national appeal was uneven: he never enjoyed great success in the USA, yet his 1940 film *Let George Do It* ran for a year in Moscow, and in 1944, according to John Fisher, 'a Russian poll showed [him] to be the most popular figure in Russia after Stalin'.[20]

Greater than Churchill, not quite so popular as Stalin: the buck-toothed, bulging-eyed, squeaky-voiced lad from Wigan was in dangerous company indeed, raising the stakes on what kinds of ideological transaction had produced such authority. The archive's ambivalence regarding just who or what this subject might have been poses another conundrum about the circu- lation of power in his performances: was this just another case of render unto Caesar that which is Caesar's, or were some other, fairer kinds of trade under way? Was this, in Hegel's terms, flattery of the monarch who substitutes wholly for the state, totally denying any rights to the people in the moment they praise him, or was some other game in play through which the 'masses' might gain some vestige of power?

Formby's film performances may be the best place to get a grip on these questions, because there he was most enmeshed in the machinations of capital as the engine of oppression. The films were offered by the industry as pure and simple entertainment, with Formby always playing the guileless and gormless anti-hero ensnared in plots of such risible contrivance that no-one could possibly take them seriously. His comical character was invariably caught in an intrigue between stereotypical 'goodies' and 'baddies' which puts him into a spiral of undeserved decline—typically losing face, friends and job—that places the object of his greatest desire, the pert and proper but suggestively sexual 'girl', increasingly out of reach. The denouements virtually always hinged on the girl recognizing his innocence and egging him on in a triumphal comeback that ends in sexual promise. The songs intersperse the plot like precious time-out in a busy schedule, and even when they drive on the narrative they are framed as 'something else'. This is particularly the case when Formby serenades the female star, the strumming of the banjulele always rising to an up-beat instrumental climax before the final verse, in patent witness to the sublimation of sex in the song. For all the surrounding flim-flam business gently satirizing ethical weakness and economic ambition, this insistent beat of ecstasy is the main undertow in the current of the drama's comic flow. The formulaic plots deliver a fantasy fulfilment.

To twenty-first-century eyes uninfected by nostalgia, though, these films almost certainly will look highly contrived and corny. They are also frequently marred by low levels of aesthetic and technical competence, the result of poor scripts, very uneven acting, clumsy editing, awkward camerawork, and more. Ideologically, they are riddled with misogyny, sexism, racism, jingoism, and other evils consequent upon their stereotypical view of the world. A common defence for this syndrome from scholars of popular culture has been that the conventional moral rectitude is required as a trigger to spark off opposing psychic forces, most commonly found in the anti-structures of the carniva-lesque, saturnalia, bacchanalia, and so forth, to create what Richard Dyer has described as a 'utopia of sensibility'.[21] From this perspective the sloppy production of Formby's films may even become a factor in understanding how their public was empowered. The list of 'faults' is so easily compiled that one wonders whether audiences even noticed them, or in noticing did not care about them because they were caring more about something else. But if that 'something else' was empowering, then it must still have been so ambivalently, for after the final reel it is back to political business as usual as Formby goes off laughing all the way to the bank. The public have flattered the monarch of perform-ance in paying their dues to the point where perhaps all passion is spent. So these further stories from the celluloid part of the archive unfortunately serve to make the extraordinary in Formby's performance even more inaccessible.

We must look a little more closely and obliquely at these shoddy items, hazarding guesses about their more fabulous resonances, perhaps in the way Formby seemed positively to revel in the denials of his fictional roles: to strength, good looks, manliness, normal physical coordination, and so on— in a word, invulnerability. There is a telling description of him at the mid-point of his career, which recognizes that he was on a kind of cusp, on the verge of international success in the balance between live and mediated performance:

> He is a broad comedian, a knockabout clown . . . and still half a variety artist in a strange element. He also has that spark of personality that breeds universal appeal and commands universal affection. His teeth and the dumb grin are his properties, like the clown's red nose and white diamond patch. *But the spirit of Formby is in the eyes.* There is a smile in them that can turn to the most touching pathos, like the eyes of a spaniel. There is also in them an unquenchable optimism that sums up the very essence of his character . . .[22]

This appeared in 1937, the year Formby made two films that were highly successful at the box office—*Keep Fit* and *I See Ice*—and in which his character was especially vulnerable. If there is a recognition of some kind of disjunction in the acute view that he is 'half a variety artist in a strange element'— a kind of filmic alien?—then there is another, more stupendous, in the perception that links the 'eyes of a spaniel' with the very 'essence of his character'. This ghosts the idea that the eyes are the window to the soul, but it fails to offset the stress already laid in the impression of an animal spirit. An animal spirit with soul? What kind of creature are we being hailed towards here?

Fascination with the eyes of film stars has a long pedigree, of course. This is partly produced by the technical achievement of the close-up, but also by the ocular structures of film itself: we are looking through two lenses, the lens of the eye through the lens of the camera, into a third lens on screen which despite its enormous visual presence is in all other respects absent. This is part of the uncanny 'magic' of film, the paradox of an infinite regression away from the 'real' of the live event now well-and-truly out of reach except through the lenses which together seem to bring it ever closer through magnification. In the archive, this is one of the strangest impressions of all, because phenomenally it appears to collapse time—between the then of one seeing and the now of another—while ontologically asserting an absolute distinction between past and present. No wonder, then, that the seeming depth of the eyes on the flat surface of the screen has attracted some inspiring writing. I am thinking particularly of Roland Barthes's short essay on 'The face of Garbo', which makes fabulously suggestive contrasts and connections:

> Amid all this snow at once fragile and compact, the eyes alone, black like

strange soft flesh, but not in the least expressive, are two faintly tremulous wounds. In spite of its extreme beauty, this face . . . comes to resemble the flour-white complexion of Charlie Chaplin, the dark vegetation of his eyes, his totem-like countenance.[23]

Soft flesh, wounds, dark vegetation, animal spirits. Are we here back at the start of civilization, the moment when, according to Vico, a decisive space was carved out of the forest, a space that led to cities and empires?[24] These images certainly call up the vulnerabilities of that space, and the fascination with what lies beyond it, the past of another world that civilization left behind (Figure 18).

So is this where the extraordinary act may have to take place, well beyond the nature of the archive? Somewhere beyond the edge of the human as we have come to know it, where incommensurates meet and mingle, animal and human, nature and culture in a combination of pleasure and pain beyond all reason? This was certainly a dimension of the sublime as conceived by Žižek in his reading of Hegel: the radical negativity of the sublime is achieved in a recognition that not only is there nothing beyond phenomena (representations, impressions), but each phenomenon itself is constituted through radical negativity. If we are honest, when we look into the animals' eyes we become aware that we are seeing nothing (not just nothing that we can know); and, as for the human, in gazing into each other's eyes we know no essence,

Figure 18. 'Whatever disaster looms the eyes always have it.' Formby Jnr in *Spare a Copper*, 1941.

however much the warm looks of desire might try to fool us of its presence. Is this the kind of sublime honesty that the on-screen eyes of Garbo, Chaplin, Formby inspired? And are they supremely flattering *us*, turning us each into a monarch of the true state of the real?

There were certainly incredible extremes actually at play around the two Formby films of 1937. As with all his leading ladies, Formby aimed to seduce Kay Walsh if he got the chance, spurred on by Beryl's distaste of sex and her incessant policing. Usually Beryl's hyper-vigilant jealousies prevented any significant contact, but towards the end of the shoot of *Keep Fit* she spent a couple of days in hospital, reportedly for appendicitis. Circumstantial evidence of Formby's success with Walsh can be seen in the final scene of the film, where as the pair are bounced up and down on a stretcher following the climatic fight, she appears to be enjoying him visibly touching her breast, albeit wearing big boxing gloves! Irene Bevan, Gracie Field's stepdaughter, also claimed there had been a successful liaison.[25] In fact, the operation that 'allowed' the affair to happen was for a hysterectomy, apparently undertaken for extraordinarily ambivalent purposes by Beryl: a childless marriage would ensure that Formby's career always had priority, and he—a confirmed Catholic—might be distracted from other women if she could offer him sex without consequences. Such strange conjunctions of deferral, a vital subtraction producing a doubling of tractable benefits. Or maybe a raising of the ante on a hiding to nothing?[26]

God is Jesus—Going for a Song

> . . . the state as the rational organisation of social life *is* the idiotic body of the Monarch; God who created the world *is* Jesus, this miserable individual crucified together with two robbers . . . Herein, lies the 'last secret' of dialectical speculation: not in the dialectical mediation-sublimation of all contingent, empirical reality, not in the deduction of all reality from the mediating movement of absolute negativity, but in the fact that this very negativity . . . must embody itself again in some miserable, radically contingent corporeal leftover.[27]

Descriptions of Formby Jnr performing live refer to how he made audiences feel 'at home' or 'held them in the palm of his hand', as if he had somehow taken them into his confidence, shared a secret with them. The columnist for the *Blackpool Gazette* described a 1940 performance for troops in Quimper, France: 'Half of this young comedian's success can be ascribed to his unaffected intimacy with the audience'.[28] It would be an elementary mistake to assign the quality of this 'unaffected intimacy', these close encounters and exchanges, to the effects of Formby's persona as an 'ordinary', down-to-earth,

easy-going Northerner, something with which audiences might easily identify. It is not through mediation that such inclusion might be produced, but
rather through some welcome deduction of that which is usually taken as real.
The star's eyes on film seemed to play this trick, while for one critic Formby's
smile may have produced a similar movement in the live events, 'a smile of
perpetual wonder at the joyous incomprehensibility of the universe and the
people in it'.[29] That 'joyous incomprehensibility' moves us closer to the positive negativities of the sublime object, but of course the archive will hardly
reveal the secrets of the extraordinary in his live performances even through
so felicitous a turn of phrase. Its 'corporeal leftovers' stubbornly defy access
to the past present, especially in their most serially seductive invitations to it
in, say, the fading photographs replete with smiles, the real Formby signa-
tures for sale on the world wide web. To adopt a phrase from Balzac: 'They
must have the defects of their qualities'.[30]

So this is where we must risk entertaining the spectral, peering for ghosts
in our final attempt at an answer to this fool's slippery question. Also this is
where archive fever poses its greatest threat, as Derrida has it: 'It is to burn
with a passion. It is never to rest, interminably, from searching for the archive
right where it slips away.'[31] And where this one slips away, perhaps most
excessively, is in the encounter of extremes meeting that we considered at the
outset, in the silence as the song ends, yes, but now maybe more so in the
silences in the midst of the song. For Formby was not especially competent
with the notes—he could not even tune his own instruments—so he might
have agreed with the pianist Schnabel's paradoxical view: 'The notes I handle
no better than many . . . But the pauses between the notes—ah, that is where
the art resides!'[32] Therefore, in the dying moments of this chapter, let us risk
all and try to follow Formby's lead when he made his greatest gamble, perhaps
hoping to allay the spectre of the father—the origin, the law—by taking on his
name.

It is necessary to listen to Formby singing, first cut on black acetate, now
're-mastered' on some CDs. The lyrics of many of his songs have been justly
celebrated for the way they capture the spirit of carnival in the everyday, especially as it appears at English seaside holiday resorts. Consider 'With my little
stick of Blackpool rock' (1937):

> With my little stick of Blackpool rock
> Along the Promenade I stroll;
> In my pocket it got stuck I could tell,
> 'Cos when I pulled it out I pulled my shirt up as well.

The world they picture has been likened to Donald McGill's postcards, full
of the kind of smutty misunderstandings of Formby's personal favourite,
which shows a doctor chastising a nurse before an agonized hospital patient:

'No, I said *prick* his *boil*'.[33] But the comparison is misleading, because Formby invested even the clumsiest double entendres with a delicacy of rhythm and timing that was literally breathtaking. Listen to the penultimate line of the fourth verse of 'Auntie Maggie's Remedy': (1941).

> Now I knew a girl who was putting on weight
> In a spot where it just shouldn't be,
> So I said to Nelly
> Now your rub your. . . ankle
> With Auntie Maggie's remedy.

The minuscule pause, like the tiniest catching of breath, before the ridiculous substitution of 'ankle', is exquisite in its poise as the word is sung with utterly

Figure 19. 'Final appearance, still singing.' Formby Jnr in *Solo Performance*, BBC TV 1960.

unerring precision on the next beat. This extraordinary control over the moment, a kind of insistent musical cliffhanger, appears in many of the songs as a brief, two-syllable interjected laugh, a 'tee hee' of knowing cod-wickedness, or a 'hee hee' of sheer exuberance. In every instance the timing is brilliantly precise because wholly unforced, apparently as natural as breathing. And here, perhaps, is a key to the success of Formby's performance, because—despite the sometimes dreadful lyrics, the monotonous beat, the narrow musical range—the singing is imbued, through the jaunty, upbeat rhythms and the light-footed lilt of the slightly throaty voice, with the rising energy of laughter (Figure 19).

It is in the momentary catching of breath to produce such energy that the special quality of Formby's silence is produced, for the laughter is directed at the world pictured by the songs and in the films, a world of everyday disasters, oddities, distortions, mistakings, excesses, extremes. A radically *ordinary* world in which, in principle and if necessary in practice, anything can be substituted for anything else: ankles for pregnant bellies, Blackpool rock for penises, ghosts for lovers, hysterectomies for love, fathers for sons. In short, a world in which nothing is anything in itself. A world that, because appearance is continually ripe for displacement, amounts to nothing. A world that *is* nothing, a radical negativity even as it is becoming something. But—and here we certainly verge onto the sublime—this is not a matter for despair, but for ridiculously reassuring laughter. The laughter in the voice, whatever the song, is urging us on to smile, to be good-humoured, glad-hearted about this nothingness in all things. So in the moments of caught breath, the tiny silences before each laugh erupts, there is a mingling of horror and joy. Yes, that's it. In his performances, Formby produced the sublime for his fans, he became a sublime object, a sublime body. This oh so ordinary corporeal body, crucified on the miseries of a hellish private life in the midst of fabulous success, was, in his way, a god. Perhaps.

There has to be a 'perhaps', doesn't there, George? Because how can we be sure that this raving about nothing is not a delusion brought on by archive fever? And what is the archive but, as Derrida tells us, a place of commencement, of origin, and of commandment, of law? Hence, in making this writing say thus, do I submit to the impression of the very authority that I have attempted to rubbish by reaching for the imprint of the live in your act. And now, only by calling up the dead, by invoking your spectre—that complex, impossible singularity I dreamed up at the outset—can I move on past it, to leave you behind. You were indeed, according even to the archive, an extraordinary performer, even among the rest that surround you here. But who can believe that, as they say, in good faith, from a professor who calls up spectres?

CHAPTER TEN

Leo Fuchs, Yiddish Vaudevillian

Joel Schechter

> Everywhere you go, you hear people yelling woe.
> These are troubled times. Trouble.
> (from *I Want to Be a Boarder*, 1937)

He was called the Yiddish Fred Astaire, and praised for his dazzling imitation of Charlie Chaplin, but Leo Fuchs was far more gifted than Astaire and Chaplin in one respect. While they could match him in physical comedy and eccentric dance, they could never sing Yiddish songs as eloquently as Fuchs. Because he performed for many years in the language East European Jews imported to the United States, Fuchs's stage art has not been widely discussed in English. He was one of the most popular Yiddish stage comedians in America, and his name deserves the same honours—admittedly limited so far—that Sigmund Mogulesko, Aaron Lebedev, Ludwig Satz, Molly Picon and Menasha Skulnik have been accorded in the annals of theatre history (Figure 20). Fortunately some of the comic performances by these Yiddish actors have been preserved on film, and now can be seen with English subtitles. Leo Fuchs is featured in a short film titled *I Want to Be a Boarder*, and his comic repartee, as well as the song and dance number in the film, amply demonstrate the vaudevillian talents that made him an extraordinary actor.

I Want to Be a Boarder is hardly the culmination of Fuchs's career, since it was released in 1937. He continued to perform in America for five decades after his New York debut in 1935. An Eastern European who emigrated to the United States, Leo Fuchs was born with the name Laybl Springer in Lemberg, Galacia (Poland), in 1911. He began acting when he was 5 years old, and won praise at Warsaw's Que Pro Quo theatre at age 17. Fuchs was still an actor at the age of 79, four years before his death in Los Angeles, when he portrayed an Eastern European immigrant in the film *Avalon*; it was a role he knew quite well and played with many variations throughout his life. The comedian spoke his lines in English in *Avalon*. Earlier in his American career, Fuchs joked and sang in Yiddish, with a few English sentences mixed in, as

Figure 20. Portrait of Leo Fuchs.

can be seen in the full-length Yiddish films *I Want to Be a Mother* (1937) and *American Matchmaker* (1940). The actor also performed in a television production of Clifford Odets's play *Awake and Sing* (1970), and the Hollywood, American-language films *The Story of Ruth* (1960) and *The Frisco Kid* (1979).

Beginning with his New York stage debut, and for many years following, Leo Fuchs won high praise from critics for his clowning in Yiddish stage plays such as *Lucky Boy* (1935), *Cigarettes* (1936), *Give Me Back My Heart* (1937), *Sammy's Bar Mitzvah* (1938), *Bei Mir Bistu Schoen* (1961), *A Cowboy in Israel* (1962), *My Wife with Conditions* (1963) and *Here Comes the Groom* (1973).

The plays themselves are not well-known, or available in print; and even at the time they first opened, they served primarily as vehicles for Fuchs and other Yiddish actors to display their comic art.

Throughout Fuchs's long career on stage, he never abandoned the songs (or *kuplêts*, as they were called) and comic turns of Yiddish vaudeville. New York and other American cities had a Yiddish vaudeville circuit which presented variety shows composed of short sketches, songs and dances. But Fuchs and other Yiddish actors did not need the vaudeville houses to perform vaudeville acts; they were able to insert their own, special songs, impersonations and comic dances within the structure of full-length plays. In a memoir, actor and producer Herman Yablokoff recalled that when Leo Fuchs hesitated to take a role in *Cigarettes*, 'to please him [Fuchs], I [producer Yablokoff] padded his part with special material suited to his own unique style'.[1] Inclusion of such 'special material' and solo turns in Yiddish plays allowed actors their own equivalents of commedia *lazzi* or circus clown *entrées*, forms of an unwritten, orally transmitted repertoire which popular theatre artists developed as signature pieces, and repeated in different shows.

Vaudeville itself receives only passing mention in most chronicles of Yiddish theatre, which focus on full-length plays, not performers of novelty songs or 'special material'. In his book *Klezmer*, historian Henry Sapoznik suggests that popular Yiddish recordings on vinyl provide 'an unparalleled glimpse of a typical Yiddish vaudeville show. These three-minute distillations of what Yiddish audiences clamored to see are dependably formulaic: a bit of a skit, a song, and some brisk closing music with which to dance off into the wings.'[2] In this respect, vaudeville and stage plays were similar for Fuchs and other leading Yiddish actors—in both arenas they sang *kuplêts* and performed comic monologues. As the critic Nahma Sandrow notes in her chronicle *Vagabond Stars*, a Yiddish musical's comic *kuplêts* often were only peripherally related to the plot of their play, and they 'took the clown out of the play framework, reasserting the primacy of the relationship between the individual and the audience. For the moment, the play resembled the vaudeville of the era, both Yiddish and American (and the English music hall), with its intense rapport between performer and public.'[3] Occasionally the audience was invited by Fuchs to sing along with him, which increased the contact between the singer and his spectators.

The insertion of vaudeville diversions into stage plays allowed Yiddish actors to carry their most popular acts into different dramatic plots and different theatres. Why give up a good routine, just because you change plays or cities? The practice of departing from the plot, in order to perform a favourite novelty song, impersonation or comic monologue, also may have developed because many Yiddish actors were wandering stars. Their circuit was widespread, as Sandrow reports; they performed 'on Second Avenue [in Manhattan], or in the Bronx or in Cleveland, Ohio, in music halls or in musical comedies'.[4] Actors like Fuchs and Molly Picon also imported their special numbers into films when the opportunity allowed. The right song and dance act would fit in vaudeville houses, stage plays, and films, too.

Fuchs the vaudevillian can be discerned in a description of his role in the Yiddish stage production of *My Wife with Conditions* (1963). *New York Times* critic Richard Shepard remarked:

> the irrepressible Leo Fuchs . . . does not let his role—a young man driven by deception into destitution and alcoholism—distract him from the business of comedy. His very presence is laugh-provoking and he tells even the oldest of jokes with style, even, as in one, when he missed a word and the audience corrected him. Mr. Fuchs doesn't stand still for a second. He slips, slides, struts, fiddles, dances, and for a too-brief second does a dazzling imitation of Charlie Chaplin.[5]

Needless to say, Fuchs was offering his audience far more than the play's text required; the fact that he staged this production allowed him certain liberties with the script, and he took them. Shepard noted that *My Wife with Conditions* had 'a plot of sorts if you want to follow a story, but you don't really have to. In summary, it's about blighted love, con men, and the decline, fall and rehabilitation of the hero who really couldn't have cared less.' Clearly the critic did not care much for the story; Fuchs, and not the plot, was the main attraction, even when he was playing the role of 'a young man' at the age of 52. (By 1963, the average age of Fuchs's Yiddish-speaking audience members may have been high enough to make a 52-year-old appear young by comparison. The Yiddish theatre audience did not grow younger, or gain many newcomers after the Second World War.)

Fuchs began to perform in New York's Yiddish theatre in the 1930s, an era when it still had a considerable following. This theatre's Golden Age ended after the Second World War, as assimilation of American Jews into the cultural mainstream and destruction of Yiddish-speaking communities in Europe sharply reduced the prospective audience. (Curiously, there has been a revival of interest in Yiddish culture among young American Jews in the past decade, marked by playwright Tony Kushner's 1995 adaptation of Ansky's Yiddish classic, *The Dybbuk*, and other adaptations of Asch's *The God of Vengeance*; but the new enthusiasm is more apparent in following for music bands such as the Klezmatics, dedicated to Yiddish songs, than in the theatre.)

Speakers of the Yiddish language began large-scale emigration from Eastern Europe to the United States toward the end of the nineteenth century. Jews left Russia, Poland and Romania to escape persecution, but they did not entirely abandon the Old World culture upon arrival in the United States. Continuing to speak in Yiddish, the immigrants sustained a sense of community and identity among themselves in North America, and so did their theatre.

Yiddish theatres in New York, Detroit, Chicago, Los Angeles, and other urban centres offered a haven to Jews who spent long hours in garment industry sweatshops, department stores, open air markets, and struggled to pay the rent for their crowded tenement apartments. They turned to theatre for relaxation; but Yiddish plays and vaudeville evenings also gave the audience reflections and celebrations of its own condition. Leo Fuchs's comic depiction of a boarding house tenant in *I Want to Be a Boarder*, for example, was inspired by the need of many immigrant families to take in boarders for extra income.

Despite struggles to pay the rent, immigrants willingly paid for theatre tickets. Yiddish theatre was popular among working-class audiences who worshipped some of the leading actors (particularly Jacob Adler and Boris Thomashefsky) and welcomed mixed forms of 'low' comedy, musical entertainment and melodrama which were sometimes described in Yiddish as *shund* (trash). Irving Howe notes in *World of Our Fathers* that: 'Jewish audiences relished the details [in Yiddish plays], often demanded that songs be repeated, took special amusement from couplets denouncing rival companies, shouted denunciations of villains, and showed no displeasure with the mixture of tragedy and vaudeville, pageant and farce—not even with the intrusion of personal affairs in the midst of performances'.[6] This was popular theatre in all its glory, and Fuchs kept some of it alive for decades through his acts.

By the time Leo Fuchs arrived on the scene in the 1930s, prominent New York artists already had endeavoured and failed to 'elevate' Yiddish theatre from the level of *shund*. Some Yiddish 'art theatre' ventures were successfully sustained, notably the Moscow State Yiddish Theatre (1919–49) and Maurice Schwartz's Yiddish Art Theater in New York (1918–50). It could be argued that those Yiddish theatre groups which shunned the popular appeal of *shund* consigned themselves to a small audience. In general, though, it was difficult to separate Yiddish theatre entirely from the comedy, melodrama and songs found in *shund*. In 1902, journalist Hutchins Hapgood reported that when two Yiddish theatre pioneers tried to create high art they 'were compelled to compromise. [Jacob] Adler is now associated with a company which presents every kind of play known to the Ghetto, and [Jacob] Gordin has had to introduce horseplay and occasional vaudeville and comic opera into his plays.'[7] Leo Fuchs was much more willing to introduce horseplay and vaudeville on his stage.

Although he later portrayed Jewish cowboys, Fuchs's comedy was not all horseplay or even all vaudeville. At its best his acting approached the surreal through comic distortion of everyday life. His depictions of characters with multiple-personalities move from realism into a dream world—which the New World was to immigrants at times. In *I Want to Be a Boarder* Fuchs portrays both a greenhorn (an unassimilated immigrant) and a successful, beloved nightclub entertainer, two distinct characters who may have represented halves of Fuchs's own life. They also represented the economic disparities many Americans experienced during the Great Depression of the 1930s, when it was not unusual for rich and poor people to live in close proximity. As Fuchs sang in his song 'Trouble', 'Everywhere you go, you hear people yelling woe. These are troubled times.'[8]

For an immigrant actor like Fuchs, the move from Eastern Europe to New York during a period of economic depression must have been troubling. (In fact, he once told Herman Yablokoff: 'I'm going back to Poland. In Poland, I'm the greatest, but in America, I don't stand a chance.' Yablokoff persuaded him to stay for his 1936 production of *Cigarettes*, which was quite popular).[9] In the New World, where immigrants once dreamed that the streets were paved with gold, Fuchs saw both great poverty and wealth, among fellow artists as well as other citizens. His own life was an extended, continuing change in character, if not a surreal dream: an unending move back and forth between the different languages, income levels and cultural identities which co-existed in Manhattan's Yiddish theatre world on Second Avenue. (His Yiddish films, such as *I Want to Be a Boarder* and *I Want to Be a Mother*, were also created in New York, not Los Angeles.)

Surreal dreams and the American dreams met in the characters Leo Fuchs portrayed: incompletely assimilated, Yiddish-speaking immigrants including a Yiddish cowboy, a Yiddish Fred Astaire, the Yiddish Chaplin, a Yiddish private eye. All of them were misfits, or at least incompletely assimilated into American culture. As they spoke Yiddish and moved like Astaire, Chaplin, or a cowboy in a ten-gallon hat, these figures comically embodied some disparities which continue within American culture, as new immigrants from Europe, Asia, Africa and South America arrive and face challenges similar to those East European Jews met in early in the twentieth century. (The African-American actor and writer Anna Deavere Smith, in the preface to *Fires in the Mirror*, a play in which she portrayed twenty-seven culturally diverse Hasidic Jewish and Caribbean American characters in 1992, noted that 'in America, identity is always being negotiated'.[10] Fuchs's roles offer earlier evidence of the ongoing negotiations.)

In his song 'Der Millionaire fun Delancy Street', Fuchs jubilantly sang about a 'millionaire' from the New York's Lower East Side, where many Jewish immigrants lived.[11] Fuchs's 'rich' character walks with Rockefeller— 'it's no joke,' he sings; as Rockefeller smokes cigars, 'I walk behind him and inhale all the smoke.' Fuchs also reports that he and the wealthy Gloria Vanderbilt talk; when he is going to the park, she asks if he'll take her little dog for a walk. Fuchs's immigrant is not exactly intimate with the upper class, but the comic song brings him closer to their way of life, even if vast financial and social differences remain. The fact that he sang in Yiddish about being 'the millionaire from Delancy Street' was part of the joke. Without a translator, Rockefeller and Vanderbilt couldn't have conversed with Fuchs, or understood his musical dream of sharing their world without giving up his language and his Eastern European background. (Now a Rothschild might have understood.)

Fuchs's vision of a promenade by millionaires on Delancy Street is not exactly what Irving Howe had in mind when he wrote that 'the streets [of New York] are crucial . . . [as] the training ground for Jewish actors, comics, and singers'. Howe observed Jewish comedians learn 'to hold an audience, first on the stoops and sidewalks, later in vaudeville and legitimate theatres'.[12] In the Delancy Street song, Fuchs holds a sidewalk audience of wealthy citizens, not Lower East Side immigrants; but he is dreaming aloud, imagining a land so friendly and golden even Rockefeller frequents the training ground of Yiddish comics.

Fuchs brought immigrant greenhorns and debonair New Yorkers closer together still, by embodying both groups within his own dramatic repertoire, and joining them in one character. Film critic Judith Goldberg sees a double world in Fuchs's Yiddish film *Amerikaner Shadchen*. She notes that its characters live in both 'the English speaking [world] outside [the house] . . . and the closed world of Jews, albeit successful ones, wherein one speaks Yiddish and may relax'.[13] Fuchs portrays a wealthy Jewish New Yorker named Nat Silver, who, like his uncle before him, has trouble finding a wife. Like his uncle, Silver becomes a matchmaker. A hybrid of Old World *schadchen* (matchmaker) and modern businessman, Nat Silver falls in love with one of his clients. A camera flashback to his uncle (Fuchs in beard) briefly suggests Silver's relative looked like him, only unshaven. The two characters even sing similar, wistful Yiddish tunes, and through this double identity Fuchs represents different Jewish generations with one body—his own—and one beard.

He wears a beard and removes it again, and two disparate worlds meet again, more fantastically, when Fuchs sings and dances to the tune of 'Trouble' in *I Want to Be a Boarder*. The song is part of a dream sequence in the film. Fuchs first portrays a Yiddish-American immigrant who looks like an early version of Nat Silver's uncle. Quite Eastern European in appearance, the character wears unflattering, overlarge eyeglasses, a false goatee and moustache, ill-fitting coat, hat and trousers, and a worse fitting marriage. After quarrelsome conversation with his wife, portrayed by comedienne Yetta Zwerling, both characters agree the husband might fare better if he were her boarder:

> HUSBAND [Fuchs]: Tomorrow, I move out.
> WIFE [Zwerling]: Wait, I have a better plan. Be my boarder. . .
> HUSBAND I'll be your boarder.
> WIFE Ya.
> HUSBAND But then treat me like a boarder, not a husband.

Zwerling, zany as Fuchs in her waywardness, briefly contemplates marital fidelity, then warmly welcomes the new boarder's overtures, and drives her husband to jealousy (of himself) with thoughts of divorce and new romance.

HUSBAND [as boarder]: Mrs, can I hope that you will be mine?
WIFE How can I? I'm married. I'll get a divorce. Or perhaps become a widow.
HUSBAND I have sleepless nights. Eating, I see you on my plate. Walking in the park, you hang from the branches. Bathing, you appear in the tub. Do you think I have no heart, no feeling?
WIFE Such dear, sweet words. My husband, I hate him. Come into my arms, my beloved boarder.
HUSBAND So, you love your boarder, eh! Beautiful, really lovely.
WIFE And you, you make love to your landlady. As my husband you never made love to me. That's why you want a divorce.

The comedienne Zwerling was a fine partner for Fuchs, even if her character, the wife, was not. She also appeared with him in the film *I Want to Be a Mother*, and in the Yiddish stage musicals *Give Me Back My Heart* (1937) and *Sammy's Bar Mitzvah* (1938). Like Fuchs, she performs delightful transformations of character; and she turns from bitter wife into charming landlady in a moment.

Comedy about boarders and landladies was not unique to this act. As Richard Shepard and Vicki Gold Levi note in their book on Yiddish culture in America, early in the twentieth century, when young male immigrants from Eastern Europe boarded in New York, 'the institution of the boarder provided an endless source of plots for novels and plays, and was equally valuable for stage comics, who would delight and scandalize audiences from Chrystie Street to the Catskills with ribald tales of intimacies between boarders and their landladies'.[14] Still, the film version is unique and especially innovative when Fuchs begins his song and dance.

After flirting with his new landlady (his ex-wife), Fuchs's character drinks some liquor, falls asleep, and dreams of himself as a debonair, clean-shaven nightclub singer adored by a crowd of young women. He still speaks Yiddish, but he is a different person, almost unrecognizable. His voice has lost its gruffness, and is now smooth; his demeanor is modest, almost bashful. It is as if Groucho Marx shaved, lost his comic stoop and leer, and assumed the top-hatted elegance of Fred Astaire. Fuchs's new character, the debonair singer, has a second lower-class identity hidden within that of the elegantly dressed entertainer (Figure 21). He serenades the nightclub women with lyrics about the Great Depression, about how the world has gone to hell, businesses are turned upside down, and all is woe and trouble. He sings of an unhappy bride-

Figure 21. Leo Fuchs dancing the dream sequence from *I Want to be a Boarder*, 1937.

groom about to marry a hunchback, and his own hand, curving from behind him in a clownish trick, appears to be someone else's, a pickpocket's, perhaps, and reveals that his trouser pocket (or, the lyrics suggest, the pocket of the bride's father) is empty. Though the singer wears a tuxedo, he temporarily becomes a destitute man, who knows the financial troubles of which he sings. Despite the high society costume he wears, Fuchs links his identity with that of the poor and forsaken—a dowryless hunchback bride and her father.

Fuchs's filmed vaudeville number is replete with dream imagery, intoxication and 'bodily innervations' which Walter Benjamin once ascribed to surrealist art.[15] The immigrant portrayed by Fuchs not only falls asleep and dreams after drinking liquor; his intoxication induces the grotesque comic song and dance which unwittingly fulfil Benjamin's calls for surrealist actions in which 'no limbs remain unrent' (or at least unstretched to their limit in this number). Several times during the song, the otherwise stately Fuchs breaks into a crazy eccentric dance, full of rubber-limbed footwork and doltish facial expressions, as if he can no longer stand still or remain calm in a poverty-stricken and chaotic world. His elegant, restrained character turns into a rubber-legged clown who dances and finds joy in the moment, intoxicated by dizzy dance steps if not by liquor. The women in his audience cheer for his dance, despite the distressed state of the world and the ill-fated wedding he describes. The number recalls Irving Howe's description of the Marx Brothers and their 'gleeful nihilism . . . [which] made a shamble of things, reducing their field of operations to approximately what a certain sort of East Side skeptic had always thought the world to be: *ash un porukh*, ashes and dust'.[16] Or as Fuchs sings, 'Everywhere you go you hear people yelling woe'. But he keeps singing. Like Chaplin's resilient tramp, Fuchs's would-be boarder cannot be kept down for long: he literally bounds back to an upright position after his legs nearly fold under him during the 'Trouble' number. Of course, the dancer superbly controls his balance in this movement. Unlike the *schlemiel* Leo Rosten once described as a simpleton who 'falls on his back and breaks his nose', Fuchs breaks his fall, and returns to a state of grace as he croons about catastrophe.[17] He is more like the *schlemiel* Walter Benjamin described, in one of his rare references to Yiddish comedy, when he wrote about the 'genius of failure' and noted: 'Chaplin or Schlemihl. The schlemihl takes offense at nothing; he just stumbles over his own feet. He is the only angel of peace suited to this world.'[18]

Whether or not Fuchs is a 'genius of failure', he finds in failure—a world of woe and trouble—something to sing and dance about. As Brecht once said, in dark times, there will be singing about the dark times. Fuchs in his double identity of suave singer and dancing dolt, and in his comic dialogue as husband who would be a boarder, is a clown who can speedily pass between high and low life, and find stately grace and intoxicated abandon in the process. His vaudeville act bridges the distance between assimilated and greenhorn Jews, and Fuchs delights in leaping between their different worlds. He plays one world against another—but both are within his character and his ample imagination—two sides of a larger American schism between dreams of luxury (or luxury itself) and the uncomfortable, entry-level struggle known to so many newcomers in the United States. The comedian moves from one extreme to the other in a few deft face, hand and foot manoeuvres, literally descending to the lower depths and rising again to high society demeanour in the course of his dance. He offers a graphic confirmation of Yiddish cultural historian Henry Sapoznik's thesis that for immigrant performers in vaudeville, 'the way to ascend the ladder of entertainment success was to portray someone farther down that ladder'.[19]

At the same time, Fuchs's transformations in character and social standing convey the possibilities of another, better life developing out of that which already exists. It has been suggested that *Yiddishkeit*, Yiddish culture itself, represented to many Jews the geographical location of a *shayner, besser velt* (more beautiful, better world); while anarchist critic B. Rivkin's reference to this better world in *Yiddishkeit* originally meant a world of socialism, it might be argued that in Fuchs's Yiddish vaudeville there is also a better world: one of humorous song, dance, community and the promise of change wrested from the throes of economic hardship and woe.[20]

When the song ends, the dreamer wakes (actually his wife wakes him) and has to choose one identity: either he will be a flirtatious boarder or an unhappy husband in his own home. The film ends with the boarder cheerfully escorting his alleged landlady out of the apartment. Their quarrelsome marriage, somewhat like the wedding in the song, has dissolved. The dream of the nightclub entertainer turned into a dancing fool, his suavely sung Yiddish lyrics about the Great Depression, and the eccentric dance cross other boundaries, too. Fuchs's contortionist twists to music are similar to dances African-Americans were performing in vaudeville and nightclubs around the same time; it suggests a crossover between Yiddish-American and African-American cultures. Fuchs was no Al Jolson, not exactly a jazz singer, but there is an uncanny confluence of interests in his eccentric dance steps and those of African-American vaudevillians of the period—Leon Errol, the Nicholas Brothers.[21] In fast-paced, comic contortionist moves, the dancers seem to be set free, or free themselves, from the culture of Old World dance steps.

Yiddish actor and producer Herman Yablokoff recalled in his memoir, *Der Payatz* (*The Clown*), that in one Yiddish theatre production, when Fuchs 'went into his eccentric dance, doing double-jointed twists and corkscrew turns . . . the crowds wouldn't let him off the stage. And, since he would not repeat his bag of tricks to satisfy them, the only solution [to end the act] was to drop the curtain.'[22] The dance was quite literally a show-stopper in the 1938 musical *Sammy's Bar Mitzvah*, which Yablokoff produced in New York. Much as the Marx Brothers decimated the logic and dignity of polite conversation through their barrage of puns, Fuchs could destroy a certain kind of social club elegance and demeanour through his wild dance. Further movement (going on with the show) became difficult and counterproductive of the sensational effect already created. All one could say in response would be *genug shoyn* (Yiddish for 'enough already').

Here I am tempted to compare Fuchs to the Elizabethan clown Will Kemp, whom that great friend of popular theatre, Peter Thomson, praised as a 'people's clown'. In his own way, Fuchs too was a people's clown. His show-stopping eccentric dances were modern sequels to Kemp's stage jigs, which, as Thomson observed, brought the Elizabethan comedian 'a playhouse status that would have been immediately recognizable in the responses of [the] audience'.[23]

In his history of Yiddish cinema, J. Hoberman describes the filmed vaudeville act of *I Want to Be a Boarder* as 'a kind of missing link between the Marx Brothers and the Yiddish stage' and 'a small classic of Jewish surrealism'.[24] Although Fuchs doesn't portray four brothers, only three different men in the film, his identity transformations recall the moment when Groucho Marx steps out of character to face the camera in *Animal Crackers* and says, 'Pardon me while I have a strange interlude'. Fuchs in *I Want to Be a Boarder* also revels in strange interludes, surreal transformations and disruptions of situation and character, as he and his partner Yetta Zwerling keep changing their identities.

The 'Trouble' number in *I Want to Be a Boarder* is a filmed version of the kind of Yiddish stage act for which Fuchs received tremendous praise in the 1930s. (A version of the routine also appears in the longer Yiddish film *I Want to Be a Mother*, made the same year.) The dances which Fuchs performed during such songs led a *New York Times* reviewer of his 1935 American stage debut in the Yiddish comedy *Lucky Boy* to say that Fuchs 'has half a dozen loose or double joints, but he is not merely a contortionist. He is a nimble dancer, but he is not only a dancer. He can put over a song; he can fiddle, and he is a subtle character actor.'[25] Two years later, another *Times* review proclaimed Fuchs 'an extraordinary comic. His clowning, contortions, dancing and miming are full of grace and esprit.'[26]

Even in *Avalon*, the Hollywood film which required more traditional, realistic acting in English, Fuchs's nimble timing stole a scene. At the age of 79, Leo Fuchs did none of his famous vaudeville dance steps in the film; but he engaged in fast-paced, vaudevillian repartee. Director Barry Levinson's portrait of Jewish family life in Baltimore shows four aged immigrant brothers sitting lazily on a couch in one scene. Sam Krichinsky (played by Armin Mueller-Stahl) asks the other brothers, 'What was the movie we saw with the stagecoach? A very good movie.' Fuchs's character, Hymie Krichinsky, responds without hesitation, '*Stagecoach*'. He is not fully understood, as the dialogue continues:

SAM [Mueller-Stahl]	The movie had a stagecoach.
HYMIE [Fuchs]	*Stagecoach.*
SAM	Very good actor, John Wayne. The movie had an outlaw, but he was not an outlaw.
HYMIE	*Stagecoach.*
SAM	That's what's I'm saying, *Stagecoach.*
HYMIE	*Stagecoach.*
SAM	*Stagecoach.*[27]

Fuchs's character, Hymie, wryly and quickly repeats the correct answer until Sam accepts it. Hymie's Eastern European accent adds a touch of humour to each repetition of '*Stagecoach*'. With his Old World knowledge of Hollywood cowboy films, accurate from the start, Hymie never wavers, and his voice sounds slightly more amused each time he correctly answers the question.

How could a Jew from the Galacia be so confident about cowboy lore? Decades earlier, Fuchs explored that question in his Yiddish stage musical *A Cowboy in Israel*. The billing for the play by Louis Freiman and Chaim Tower credited Fuchs as the author of 'special material', and his opening line, 'Shalom, Partner', was also the title of a Fuchs record album. He sang about a Jewish cowboy named 'Hop Along Knish'; although Knish, named after a special Eastern European dumpling, was not as famous as television's Hopalong Cassidy, his lyrics promised that 'My reputation's getting bigger, I can even outsmart Trigger' (Roy Rogers' horse). The actor also once performed a role on the television series *Wagon Train*. Fuchs knew Yiddish cowboys, although in the 1962 musical the American cowboy he portrayed ended up in Israel raising a herd of Goldsteins instead of Holsteins. The actor found comedy in the meeting of Old World and Wild West, and Hollywood cast him accordingly. Before *Avalon*, Fuchs portrayed a Chief Polish Rabbi in the film *The Frisco Kid*. From within his huge white beard, the Rabbi called one of his least learned Talmudic students (played by Gene Wilder) 'cowboy', and sent the young man from Poland across the American plains to San Francisco. (In this film role, Fuchs was permitted few lines and gestures; he was much freer on the Yiddish stage.)

Besides Yiddish cowboys, his repertoire included a Yiddish detective, the 'Private Oy' named Friday in William Siegel's parodic play *Yiddisher Dragnet*. Later in his career, between films in Los Angeles, he also took some stage roles in American, English-language musicals and comedies, including a 1956 parody of Tennessee Williams titled *Katz on a Hot Tin Roof*. (Fuchs portrayed Danny Katz, a character who marries his landlady's daughter in Havana, and then discovers that one of his ancestors was an Irish 'Leapracohen', with emphasis on the Jewish name Cohen.) But in his finest hours on the Yiddish stage and on film, Fuchs displayed the gifts of a popular variety artist. He excelled in parodies of film genres, jokes based on ethnic identity, as well as songs, dances, circus-like contortions and impersonations, all part of his vaudevillian repertoire. This genre of live entertainment lost much of its audience as film culture became more prevalent in the United States. Ironically, when Fuchs's film *Amerikaner Shadchen* (*American Matchmaker*) opened in 1937 at a Yiddish theatre in Brownsville, New York, it could be seen daily along with eight live Yiddish vaudeville acts.[28] Even if Fuchs was not on stage in person at the time, he was still playing to a vaudeville house.

On stage, live in front of a Yiddish-speaking audience, Fuchs was able to improvise each night, and perform in and out of character more freely than he could on film. (As noted earlier, the Yiddish plays in which he appeared did not all have compelling plots to begin with; it may be no accident that he was tempted to digress from their plots, or forget the plot completely, as subsequent generations have.) The absence of a compelling plot, and his delight in digressions, probably led Fuchs to step out of character late in his career, and offer his stellar impersonations of Maurice Chevalier, Menasha Skulnick and Jimmy Durante in a stage play titled *Here Comes the Groom* (1973). But earlier in his career, Fuchs was just as prone to step out of one character and into another, to play multiple roles within plays and films.

In 1962, when Fuchs stepped onto a New York stage in a ten-gallon hat and said 'Shalom, Partner!' he was still a half-assimilated American, half Yiddish immigrant in his opening line, two cultures at once, three decades after leaving Eastern Europe. Here too, he was incapable of leaving behind his vaudeville custom of offering the audience a novelty song, even if it had no special relevance to the play on stage. Fuchs was reported by *Times* critic Richard Shepard to have left the script 'when needed, as in his seizure of the happy chance to do his popular chicken-flicker song in which he is unable to dissociate any thought or dream from his job of plucking chickens'.[29] The Yiddish cowboy Leo Fuchs was still a vaudevillian in 1962, perhaps the last Yiddish vaudevillian able to stop a show with a song about chicken-flicking.

As S.J. Perelman once said in praise of a talking chicken, it might be said of Leo Fuchs, too, that as a comedian versed in Yiddish humour, chicken-flicker songs and vaudevillian variety acts he 'reached a pinnacle undreamed of in poultrydom'.[30]

CHAPTER ELEVEN

Peter Lorre (and his Friend Bert Brecht)

Entfremdung in Hollywood?

Christopher McCullough

The term *Verfremdung(seffekt)* is often employed to describe the so-called 'alienation effect' at the centre of much of Bertolt Brecht's theories and practices. The word is a difficult one to translate into English and the ubiquitous use of 'alienation effect' does little service to what we understand Brecht to have meant. Problems arise when people attempt to attribute to Brecht a single meaning, or even a single theory. Whereas *Entfremdung* is translated into English as 'alienation', or 'estrangement' (and even in American English 'to antagonize'), *Verfremdung*, it would seem, is a term that Brecht employs to describe a specific action in performance that produces in the audience a particular level of insight through making strange the familiar. While *Verfremdung* is etymologically related to *Entfremdung*, it seems to have as its function a development beyond alienation or estrangement, that of encouraging the audience towards a new way of seeing and thinking. A simple example that I often employ is to consider seeing your mother as your father's lover. The familiar, and often possessive, image of one's mother takes on a new dimension when we realize that she is also the lover of your father. It is not enough to be 'estranged' from the familiar possessive image of your mother; we also need to see her in other ways. Nowhere is this more clearly exemplified than in *Mutter Courage Und Ihre Kinder* (*Mother Courage and Her Children*), where the defamiliarization of the mother figure forms the central irony of the play. Irony is the engine that drives the concept of *Verfremdungseffekt*. A useful example is to be found in Brecht's notes (translated by John Willett) entitled 'Alienation effects in the narrative pictures of the Elder Brueghel'. The second paragraph focuses on Brueghel's painting *Dulle Griet*: 'Such pictures don't just give off an atmosphere but a variety of atmospheres. Even though Brueghel manages to balance his contrasts he never merges them one into another, nor does he practise the separation of comic and tragic; his tragedy contains a comic element and his comedy a tragic one.'[1] In this essay, I am deliberately employing both terms, *Verfremdung* and *Entfremdung*. In the early part of this essay, the purpose is to understand the work of both Brecht and Lorre and their struggle to define a new 'materialist' aesthetic. Later in the essay, when considering Lorre's (and Brecht's) careers in the United States of America, *Entfremdung* seems to be more appropriate in describing their various estrangements from that culture.

The Austro-Hungarian László Löwenstein, after running away from home and working as a bank clerk, undertook actor training in Vienna and became the stage and film actor Peter Lorre. Such changes of name and profession are not unusual; indeed they are often a necessary part of the cultural transformation that is intrinsic to both the social and professional progress of an actor. However, when that transformation is further extended to a move from one continent to another (pre-war Germany via Paris and London to the US), and that in its turn also engenders a radical transformation in the work of the actor, our curiosity may be aroused. The career of this extraordinary actor Peter Lorre may serve as an exemplar by which to assess the transposition of European theatrical and filmic experimentation to the theatrical culture of the United States of America. To the casual observer, his work may seem to shift from the sublime to the, mostly, ridiculous. However, the complex picture of Lorre's career allows space for a discussion of attitudes towards certain kinds of actors and the general expectation of the roles they may, or may not, be considered appropriate to play.

Any discussion focusing on Peter Lorre's career cannot avoid involving his personal and professional association with Bertolt Brecht. After about seven years acting in Germany, Austria and Switzerland, during which time Lorre made his name initially at the Volksbühne as Moritz Stiefal in Wedekind's *Frühlingserwachen* (*Spring Awakening*) and as Saint-Just in Büchner's *Dantons Tod* (*Danton's Death*), he encountered Brecht and performed in *Happy End* and notably as the packer Galy Gay in Brecht's 1931 production of *Mann ist Mann* (*Man Equals Man*) at the Staatstheater. In the same year Fritz Lang cast him as the psychopathic child killer in the film *M*. This dual film and stage career was to be significant in his later work in Hollywood. Lorre's performance as Galy Gay, while arousing a mixed reception in the audience, formed the basis of a personal and professional relationship between the two men that lasted until Brecht's death in 1956 and, if certain evidence is to be accepted, lived on in Lorre's mind until his own death in 1964.

> I saw many friends, and among them the friend I loved most
> Helplessly sink into the swamp
> I pass by daily.[2]

This quotation is the first stanza of a poem by Bertolt Brecht reputed to be about his friend Peter Lorre. It was written in 1947 not long before Brecht left his exile in America in order to make his circuitous way back to what we came to know as East Germany. Although we cannot be certain that the poem was about Lorre (the swamp being Brecht's image of the Hollywood film industry into which Peter Lorre had sunk), according to James K. Lyon, while Brecht was non-committal when asked, the poem was discovered among Peter Lorre's posthumous papers in 1977.[3]

Whilst it may be unorthodox to begin on such a personal and anecdotal level, the personal journeys of Lorre and Brecht, from the 1931 production of *Man Equals Man*, are simultaneously ones of culture and ideology. The lives of artists such as Brecht and Lorre, as well as those of the many other Europeans forced into exile by the political climate of pre-war Germany, reveal a conflict of ideas and ideology focused on the conventions of acting and the function of theatre. While there were, undoubtedly, tensions in the critical reception of Brecht and Lorre's work in pre-war Germany, those tensions were intensified by the encounter with the commercial film industry of Hollywood and the left-wing theatre of pre-war New York. It is important to note, though, that Lorre's emigration to the United States was as the result of an offer of a contract made by Harry Cohn, the chief of Columbia pictures, rather than as a direct result of the political situation in Germany. Nevertheless, I contend that the complex cultural clash was no less intense.

Nor was the tension between theatrical forms a simple conflict between the experiments of European modernism and the North American adherence to a version of Stanislavki's American interpreters. The more the full picture is revealed, the more evidence there is that Brecht was as alienated from the New York left-wing theatre's Soviet Union-inspired form of Socialist Realism, as he was from Hollywood. Lorre's encounter was more damaging. While he was relatively easily absorbed into the West Coast film industry he was reconstructed by that culture as a professional foreigner. The 'strange' voice and the actor's *Gestus* were read as 'other' and were perceived as mannerisms, which at best served to add interesting dimensions to *The Maltese Falcon* (1941) and *Casablanca* (1942), but eventually became the source for Warner Brothers' animated cartoon, voiced by Mel Blanc.

In order to understand the genesis of Lorre's acting style we may usefully look back to Brecht's own notes reflecting on the mixed public reception of Peter Lorre's acting in the 1931 revival of *Man Equals Man*.[4] A close reading of these notes (in translation) suggests that Lorre's acting—and Brecht's concern—was not a simple case of prosecuting the arguments for 'epic acting' in its widely understood form, but was closely intertwined with decisions made by Lorre within the broad aims of the conventions of the production. It is particularly important at this juncture to avoid the broad classifications and delineations of what 'epic acting' in Brecht's work is, or is not. Such general definitions are more often than not misreadings and, by their very generality, simplistic appropriations of the specific material, performative and ideological conditions of production. In this case, Brecht appears to be formulating the acting conventions in an empirical manner that derives as much from decisions made by Lorre, as it adheres to any broad theoretical premise. This may be seen by theoreticians as a form of heresy and does require some explanation. Theory in contemporary usage may be understood as implying objectivity (or maybe it is inferred as such) and the cry will go out from theoreticians 'that theory is its own practice'. I have to admit that I have never quite understood what that statement meant. However, in respect of political theatre—and clearly when we think about Brecht (and Lorre at this stage of his career) we are thinking about political theatre—theory without action is of little use. Graham Holderness argues that some theatre may be political without becoming political theatre:

> a play may represent political matters or address political issues, in exactly the same way as a play can represent love, or old age, or poverty, or madness: if, that is, the play performs that representation of politics in an *objective* way, without taking sides. Such drama is in a sense political by accident. Politics proper is surely, however, incompatible with a detached, objective perspective: politics is about making choices, taking sides . . .[5]

Lorre and Brecht (apart from the many other collaborators over the years) were working out, through the material practice of theatre, the models by which the partisanship of their politics could be articulated in performance. The theoretical, or more precisely the ideological purpose was in part created through the materiality of theatrical practice. The 'side to be taken' was inextricably linked with the development of epic theatre in practice. Real problems only arise when teachers, readers, scholars attempt to create a single definition of epic theatre, which by the political forces that drive it should, necessarily, be in a constant state of flux.

The notes reveal, clearly, a degree of uncertainty in Brecht's mind regarding the process by which he and Lorre were to achieve their desired aims in this production. The final paragraph is shaped in the form of a series of statements of productive enquiry, rather than a reflection on the failure of a formulaic model for the production of the new epic theatre.

> It is possible that the epic theatre may need a larger advance loan than the ordinary theatre in order to become fully effective; this is a problem that needs attention. Perhaps the incidents portrayed by the epic actor need to be familiar ones, in which historical incidents would be the most immediately suitable. Perhaps it may even be an advantage if an actor can be compared with other actors in the same part. If all this and a good deal more is needed to make epic theatre effective, then it will have to be organised.[6]

Given the period in which this production was performed, and the stage that Brecht's thinking about the future of theatre had reached, we should not be surprised. The first sentence is completed with the clause: 'this is a problem that needs attention'. Likewise, the final sentence declares the same level of self-imperative: 'then it will have to be organised'. *Man Equals Man* is one of those plays that may be described as either a late Lehrstück, or as a part of the transition from the early Lehrstücke to the later plays. We may assume that Lorre was wrestling with similar problems in his approach to the performance of Galy Gay and that the audience may have perceived this level of experimentation as unformed acting.

The problem (for certain sections of the audience) was Lorre's departure from generally accepted criteria for 'good' acting, namely 'his habit of not speaking his meaning clearly, and the suggestion that he acted nothing but episodes'.[7] Brecht's notes, at this stage, are complex and the impression is that he is working out the problem as he writes. If we approach the problem, as it were, from the other end and consider what expectations the audience may have had of the actor, we may achieve some degree of clarity regarding the nature of Lorre's acting. Brecht raises the questions of how 'old' acting and actors satisfy expectation (on the part of the audience) through carrying the tempo of the play, creating a clear flow of character development largely through emotional and empathetic engagement with the character and his/her relationship with other characters. Instead, we have a situation where the emphasis is on the character's mental (and social) processes, rather than emotional processes. 'Mental processes demand quite a different tempo from emotional ones, and cannot stand the same speeding-up.'[8] What is apparent, to this reader, is that Lorre was associating each line, passage and scene with a *Gest*. Brecht describes four phases for which four masks are employed, 'the packer's face, up to the trial; the "natural face", up to his awakening after being shot; the "blank page", up to his reassembly after the funeral speech; finally the soldier's face'.[9] This may seem to us to be a familiar episodic technique of acting, but to Brecht the four phases, or masks, were something quite different, and we may hazard a guess that this was linked to particular qualities in Lorre's performance, as well as the juxtaposition of seemingly disparate images derived from early twentieth-century experiments in film (Eisenstein) and painting (Braque).[10] Apart from that level of speculation, it is clear from Brecht's notes that the phases/masks were more connected with an alternative (alternative to dramatic acting) form of character development and construction of meaning.

The most notable and often quoted third phase involving Lorre's performance as Galy Gay was the moment in which he chose to turn away from the audience while he whitened his face with chalk dust before turning back to the audience. By so doing he chose to demonstrate the moment, rather than 'live' it. In Brecht's words, 'Between fear of death and fear of life he chose to treat the latter as the more profound'.[11] The technique is to choose two seemingly disparate images and, by juxtaposing them, produce a new meaning created in the audience's perception of what may lie between the images. This should not be read as a simple binary tension, as any theory of the *Gestus* must also involve a more complex arrangement of imagery that takes account of the past (residual ideology) and future (emergent ideology) in tension with a given (present) hegemonic structure.

By way of example I remember clearly being taught at Art College to draw the 'negative' shapes between objects, rather than the outline shape of the objects in question. By so doing, the 'positive' objects appear in the drawing by the perception of the shapes in between. I cannot be certain if this is a technique drawn from modernist montage theory, but I have little doubt as to the effect it has on the way we perceive the image or theatrical event. The concept of 'negative' images in between overt narrative/dramatic moments (the positive image) carries with it the potential to be read semantically as well as visually (*gestically*). We may consider such space, which is social and dramatic, as well visually gestural, as liminal: a space in performance that exists in between actor and character / off stage and on stage. The notion of the liminal and gestic space in between would seem to bear out Brecht's denial that Lorre was simply acting in and within episodes. The concern here is with what happens between the episodes. The concept of an episodic structure, while clearly relating to indicators of performance, relates more to narrative structure. In this instance I am sure that the problem being tackled is more concerned with the actor's performance, which reaches beyond the template of the dramatic script. Even in the less memorable film performances by Peter Lorre, such as many of the thirty-seven films he appeared in before *The Maltese Falcon*, there is still that sense of a dislocated image in what may only be a residual echo of the early theatrical experiments.

A further dimension that may help in the attempt to understand what was both disturbing and extraordinary about Lorre's work in *Man Equals Man* is to be found in Joel Schechter's essay 'Brecht's clowns: *Man is Man* and after'.[12] Schechter argues that Brecht was not a great comedian 'but several of his friends were'.[13] The sense of this statement is that Brecht did not write comedies in the populist sense of the term. However, Brecht claims in epigrammatic form in *The Messingkauf Dialogues* that 'A theatre that can't be laughed in is a theatre to be laughed at'.[14] One may assume that a theatre that engenders critical thought because the audience is able to observe not only effects, but also a multiplicity of causes, carries with it the potential to engender a subversive perspective of the status quo. This analysis sounds somewhat dry, particularly when we consider the second scene, for example, of *Man Equals Man*, 'Street Outside the Pagoda of the Yellow God' (I am reminded of *The Green Eye of the Yellow God*, a nineteenth-century parlour ballad minus Brecht's sense of humour[15]). The soldiers' attempts to break into the Yellow

Pagoda in order to steal money with which to buy alcohol are nothing less than a series of pratfalls each containing their *gestic* spaces 'in between' lines as I have argued earlier with regard to Lorre's own performance as Galy Gay. The idea that Brecht was not a great comedian rings less and less true if we consider scene 11 of Brecht's great (anti-tragic) late play *Mutter Courage Und Ihre Kinder* (*Mother Courage and her Children*). This is the scene where dumb Kattrin attempts to warn the city of impending attack by drumming from a rooftop. There is a tedious inevitability in most readings of this scene that seeks out proof that Brecht did, in the final analysis, write a tragedy. As I have argued elsewhere,[16] a straightforward analysis of the *gestic* moments when the soldiers attempt to be quiet in their heavy armour and simultaneously shoot Kattrin (which of course they do in the end) is as much a series of pratfalls as the four soldiers in *Man Equals Man* or Charlie Chaplin in *The Gold Rush* (a film we know Brecht saw).

Joel Schechter does quote Brecht's 'jolly business' by which the character/actor Galy Gay surrenders through music-hall numbers and songs.[17] The point is that Galy Gay/Lorre wins in the end despite the seemingly insuperable odds stacked against him. Brecht summons up the image of the similarity between Galy Gay and Charlie Chaplin's 'little tramp'. Of course we must not fall into the trap of believing that we are dealing with a comedic form that necessitates the re-assertion of a status quo by the end of the play. The pratfall element leads us nearer to a dark form of farce in *Man Equals Man,* which is borne out by the farcical quality in Lorre's use of the white mask applied on stage. This dark quality of image is further reinforced by Lorre's performance as the psychopathic child murderer in Fritz Lang's film *M*, which was made in 1931, the same year in which Lorre played Galy Gay in Brecht's revival. While Lang's film owes more to expressionism than it does to any sense of 'epic' theory in film, there are intriguing elements in Lorre's performance which, it may be argued, echo his performance in *Man Equals Man*.[18] The final twenty minutes or so of *M* focus on the pursuit of Lorre's character by the gangsters who are determined to capture him because the intense police search for the child killer is endangering their own activities. They corner Lorre hiding behind some crates, and as their flashlight catches him in its glare, he shoots upright. Lorre's face in that moment, in the intense glare of the flashlight (of course intensified by studio lighting), is a white rictus of a facial mask. I am not claiming a direct link with Galy Gay's white mask, but the moment in the film creates a similar suspension of illusion in what may be read as a *Gestus*. Lorre's big final scene in front of the gangster kangaroo court is, in part, an exemplar for expressionist acting, but equally Lorre's acting carries with it all the hallmarks of *gestic* liminal moments that may be deduced from his performance as Galy Gay, and persist later in life as a residual echo in his Hollywood film performances. Lorre's career in Hollywood bears little resemblance to his career in Europe, although, as I hope to demonstrate, we may still perceive that, even in the nadir of his decline into the strange little 'middle-European' player in thrillers and horror movies, the residual echoes of the experiments of the 1930s can be observed in what a number of directors referred to as duality in his work.

We may observe certain tensions between the theatrical cultures of Western Europe and North America. These cultural differences were not simply a matter of the conflicting aspirations between what we might call the values of a theatre of commitment in Europe and the commercialism of the United States. A powerful left-wing theatre existed in the America of the 1920s and 1930s, which thrived up until its demise under the growing power of the right-wing movement led by Senator McCarthy and the House Un-American Activities Committee. A brief account of Brecht's initial encounter with the New York Theatre Union's production of *Die Mutter* (*The Mother*) in 1935 will serve as a useful vehicle by which the tensions between the theatre of Brecht (and Lorre) and that of left-wing practitioners in New York may be demonstrated. A cursory glance at the body of work that emerged from the left-wing (socialist and communist) theatre groups at work in the 1920s and 1930s in the US is enough to suggest that the predominant form of this work may be described broadly as Socialist Realism. The radicalism of such theatre seemed to be embedded in the content, rather than in a radical re-assessment of both form and content, as was the case with the work of Brecht, Piscator, Meyerhold and others in Europe.

Lee Baxandall's excellent account of Brecht's visit to New York in 1935, at the invitation of the Theatre Union during the rehearsals of *The Mother*, gives the strong impression that the enterprise was a disaster from beginning to end.[19] This cannot be assigned simply to Brecht's irascible character, although the image of Brecht leaping onto the stage during a 'run through' with an invited audience, 'screaming: "Das ist Scheisse! Das ist Dreck! Ich will es nicht haben!" ("That's shit! That's crap! I won't have it!")' is irresistible.[20] The real problem was deeper and ideological. As Baxandall points out, the Theatre Union's enthusiasm was for Gorky's novel as an excellent example of Socialist Realism, rather than for Brecht's innovations in playwriting and theatre practice. The many scholarly accounts of the transition of left-wing radical theatre in the Soviet Union from the experiments of Meyerhold to state control in the form of Socialist Realism as approved by Stalin and prosecuted by Gorky are well documented, and I will not dwell on them in this context. The salient point is that both Brecht and Lorre found themselves alienated (*Entfremdung*) both from the Gorky-inspired Socialist Realism of left-wing theatre groups in the United States and from the commercialism of 'the swamp' of Hollywood. We should, however, be wary of generalizations that, while serving a useful purpose in opening a debate about the difficulties faced in the transposition of theatre from one culture to another, ignore those instances where similarities of intention and form coincide. Such examples not only illuminate, but also expose the complexities of cultural exchange. For example, we do know that Brecht, during his visit to New York in 1935 and 1936, admired a performance of Clifford Odets's play *Waiting For Lefty*. This play about a taxi drivers' strike is structurally curious, containing a number of vignettes of 'naturalistic' scenes inserted as illustrative moments in a union meeting that carries all the influences of the *Living Newspaper* agit-prop convention, which we may assume appealed to Brecht.

While Brecht's relationship with life in the United States was uneasy both in his initial visit to New York and in his later enforced exile predominantly in California, Lorre acclimatized to California with relative ease. However easy this was for Lorre, he brought with him a reputation for being a horror movie actor that he resisted, but was to have to live with for the rest of his life. Apart from his early work with Brecht and Lang, Lorre had worked with a number of directors, and from reports of these experiences we may observe the split between Lorre's own wish for his comedic talent to be recognised (an aspiration that reinforces the later comic aspects of Galy Gay) and his reputation as a 'horror' actor that, even in these early days, seems to have been assigned to him. Leo Mitler gave Lorre theatre work in Breslau in the 1920s and Lorre's own reports of his experiences make it clear that he saw himself as possessing an emergent comic spontaneity. 'I was a spear carrier then and I might have bettered myself if it had not been for my habit of clowning at the wrong time.'[21] However, his reputation as a 'horror' actor was reinforced— apart from his success in *M*—by a report by Kurt Pinthus in Berlin's *8-Uhr-Abendblatt* of his performance in *Pioneer in Ingolstadt* at Theater am Schiffbanard in 1929:

> And a new face was there, a terrifying one; the hysterical bourgeois son, whose bug eyes, corpulent head poured forth in a yellow manner from his suit; as this young lad staggers between sluggishness and hysterical breakdown, as he so timorously goes and grabs and sometimes greedily fumbles, such have also older ones that I have hardly seen presented in such an uncanny manner in the theater. This person is Peter Lorre.[22]

Up until the later stages of his career, Lorre always maintained that he had only once performed in a horror film, a film of little note entitled *The Beast with Five Fingers* (1946). His argument was that many of his so-called horror films were in fact psychological thrillers and that his purpose was to expose the psychology of evil. Lorre, indeed, disliked intensely the term horror as for him such performances, whether on the stage or in film, merely appealed to the sadistic emotions of the audience.

It would seem that Lorre's commercially perceived persona as an actor specializing in horror on both stage and screen (he was received as a celebrity in Hollywood and that status promised commercial viability), combined with his own desire to be accepted as a serious actor (comedic or otherwise), created a sense of duality in his performances. This perception of duality, while held by two eminent film directors, was not simply a recording of Lorre's own wish to break away from the popular image that had been created for him, but signalled a deeper and more complex form of acting that cannot be divorced from his early work in Germany.

Shortly after Peter Lorre's arrival in the United States, Alfred Hitchcock invited him to London to work on the film of *The Secret Agent*. Comments on Lorre's performance are worth recording:

> Lorre's portrayal expressed a deliberate harmony of image and actor, playing on his aptitude for understatement as well as his ability to project a duality of human existence. This admixture of the antithetical—innocence and malevolence—had become Lorre's trademark.[23]

This is a curious observation, in that while supporting the view that Lorre's acting was complex in its antithetical nature, it seeks to present this as a harmony, whereas the contradictory nature of this 'duality' would seem to point more towards the notion that Lorre was carrying with him the residual echoes of past acting conventions. John Huston directed Lorre in *The Maltese Falcon* and 'sought the duality that Lorre so naturally projected, of doing two things at the same time and of thinking one thing and saying something else'.[24] Huston's view of Lorre's acting in *The Maltese Falcon* encapsulates an important aspect of what we understand by the term *Gestus*. Whereas Hitchcock perceived Lorre's duality as a form of harmony, Huston recognizes the potential for complex playing as a mode of defamiliarization. We are able to see how Lorre's work may have flourished in Hollywood under the direction of someone of Huston's ability. However, as the records of his career in Hollywood demonstrate, the performances were more often dissipated into what I term residual echoes. The work loses clarity and we are only able to observe the potential 'through a glass darkly'.

All Lorre's work from the early days in Berlin—and particularly with Brecht—through to the many and varied roles he had to play on and off screen in Hollywood suggest this concept of duality. This duality (multi-layered may be a more appropriate model) is not one simply constructed from the tension between the comedic and the horror, but also contains a tension between the Hollywood constructions of the 'celebrity', which would seem to be akin to, but culturally subordinate to, the 'star'. Furthermore, the model is complicated by what may be termed the residual echoes of his work with Brecht and the simple fact that physically and culturally he would always be perceived as 'other'. To be obviously foreign in such a white North American (and claimed heterosexual) hegemony, with all of its glaring inconsistencies, as was mid-twentieth-century Hollywood, was to be a disruption to the accepted cultural norm. It would seem that the method of containment within Hollywood's cultural hegemony was to create Lorre as a commercially viable 'personality' that would serve to play the marginal 'others' in films where the protagonist, no matter what the dramatic narrative, was an extension of her or his accepted celebrity. Even so, there is the continuing sense that this presentation of Lorre as a commodity always seems to be out of joint with the acceptable commercially viable model as 'other'. Ironically, the reason for this sense of being out of joint may be due as much to the complex nature of his resistance to the hegemony as to his concessions to it. However we may define the cultural hegemony of Hollywood—and there is neither time nor space in this context to pursue the matter—there was clearly a need in a society of immigrants that strove for an 'American' identity to also create some foreigners as 'other'.

There is little doubt that Lorre's relationship with Hollywood was complex in that he became a part of the culture, but on its terms. His assimilation was, simultaneously, a factor in his being marginalized as 'other' by being clearly foreign in a society made up of immigrants of whatever generation and by the constant references to his physical appearance (e.g. bug eyes and corpulent head). His increasing addiction to morphine did not help, and as well as affecting his physical appearance the addiction reinforced Brecht's view that his friend was sinking into 'the swamp'. However, the evidence would seem to suggest that the morphine addiction, while being real, was not the result of decadence. The addiction, it has been pointed out, had its origins not in his life in Hollywood, but was due to morphine being prescribed for a chronic gall bladder complaint and appendicitis when he was living and working in Berlin. The drug was freely available on prescription in Berlin, and while the addiction may well have been real, as was deterioration of his health throughout the 1940s and 1950s, the cause was ill health.

The matter of Lorre's ill health is germane to the general question of his reception in Hollywood. His admittance to that culture as a 'celebrity' (rather than as an actor) places him clearly in that convention whereby the star/celebrity is playing him or herself in relation to the character. This convention may have changed to a certain degree in recent decades, but was the case in the early and mid-twentieth century when a clearly defined star system (or hierarchy) was established. The cinema audience, more often than not, went to see a star in a film. Of course the narrative of the film engaged the audience, but any narrative, or indeed characterization, was in competition with the persona of the star, no matter what place that individual featured in the hierarchy of the firmament. Lorre's assimilation into the culture of Hollywood was as a celebrity who specialized in horror films. His appearance as a foreigner, with an unusual physical demeanour and voice coupled with, by the 1950s, the visible deterioration of his physical health and the decline in his career, simply reinforced the categorization of him as film monster (to his horror he was classed as 'one of the horror boys along with Boris Karloff—a pint-sized Karloff').[25]

Aside from his categorization as a 'horror boy' there was the obvious exploitation of him as a foreigner. His portrayal of the eponymous hero of the eight *Mr Moto* B-category films between 1937 and 1939 played not only on Lorre's European foreignness, but took the cultural process even further, transposing his screen presence into the Japanese detective. While the *Mr Moto* films deserve closer scrutiny, suffice it to say in this context that Lorre would have seemed to have survived this experience by exploiting his own comic propensity to play the character tongue in cheek, and we may hazard the view, thereby subverting the series. The degree to which he succeeded in using his comic abilities for subversion is open to question, but certain anecdotal reports offer fascinating glimpses into the actor's ability to turn solemn moments into farce. According to Vincent Price (with whom he collaborated late in his career and who read the eulogy at Lorre's funeral), when he and Lorre went to view Bela Lugosi's corpse at his funeral, upon seeing Lugosi dressed in his famous Dracula cape, Lorre remarked, 'Do you think that we should drive a stake through his heart just in case?'[26] Whatever ability Lorre may have had to exercise his humour against all the odds, the system exploited and demeaned him even after his death in 1964. His voice and physical appearance were caricatured in many animated films, including a commercial for the Dairy Council in the US where he was portrayed as mad scientist Bela Lugosi's assistant, 'pushing milk rather than mayhem'.[27]

The cultures of the West create and categorize an expectation of the appearance of theatrical characters in certain clearly defined ways that conform to hegemonic systems. Nowhere is this more evident than in the portrayal of Hamlet. Despite a number of variations, the image of Hamlet owes more to a Romantic vision of the Danish philosopher prince, reinforced by Laurence Olivier's portrayal in the film under his own direction (1948), than it does to any sense of how Hamlet may have been experienced in Shakespeare's own life time. Certainly, the possible self-portrait of Richard Burbage, presently in Dulwich College, indicates that the first player of Shakespeare's *Hamlet* was not an ethereal figure.[28] The original working title of this essay was, 'Should or could Peter Lorre have played Hamlet?' It is interesting to note, by way of an epilogue, that Brecht, in the last seven years of his life, was planning a number of projects. One of these projects was a production of *Hamlet* with Peter Lorre as the prince.[29]

CHAPTER TWELVE

A Star in Two Halves

The Democratic Comedy of Morecambe and Wise

Richard Boon

WISE:	You're turning the whole thing to ridicule!
MORECAMBE:	What d'ya mean?
WISE:	Well, you're making us look like a cheap Music Hall act!
MORECAMBE:	We *are* a cheap Music Hall act!

On 25 December 1977, an estimated 28,835,000 people—slightly more than half the total population of the United Kingdom, and rather more than half the television-owning population—sat down to watch Britain's best-known comedy double act, Eric Morecambe and Ernie Wise, perform the latest in what had become a tradition of annual Christmas television shows. That audience remains the largest in the history of televised 'light entertainment' in Great Britain. In demographic terms, there were no obvious divisions of class, age, race or gender within the viewing public: the appeal of the show cut across all boundaries.[1] If ever television achieved its ambition of becoming a genuinely popular, mass medium, then this was the moment, and, given the subsequent fragmentation of the medium into multi-channel satellite and cable provision, it is unlikely ever to be surpassed.

Morecambe died in 1984. In 1999 (the year that his partner, Wise, died) the Queen unveiled a statue of him in the hometown—an ailing seaside resort in Lancashire in the North of England—from which he took his name. The statue was subsequently credited with a 40 per cent increase in the town's tourist trade (and with the hasty development of its car-parking resources). In the same year, respondents to an internet millennial poll voted Morecambe the funniest Briton of the twentieth century. Morecambe and Wise shows continue to be repeated on British television (albeit often in the form of re-edited compilations, the carelessness of which is a source of considerable distress to their fans), and still attract remarkably large viewing figures.

If the double act lives on in the minds of the British public, then the same is true for one, at least, of its writers. Eddie Braben, whose scripts from 1969 onwards formed the foundation of their best years as performers, found himself writing sketches for them long after Morecambe's death: '[I've] always had Morecambe and Wise lines running round in my head, but there was nowhere for them to go'.[2] One such *post mortem* sketch is typical of the kind of material he had produced for them in their heyday:

ERIC   How many today?

ERNIE How many what?

ERIC   How many epic plays have you written today?

ERNIE Twenty-seven epic plays.

ERIC   And it's still only a quarter past ten! You could be another Brontë sister—you've got the legs for it.

ERNIE Please! I am trying to create.

A long pause

ERIC   Ern?

ERNIE Yes?

ERIC   Good.

Pause

ERIC   The Bard.

ERNIE Who?

ERIC   William Shakespeare.

ERNIE Oh, the Bard.

ERIC   Barred from every pub in Stratford-upon-Avon!

ERNIE I am trying to finish a thriller.

ERIC   At your age that might take some time!

Another pause

ERIC   I've never told this to another soul, Ern, but I'll tell you. I once appeared in *King Liar*.

ERNIE *King Lear*!

ERIC   No—*King Liar*. I told them I could act!

A long pause

ERIC   Do you remember when we were at Milverton Street School?

ERNIE I'm *trying* to write . . . How many 'f's are there in 'physicist'?

ERIC   The Chinese kids were very clever at school.

ERNIE They were good at sums.

ERIC   Especially take-aways.

      Laughs

      That was a belter, that one! You walked right into that one! It was like reeling in a clapped-out salmon![3]

In fact, Braben eventually found somewhere for his lines 'to go' when he

contributed to the script of *The Play What I Wrote*, an intelligent, affectionate—and genuinely funny—tribute to Morecambe and Wise, co-written
and performed by Hamish McColl and Sean Foley, which ran at Wyndham's
Theatre in London in the winter of 2001–2. Unsurprisingly, perhaps, the
play's box office was among the theatre's best-ever.

The particular sketch I quote above did not form part of *The Play What I
Wrote*, but it contains many of the elements that were central to Morecambe
and Wise's act in the 1970s. The humour is childlike in its innocence, and
takes unashamed delight in that. (Indeed, by the pair's own admission, their
scripts often appear child*ish* on paper.) With Wise in the character of the self-
deluded 'literary giant' that Braben had created for him, and the restless,
quick-witted, devious Morecambe ever ready to deflate his partner's
pomposity, the schematics of their relationship seem to fall straightforwardly
into the conventional stooge/comic dynamic of earlier double acts. Yet there
is also an atmosphere that sets the scene apart from a simple piece of traditional cross-talk. The setting is domestic, even intimate, the sketch working
in terms of a mini-situation comedy: it imagines them together in bed (like
Laurel and Hardy, they were able to share sleeping arrangements without any
hint of sexual involvement; as the playwright John Mortimer observed, theirs
was 'an English marriage, missing out the sex as many English marriages do'),[4]
and a stronger than usual sense of character, created in part through what was
only a semi-fictionalized sense of personal biography. More than anything,
there is the careful and sophisticated use of the pause, which lends the piece
a particular quality of energy unlike anything that, say, Abbott and Costello
ever found; indeed, the snatch of dialogue that follows the first *long pause*
('Ern?/Yes?/Good.') is almost Beckettian in its meticulous suggestion of a
deeper interdependency, and potential for loneliness, than might be expected
of a pair of popular television performers. Yet it is here that the clue to
Morecambe and Wise's extraordinary popularity, the extent to which they
appear genuinely to have been *loved* by millions, might be found.

Making the Double Act

If Morecambe and Wise can be described (and they often have been) as a
'British institution', then that is at least in part because the history of the act
is in many ways the history of mass popular entertainment in twentieth-
century Britain. Their origins lie in the last, pre-war days of variety (which
still carried within it traces of Victorian music-hall), and they moved on into
radio in the 1940s, television in the 1950s and cinema in the 1960s. Radio did
much to heighten their profile; their three feature films (*The Intelligence Men*,
That Riviera Touch and *The Magnificent Two*) were, on the other hand, largely
unsuccessful. Television, however, proved to be the medium which they made

their own, though their initial foray into the medium was deemed a failure: one reviewer of their first venture, a six-show series called *Running Wild* made for the BBC in 1954, famously defined the television set as 'the box in which they buried Morecambe and Wise'.[5] From 1961, however, they embarked on a television career that saw them make six series of shows for independent television (ATV, 1961–68), nine for the BBC (1968–77) and four more for the independent company Thames (1978–83). In all, this amounted to nearly 170 shows, the shortest of which were thirty minutes long. At the same time, they kept a theatrical presence alive with appearances in pantomime and summer season, and, increasingly, with one-off stage shows (gleefully referred to as 'bank-raids'). It is worth stressing the sheer volume of their output, not least because the growth of television in the late 1950s had driven the last nail into the coffin of theatrical variety. Acts similar to Morecambe and Wise, which may have spent decades refining ten or twelve minutes' worth of material for a 'spot' in a theatrical variety bill, confident in the knowledge that by the time (usually about four years) the tour brought them back to a particular theatre audiences would have forgotten the jokes, now found that material 'used up' by one appearance on national television. How, then, did Morecambe and Wise not only survive the transition from variety to television, but achieve such remarkable success in doing so?

The answer, I think, is threefold. First, they were lucky, and knew how to maximize their luck. Throughout their television career, they found good writers (Sid Hills and Dick Green, and later Braben) and good producers (particularly John Ammonds and Ernest Maxin), and demanded professional standards and disciplines (they insisted, for example, on three-to-four week rehearsal periods) that few others applied. Even so, their real breakthrough on television came only well into their first series for ATV. Hills and Green's scripts initially populated sketches with large numbers of extras, amongst which the peculiar professional and personal intimacy of the double act was lost; a strike by the actors' union Equity forced the duo back on to its own resources, and, giving them space to flower, set the pattern for subsequent work.

Secondly, their appearance on television coincided with the full and increasingly confident expansion of the medium into a national institution: as its audiences grew, so did Morecambe and Wise's. Moreover, not only did television begin to find technical ways of accommodating variety acts that had eluded it in the past (early experiments failed because, unlike in the United States, the medium struggled to adapt to the 'size' of theatrical variety performances, often leaving them to appear stilted and overblown), but its hunger for material led it to exploit resources it had hitherto treated with caution. It is a peculiar feature of the then British class system that entertainers from the North of the country were held to have little appeal in the supposedly more sophisticated South. Aside from George Formby (who appears elsewhere in this volume), and one or two others such as Frank Randle, representatives of that great Northern tradition of working-class humour, often characterized by its peculiarly odd combination of down-to-earth homeliness and exotic surrealism, had struggled to achieve national recognition. Certainly Morecambe (from Lancashire) and Wise (from Yorkshire) had felt held back in their earlier career; now, helped further by the sudden fashionability of all things Northern, as evidenced by developments in pop music (The Beatles), theatre and film ('kitchen sink' drama) as well as elsewhere in television (the Manchester-set 'soap' *Coronation Street*, for example), there was a tide to be ridden.

Thirdly, and most significantly, Morecambe and Wise survived the transition from theatrical variety to television because they brought theatrical variety *to* television with them, and did so in increasingly complex and sophisticated ways. What became the established format of their shows was essentially a variety format: the duo appeared on stage, introduced guest stars (who might then appear in one or more short sketches), and ended with a song and dance number before returning for a curtain call. Despite the technical difficulties involved, they worked (to a live audience) from a two-foot high-stage specially built in the studio, and in front of the plush drapes of old music hall:

> The difficulty in finding the split in the curtains, the belated appearance, the eavesdropping, the mime of the mad throttler—each of these makes the viewer comprehend the curtains. They salute and insult their audience good-naturedly; they end with a song and take a curtain call. They swap straight duologues with costume sketches, and normally demonstrate their dancing prowess. They are 'Lords of Misrule', and it has become almost another kind of award for the great ladies and gentlemen of the theatre and the arts, like Glenda Jackson as Ginger Rogers, to have found themselves in a musical burlesque or in one of Ernie Wise's smug little plays.[6]

Those 'great ladies and gentlemen' effectively stood in as 'top of the bill'; they included actors such as Vanessa Redgrave, Dames Flora Robson and Judi Dench, Sir Ralph Richardson, Sir John Mills and Lord Olivier, pop stars such as The Beatles and Sir Elton John, the political journalist Sir Robin Day, and former Prime Minister Lord Harold Wilson. Each was mercilessly, if gently, humiliated, and with unerring comic instinct. The principal conductor of the London Symphony Orchestra, André Previn, in what Morecambe himself believed to be the funniest thing the duo ever did, was forced to endure the slaughtering of Grieg's Piano Concerto,[7] whilst Shirley Bassey, the lurexed golf-club diva, found herself hobbling down stage in a single, size 10 hobnail boot whilst the set collapsed around her rendition of Jerome Kern's *Smoke Gets in Your Eyes*. No less important, though less famous, were the harmonica-player Arthur Tolcher, with whom the duo had first worked on the variety circuits of the 1940s, and who frequently tried to interrupt the television shows with his enthusiastic rendition of the 'Spanish Gypsy Dance' only to be thrown off stage a few bars in ('Not *now*, Arthur!'), and Ann Hamilton, a regular female presence in sketches (usually greeted with 'Hello, young sir!'), who had worked at the Windmill Theatre where in the 1950s Morecambe and Wise had provided unwanted comic relief between the notorious nude tableaux. Here, an overt and direct acknowledgement of the double act's variety training was being made, but the debt to variety days ran deeper than that: indeed, the very substance of Morecambe and Wise's double act was mined from their earlier professional—and to an extent personal—lives, and that in itself is a further clue to their remarkable success.

They had met in 1939, when Wise was already an established juvenile performer (known as Britain's answer to Mickey Rooney) and Morecambe was taking his first tentative and to some degree unwilling steps into performing; both had been 'discovered' by Bryan Michie's *Youth Takes a Bow* variety show (where they first met Tolcher), and it was the variety circuit in the North of England that provided them with their apprenticeship. Their first appearance as a double act was at the Liverpool Empire theatre in 1941 when they were both in their mid-teens, but it was not until after the interruptions of war that they had the opportunity to establish themselves. Even then, their beginnings were uncertain; Wise was originally the comic, Morecambe the feed, and one of their early engagements was as part of Lord John Sanger's touring variety and circus show, a misconceived attempt to marry two popular entertainment forms that ended in abject failure.

The 1930s and 1940s were the golden age for variety double acts in Britain. Typically, such acts opened or took second spot in each half of variety shows on seaside piers (most famously at Blackpool), or which toured on national 'circuits'; one such was the 'FJB' circuit, created by Freddy Butterworth through the purchase of failing cinemas and their reconversion to music-halls. (Another, far bigger and more powerful, was the Moss Empire circuit, which controlled twenty-four major theatres, including the prestigious London Palladium.) Similarly, *Music Hall*, the centrepiece of Saturday evening radio, customarily began with a double act, such as Bennett and Williams, Clapham and Dwyer, Morris and Cowley or Scott and Whaley. Arguably the most popular act of the time was 'The Crazy Gang', which, aside from 'Monsewer' Eddie Gray, was made up of three double acts: Naughton and Gold, Nervo and Knox and—perhaps most influential on Morecambe and Wise— Flanagan and Allen. The great exemplar, however, was Murray and Mooney, who did much to enshrine, even codify, the principles of the format. Murray, 'serious' and a little pompous, might begin by announcing 'a little monologue', only to be immediately interrupted, to his great frustration, by the wise-cracking, anarchic and irresponsible Mooney. Thus was set in train an escalating cross-talk routine of gags and misunderstandings, with Murray forever trying to get Mooney off the stage and apologizing to the audience for his partner's attempts to destroy the intended 'real' act. It is a stratagem instantly recognizable to viewers of the classic Morecambe and Wise shows thirty years later.

By their own admission, however, the Morecambe and Wise of the post-war years primarily looked across the Atlantic for inspiration. Both had been seduced by the Golden Age of Hollywood, particularly Wise (whose 1990 autobiography was entitled *Still on My Way to Hollywood*).[8] The infatuation was evident throughout their career, reflected in Morecambe's (very bad) impressions of James Cagney and Jimmy 'Snozzle' Durante (gags which ran for years) and most notably in the show-stopping comedy musical numbers of their great years at the BBC. (Most memorable were 'There ain't nothing like a dame', from Rodgers and Hammerstein's *South Pacific*, with a chorus of well-known news- and sports-casters performing unlikely acrobatics, and 'Singin' in the rain', performed by Wise on a set lovingly recreated from the MGM original in every detail bar the fact that, to the bewilderment of Morecambe's watching policeman, it wasn't actually raining.) In the formative stage of their careers, however, the most important, if slightly unlikely, influence was that of the American double act Abbott and Costello, whose films formed a staple of British filmgoers' diet during and after the war. Morecambe and Wise freely and openly stole from their American counterparts, even going so far as to adopt American accents (a not entirely uncommon practice at the time; infatuation with all things American was a characteristic of acts other than Morecambe and Wise, and, indeed, the usurpation at the top of the bill of native performers by American stars was another damaging blow to British theatrical variety). The tall, bullying, know-all Abbott and the short, tubby, anxiety-raddled Costello have not, it must be acknowledged, gone down in comedy history as 'greats'; they may have had their moments (Wolf Man: 'You don't understand. Every night when the moon is full, I turn into a wolf.' Costello: 'You and twenty million other guys!'),[9] but one critic perhaps sums up the limits of their appeal when he refers to their 'moderate custard pie routines and silly double-talk'.[10] Nonetheless, for a period of two or three years in the early 1940s, Morecambe and Wise copied Abbott and Costello to an extraordinary degree, mimicking not only their characters and aggressive style of delivery (including a large amount of plain slapstick) but wearing the same hats and using the same catchphrases. They revived one of their early routines for a television show:

> ERIC   Lend me two pounds. One'll do—now you owe me one.
> ERNIE I don't understand.
> ERIC   Lend me two pounds. One'll do—now you owe me one.
> ERNIE I don't understand.

ERIC   Well, I'll show you. Ask me for two pounds.

ERNIE   Lend me two pounds.

ERIC   There's two pounds. How much have you asked for?

ERNIE   Two pounds.

ERIC   How much have I given you?

ERNIE   Two pounds.

ERIC   How much do you owe me?

ERNIE   Two pounds.

ERIC   Thank you.

In terms of essential, if simple, clarity of characterization and dynamism of delivery, there was something to be learned here (not least the brazen, quick-fire qualities needed to survive in front of what could be demanding, even hostile audiences), but the Abbott-and-Costello template quickly proved limiting for Morecambe and Wise. For one thing, Morecambe grew to dislike the ultimately cretinous model of the comic that Costello offered. More significantly, the American double act's relationship seemed to be founded on a deep, underlying dislike of each other (when Costello died, Abbott was suing him for over $200,000) whereas there existed between Morecambe and Wise a genuine and close friendship. Abbott and Costello talked *at* each other; Morecambe and Wise wanted to talk *to* each other. As their confidence grew, and they learned to trust their instincts, allowing that human warmth to be seen on stage became crucial to the development of their act. In that sense, the more important—and profound—American model was Laurel and Hardy.

Although Laurel and Hardy were past their best by the time Morecambe and Wise began their career, they remained the benchmark for double acts everywhere. Morecambe and Wise's debt to them may be traced simply in Morecambe's borrowing of Hardy's blank stare to camera, and its way of making the audience complicit in the preposterousness of the situations their partners had landed them in. But the debt runs deeper than that, as John Fisher points out:

> Here are not merely the individual parallels, Stan and Eric sharing a Lancastrian warmth and simplicity, Ollie and Ernie a fastidious but never objectionable concern for their own self-importance, all four representing a degree of idiocy to which Abbott himself as straight man of the other duo would never have been party; but also the ability to reconcile a simple homely style with the most surreal flights of fantasy.[11]

In the conventional double act, the straight man often shares a sense of quotidian reality with his audience, a shared world into which the lunacies of the comic briefly intrude. With Laurel and Hardy, and increasingly as their career wore on with Morecambe and Wise, both partners are fools, albeit of different kinds, and the lunacy of their world is made the lunacy of the audiences' world. In both cases, the question may be asked: which one is the comic? Although with the British pair it remained unarguably the case that Morecambe's was the greater genius, the comic engine of their act was driven, as it was with Laurel and Hardy, by the proposition that 'one-doesn't-know-the-other-doesn't-know-who-is-the-bigger-idiot'. It was the *relationship* which was ultimately the powerhouse of the comedy. In both cases, comic partners are locked together in a sexless bachelorhood, in an ever-lasting, innocent childhood, pitted against a baffling and absurd world, and they draw their strength from a relationship of shared affection and loyalty that made audiences *care* about them. It is inherently a warmer, more caring and humane comedy, and one which draws the viewer into a comforting embrace. It was this that laid the foundation for Morecambe and Wise's development, through the 1950s and 1960s, into Britain's most successful double act, and their emergence as a 'national institution'.

'You Can't See the Join'

The apotheosis of Morecambe and Wise as that national institution was trumpeted by an article by the theatre critic Kenneth Tynan in 1973. Tynan wrote that:

> There comes a point at which sheer professional skill, raised to the highest degree by the refining drudgery of constant practice, evolves into something different in kind, conferring on its possessors an assurance that enables them to take off, to ignite, to achieve outrageous feats of timing and audience control that would, even a few years before, have been beyond them. Morecambe and Wise have now reached that point. In their last TV series, written by the intuitive Eddie Braben, they came on as masters, fit to head any list of the most accomplished performing artists at present active in this country.[12]

Tynan's view is confirmed (in a peculiarly apt metaphor) by the actor William Franklyn, who appeared regularly in the show. Morecambe would:

> make a line that you'd seen him rehearse and rehearse and rehearse seem like an ad-lib when it came to the recording. That's brilliant technique. It's rather like a great cricketer who can play his shots very late. Eric could lean back and think to himself, 'Right, I'll pick this off with my eyebrows and get a laugh', and he'd do it with such *grace*.[13]

Those critics who doubted the importance of Wise's contribution to the act need only have examined his performance in the 'André Previn' sketch I described above. Because of its star's other commitments, this was a routine for once seriously under-rehearsed. Morecambe's anxiety is quite visible at its beginning, but his sudden leap into confidence and brilliant comic inventiveness is enabled in no small part by Wise's careful, ad-libbed and above all professionally generous support: 'grace' of another kind, perhaps.

Tynan goes on to identify three versions of Morecambe and Wise's act. These equate roughly to its historical development: 'Mk I' is the post-war, pre-television work, 'Mk II' is the early, Hills-and-Green scripted television work, and 'Mk III' is the later, fully mature television shows written by Braben. In 'Mk I', they are essentially a classic, though essentially conventional, double act, with Wise as the feed and Morecambe the comic. By 'Mk II', that relationship was beginning to alter:

> They were no longer comic and feed, but two egotists in more or less equal competition. 'In old-fashioned double acts,' Eric says, 'the straight man would do something right and the comic would get it wrong. With us, Ernie would probably get it wrong as well. You get the same kind of thing with Laurel and Hardy.'[14]

'Mk III' represented less a further change of direction than a subsuming and further development of earlier versions of the act, earlier versions which remained visibly present in the mature work. The revival in a later television show of the Abbott and Costello-influenced con-trick routine—a 'Mk I' piece—has already been mentioned; indeed, the 'Mk I' Morecambe and Wise remained, essentially, what was performed at their live stage shows. More than this, material from their variety days was constantly revived, recycled and developed in their later careers, and it was by no means always their own. A sequence in which Wise attempts to teach Morecambe to play the bongos as accompaniment to his impression of Sammy Davis Junior was clearly influenced by the brilliant golf and billiards sketches of Field and Desmonde. Wise's version of *Antony and Cleopatra* involved the recreation of the famous 'sand dance' of Wilson, Kepple and Betty, with Glenda Jackson in the Betty role. An appearance in the Royal Variety Show in 1966 included the pair as 'Marvo and Dolores', an affectionate nod in the direction of every third-rate magic act to have filled a post-war variety bill. Perhaps the most important of these 'lifts', however, and the one which best illustrates how material was recalled, re-presented and developed (and which is its own version of the double act) was the ventriloquist routine, and its many variations, which became a staple of the Morecambe and Wise repertoire.

The origins of the routine lie with the Northern comic Sandy Powell, whose harassed 'vent' wrestled hopelessly with a recalcitrant and physically disintegrating dummy. Morecambe's version borrowed the love–hate relationship between vent and dummy, but also raised the vent's incompetence to dizzying heights:

> Good evening, little man, and how are you?
> I'm very well, thank you.
> And what are you going to do for the ladies and gentlemen?
> I'll sing a song.

The patter is spoken at dictation speed, with Morecambe's lips moving acrobatically and the dummy's not at all. When Wise eventually points out that he can see his partner's lips moving, Morecambe replies with exasperation that 'Of *course* you can see my lips moving!'. Finally persuaded of the need to make the *dummy's* lips move, Morecambe succeeds only in detaching its head entirely, and is left clutching it by the neck ('A throat with knuckles—they've never seen that before!'). As Tynan observes, 'Any other comic would ventriloquise *badly*; only a Morecambe would take the wild imaginative step of not ventriloquising *at all*.[15] The sketch formed a key part of the duo's stage act for many years, and was often used by them when they did their own, pre-recording 'warm-ups' for television audiences. But endless variations on it also found their way into the television shows themselves: on one occasion, the dummy was three times Morecambe's height, and rather heavy ('Solid oak! You know that clearing in Epping Forest? This is him'), and required a stepladder to work the lips. More generally, the sets for costume sketches and burlesques often contained a strategically placed marble bust or moose's head up to which Morecambe would surreptitiously sidle and insert his arm before asking 'What do you think of it so far?', invariably getting the answer 'Rubbish!'. In the *Antony and Cleopatra* sketch I mentioned earlier, Morecambe's arm took the place of the asp, appearing from its basket agog at the prospect of biting Glenda Jackson's breast. More subtly still, in three-way patter Morecambe would contrive to turn his back to the speaker, then, startled, exclaim to the silent figure facing him, 'You said that without moving your lips!'

In many ways the mature act of Morecambe and Wise depended entirely on this kind of recycling of material, their own and that of others, from variety days. The playwright Dennis Potter noted that their genius consisted 'precisely in knowing how to salvage material from a yellowing stock of back numbers of *Dandy* and *Beano*: they do not so much deliver their lines as resuscitate them'.[16] Potter notices the childlike innocence of their humour, which avoided politics altogether and dealt with sex only through an unobjectionable innuendo ('My mother had a Whistler', 'Now there's a novelty') that harked back to the 1930s of George Formby (not Max Miller), and through that strange working-class surrealism identified elsewhere in this book as 'the

Northern sublime' (how else can one account for 'a little bit of hello-folks-and-what-about-the-workers' as a euphemism for the sexual act?). But his main point is to do with the *familiarity* of Morecambe and Wise's material, and the way in which it consciously tapped into and exploited audience expectation. Running gags, verbal and visual, ran across decades. One sketch had the duo performing as quiz-master and contestant, with the former trying to help the clueless latter by providing badly disguised answers to the questions: 'Who won the FA Cup Final in 1936?' was followed by an explosive cough very obviously containing the word 'Arsenal'. For years after, and long after the originating sketch had been confined to history, any cough on stage or in the auditorium would be greeted with a triumphant cry of 'Arsenal!!'. In this sense, the material became self-sustaining. Morecambe's repertoire of catch-phrases ('There's no answer to that', 'Oh yes, little Ern', 'This boy's a fool'), insults to his partner ('short fat hairy legs', or, referring to Wise's imagined wig, 'you can't see the join') and visual jokes (running his glasses up and down his leg or wearing them on the back of his head) were a vital and *expected* part of any show, and a large part of the viewer's pleasure lay not simply in the inherent humour but also in the particular enjoyment of watching craftsmen at work producing new laughs from old material. The extent to which Morecambe and Wise were aware of this is nowhere more evident than in a front-of-curtain 'stand-up' routine where Wise comes on to confess that he is 'worried' about Morecambe's increasing 'predictability'. Morecambe enters, after his customary wrestle with the drapes, to run through the familiar repertoire, each element of which is confidently, if sadly, predicted by Wise ('Now it'll be the "short fat hairy legs" . . .'). The punchline is the visual gag Wise forgets: the double-handed slap to his partner's face that Morecambe worked into almost every show. What is significant is the way in which expectation, 'predictability', so often the death of comedy acts, here becomes a source of new material. The act is effectively being deconstructed before the viewers' eyes: what is seen here is not simply two performers doing their act, but two people performing *and demonstrating* an act with a visible subtext that articulates both a personal and a general historical context and the sometimes difficult and always complex personal and professional relationship that is the substance of the double act.

This sense of self-reflexivity, of the duo exposing and guying its own act, is reflected in the treatment of celebrity guest stars, where the conventions of the wider profession are systematically taken apart. Its trigger was any sense of professional vanity, in their own work or that of their (often very distinguished) guests. It lent an extraordinary feeling of *transparency* to the work, and bred in its audiences a confidence that what it saw, it got. Eddie Braben, when he first began writing for the duo, was struck by the fact that their on-screen *personae* were less artificial constructs than exaggerated versions of their off-screen selves. (It is certainly true that, unlike the cases of other comedy favourites such as Frankie Howerd, Kenneth Williams and Tommy Cooper, the tabloid press was never able to besmirch the private lives of Morecambe and Wise.) The mutual affection visible on screen was *real*. It was from this perception that Braben made his input into Morecambe and Wise 'Mk III':

> You see, one of the first things that struck me about their relationship was its *closeness*. Like I said: there shouldn't have been an 'and' in 'Morecambe and Wise', it should've been 'Morecambewise', because they were *so* close. So my idea was to put these two people into an enclosed space—the equivalent of being inside a music-hall horse-skin—so that they couldn't escape each other, they were closeted together, and that way I could develop the characters and the dialogue the way I wanted them to go. That was how the 'in-bed' and 'at-home' situations came about. I think, at the start, they weren't too sure about this idea of two men being in bed together, and they were quite wary, but they also agreed that the situation was too good to lose. They feared that people might read something into it that wasn't there. I remember that I said to them, 'Well, if it's good enough for Laurel and Hardy, it's good enough for you!' That did it. Eric said, 'Sod 'em! We'll do it!'. And they did.[17]

The 'in-bed', 'at-home' sketches became an integral feature of the shows, taking their place amongst the stand-up and song and dance routines. They were, in effect, mini-situation comedies, though—crucially—with *character* rather than plot or narrative driving the 'situation'. Braben's development of the performers' *personae* drew on their shared, impoverished Northern backgrounds to create individual biographies that were cartoon-like, but only semi-fictionalized: he imagined them at 'Milverton Street Infant School' together, their essential characters already fully formed in miniature, and as entertainers in circus or second-rate end-of-the-pier shows, and all in the context of a bleak, Northern working-class town of fish 'n' chips, ferrets and lines of washing hung out to dry in 'Tarryassan Street' (a location almost as vivid as Tony Hancock's '23 Railway Cuttings'). 'We had roast duck on Sundays', said Braben's Eric, '. . . if the park was open'. Just as Morecambe and Wise already drew on their earlier variety days, so Braben drew on their earlier personal lives. Moreover, he further developed their individual characters, pulling out personal traits and making the performers still more into *people*:

> Braben's 'Eric' is the fast-talker, the freethinker, the face-slapper, sharp-witted but unfocused, naughty and saucy, an irresistible misfit—an altogether more devious and dangerous creature than the earlier, somewhat fatuous, incarnation from the ATV days. Braben's 'Ernie', on the

other hand, now became an even smaller man bewitched by even bigger dreams, a simpleton posing as a sophisticate ('A man of great education like what no other man has got'), the suppose worldliness of his gestures forever belied by the homeliness of his vocabulary.[18]

The effect was further to enrich what was already a shifting and complex double-act relationship: from beginning as basic comic and feed, and moving to 'one-doesn't-know-the-other-doesn't-know-who-is-the-bigger-idiot', Morecambe and Wise now found themselves, as Tynan points out, in a reversal of roles that was far from simple: 'Ernie today is the comic *who is not funny*. And Eric—the dominating character who patronises the comic— is the straight man *who is funny*.'[19] Only Laurel and Hardy, perhaps, have matched this degree of performative sophistication as a double act, and, as with the American duo, what was enabled was a three-dimensional richness of characterization that transcended the limitations of lesser acts. Crucially, an unexpected sense of compassion could creep into sketches. Take for example 'Ern' reading aloud from his latest masterpiece: 'Rocky felt a tingle of excitement as his executive jet touched down in Amsterdam. It was his first visit to Italy.' Far from pouncing on his partner's vainglorious stupidity, Morecambe turns away, winces to camera, then turns back: 'That's knock-out, that, Ern', betraying a caring, instinctive protectiveness (characteristic, perhaps, of Northern working-class families) that speaks silently of deep affection. A comparable moment occurs, as McCann suggests, at the end of Laurel and Hardy's *A Chump at Oxford*, where Ollie, having been humiliated even more than usual by a Stan afflicted with temporary amnesia, is finally about to leave. Stan, however, suddenly regains his memory: 'Hey, Ollie! Aren't you going to take me with you?' Hardy rushes back to embrace him: 'Stan! You *know* me!'[20]

   That moment also reveals another shared characteristic of two great double acts, a characteristic Beckett drew on with his own tragi-comic pairing, 'Didi' and 'Gogo' in *Waiting for Godot*: that of a sense of the mutual dependencies of friendship as a necessary if problematic defence against a terrifying lone-liness. I do not suggest that either Laurel and Hardy or Morecambe and Wise fully articulated or even knew the horrific bleakness of Beckett's world (although Morecambe's 1981 novel about a failed club comic was called *Mr Lonely*),[21] but there were moments when they at least suggested it. Left alone on stage after a 'row' with his partner, a bereft Morecambe pleaded to the audience that he'd 'never worked on my own before', whilst one full routine involved Wise 'sacking' Morecambe and replacing him with a new partner identical in all respects save his greater youth and less troublesome nature: a partner, of course, who, inevitably and desperately, could not spot the feeds, tell the jokes or time the responses.[22] Nor is it too far-fetched to sense in the strangely anonymous, bland and schematic flat which was the scene of the 'at-home' sequences, where the old routines—of schooldays, touring days, old theatrical landladies and the imagined delights of 'Ada Bailey's knickers'— punctured listless silences, something of what Fisher calls the 'time/space vacuum' bred by working together in intimate partnership for over forty years.[23] *Fear*, Morecambe always insisted, was what motivated their act. He meant, I think, fear of the misfiring joke, the failed show or the flagging career; but also, perhaps, the fear of partnerlessness, of friendlessness, of being alone. He was surely aware that one of his favourite insults to Wise—that he was only 'half a star'—was double-edged.

Morecambe and Wise were at their creative peak at a time when Britain was undergoing deep and unsettling social and cultural change. It is arguable that their immense popularity arose in part because the very familiarity of their routines, and their nostalgic appeals to real and imagined pasts, offered a point of reassurance and stability. To that extent at least theirs was a conservative humour, though there is little that is conservative in the liberations of brilliant, imaginative comic invention, with its surrealistic revisions of mundane reality. In the innocence of their material and in the way they exploited it—with humble self-awareness and supreme professionalism—they provoked a laughter that was human, humane, and deeply democratic.

CHAPTER THIRTEEN

Playing on the Front Foot

Actors and Audience in British Popular Theatre, 1970–1990

Colin Chambers and Maggie Steed

The following is a conversation between actress Maggie Steed and theatre writer Colin Chambers. They first met when they were both working for the Royal Shakespeare Company in the 1980s. She had established her reputation as a performer in political theatre; he, after a brief spell with a street theatre group, had written about political theatre as a journalist before becoming the RSC's Literary Manager.

CC: How did you become an actress?

MS: I went to the Bristol Old Vic Theatre School in the mid–1960s when I was very young, probably too young. It was run by a man called Nat Brenner, who I only discovered much later had been a member of the Communist Party.

CC: He'd been active in the 1930s in the left-wing Unity Theatre.

MS: Yes, but he kept all that completely hidden, in a very principled way. I remember from the training that we had to judge a play and then forget our judgement on it, as though as actors we weren't supposed to have any judgements about anything in the play.

CC: You were encouraged to be neutral.

MS: As though you were a blank board. It was a useful way to approach a text. You did your research and you worked out what was required, but the idea that you as a person—that your history, what had happened to you, and your ideas about the world—could impinge on the work was absent.

CC: You had to separate yourself from the play and become a walking bag of technique.

MS: Exactly.

CC: Were you political at this time?

MS: No. I thought that theatre could do 'good'. I remember having arguments about that, but there was nothing in the training that gave us any notion beyond this. I don't think we even dealt with Brecht. We did look at Expressionism, so we did *The Silver Tassie*.

CC: What happened when you left drama school?

MS: I was tall, nineteen, with very gappy teeth and it was the time of 'dolly birds'. I didn't fit in and I couldn't get work. Nat Brenner had told me I wouldn't. With tears in his eyes, he'd said, 'You know you won't work till you're thirty'.

CC: Glenda Jackson was told the same thing at RADA: 'You're not pretty, you'll be a character actress, so forget working for another ten years'.

MS: And Julie Christie was told the complete reverse. 'You do realise you'll only work until you're twenty-five.'

CC: You weren't put off by this?

MS: No. At that age, you can't imagine being thirty and I thought he was wrong. But he wasn't wrong really. And I was ill-prepared for living in London, where there were in fact a lot of very interesting fringe theatres starting up.

CC: Did you think, 'I'm not going to make it as an actress'?

MS: Yes. I gave up and I became a secretary. Then I suppose I sort of grew up. After a few years, I wouldn't say I'd become politicized but I could see that there were a lot of things wrong. And then I started working for a kids theatre workshop in south London, during the evening. A friend of mine was working there and I used to go down and help her run it. I thought I just can't go on with being a secretary. I was only twenty-five, and I had to get work back in the theatre. I did a three-month tour with Brian Way . . .

CC: One of the pioneers of theatre for young people . . .

MS: and then I went to work at Coventry Theatre-in-Education at the Belgrade Theatre.

CC: How did that happen?

MS: I met them through being around that network in London. They asked me to audition and I joined. That was the beginning of it all for me, because Coventry TiE was fascinating, a very influential company, and highly political.

CC: Yes. First the Midlands, later the world. The TiE movement began there in Coventry.

MS: They knew that you informed the work with your own history, not necessarily consciously, but that you have no alternative but to do so, and it's got to be acknowledged. The cry used to be that it was not going to be about flopsy bunnies, but it was going to be about the real world. Particularly with kids from junior school—they can take so much. They can make all the connections. It was at a time of team teaching and cross-curriculum teaching, which is now derided, but was, I think, very stimulating for the children. We did programmes about pollution and the local industries, like weaving, coal, and the railways. There were books published about Coventry TiE and we felt sure that it was important work. In fact, the programmes we initiated have been performed to children all over the world.

CC: It was a departure from the emphasis on self-expression and personal development of children's theatre to more 'content' based drama, and there was proper preparation and follow-up by the teachers in the schools, all of which was new then. Were you involved in a mixture of devised work and scripted work?

MS: We had a writer called David Holman, and if he was on a show he would write it, but it would be group devised. Other shows were scripted by the performers.

CC: It was a different method of working, and nothing at drama school had prepared you for this.

MS: No, nothing. We had to work out what the aim of the piece was, what sort of narrative the piece would need, and what were the conflicts that would best serve its aim. We'd go off and write our own scenes or improvise. We were completely thrown in the deep end. It was difficult but exciting.

CC: Did you get the sense that you were part of something bigger?

MS: Yes. There were lots of other professional TiE companies, and they came together to form the Standing Conference of Young People's Theatre that goes on today. It was a forum about the work: a lot of argument, a lot of blood spilt, a lot about the wrong ways to do things, and the right ways to do things, but it was very lively. All the companies were publicly funded. Some had funding from local education authorities, some from arts councils and some from arts associations. There were a lot of actors from my generation who worked in those companies.

CC: It was an important training ground for a particular generation.

MS: Yes.

CC: Did you come to a point when you thought 'I can use this experience elsewhere'?

MS: I still wanted to get on that stage. So eventually I went away from TiE.

CC: Where?

MS: I'd seen the work of the Belt and Braces Roadshow since they'd begun in the early 1970s. They were formed by Gavin Richards and a couple of other people. I'd been at drama school with Gavin, who was really the inspiration in the group, and we were very old friends. I said to him, 'I've really got to work with the company', and one day—in 1977—he asked me to join him playing *The Mother*.

CC: So by this time you *had* discovered Brecht?

MS: Indeed.

CC: It was quite a jump in one sense. Gavin had set up Belt and Braces as an explicitly socialist theatre company whose very purpose was to perform to a working-class audience.

MS: It was a logical move to go from Coventry TiE to Belt and Braces.

CC: The theatrical demands were of a different order. Did you feel prepared for it?

MS: No, but I felt ready to have a go at it. There were more things in common than were different. Our performing style—if there was a style at Coventry— was very full blooded, and we sang and did all sorts of different things. Naturalism was a dirty word.

CC: Did you learn from the kids and the responses you got?

MS: If they weren't responding, we did think we were doing it all wrong. We'd go away and change things and rewrite them and cut them. And sometimes we did think that we were frightening them. But usually it was passionate work and the kids responded.

CC: You had a sense of confidence about yourself as an actor.

MS: But not a sense of confidence that I was able to go off and do any kind of theatre.

CC: In that sense Belt and Braces was not so much of a change. It was doing the same sorts of things but in a slightly different context.

MS: With more resources, and pushing it further.

CC: That was your first show with them, *The Mother*?

MS: Yes. It was a touring show, directed by Paul Hellyer. I remember he said, 'This is the school of tasteless acting. No good taste on this stage.' And that seemed marvellous to me.

CC: Which is interesting because Brecht was keen on good taste, the shades of colouring of certain things and the detail, the way that objects were made.

MS: I think he was interested in good choices, choices that would serve the purpose of the piece. That's about craft and about developing your craft so you can make the right choices, and that's what Paul was talking about. He'd seen a production of *The Mother* by the San Francisco Mime Troupe, who had used all their craft to do a marvellous production.

CC: Critics often look back at what was called the fringe and damn it as not being that interested in the nuts and bolts of the business.

MS: I don't think that's true of Belt and Braces at all. For a start it was run by a complete martinet. (*Laughs.*) You'd ask, 'Why isn't that scene working?' and Gavin would reply, 'It's just bad acting'.

CC: You were dealing in concepts like good and bad acting.

MS: It was tough. No one let you get away with anything. Left-wing theatre was deeply unforgiving.

CC: You had to be strong to cope with it all. No wilting flowers. And touring was physically demanding.

MS: I saw someone the other day loading musical equipment into a van, and I thought, 'I know what that's like'.

CC: Everyone lent a hand. It wasn't, 'Oh I don't do that. I'm an actor.'

MS: Absolutely not.

CC: Was there much discussion of the nature of the audiences and the venues, or was that just a given?

MS: It was always a real problem. You had a grid of arts centres, and to fulfil your grant conditions you had to get a certain number of bookings from this grid. But of course you really wanted to be playing to workingmen's clubs or community associations on top of that. You'd be desperate to get different gigs away from the grid but it was hard to plan a tour. You might be going up to Newcastle one night, then Bristol, and back up to Huddersfield—all one night stands—but you'd do that to play good working-class gigs.

CC: How did you get those gigs, as opposed to the arts centres?

MS: Through word of mouth mostly. We had somebody who went out looking for those gigs and other groups would share information.

CC: Wanting to appeal to a different sort of audience meant performing a different sort of theatre, something you could play in a workingmen's club and to which they would respond.

MS: That's where the whole commitment to musical theatre came in. It was very important in Belt and Braces.

CC: And for companies like Monstrous Regiment and 7:84—which is why John McGrath, out of his experiences with 7:84, called his book on making popular theatre *A Good Night Out*.

MS: Getting it right was difficult. Belt and Braces tried different styles. Their shows weren't all the same.

CC: Gavin had worked with Ken Campbell, who was popular but not to Gavin's mind political, and Gavin wanted to capture something of his appeal but with the politics as well. That must have been difficult as Belt and Braces were having to play to quite separate audiences, sometimes middle-class students . . .

MS: . . . a lot of the time to middle-class students . . .

CC: and then you'd play to . . .

MS: . . .housing estates outside Glasgow or Edinburgh.

CC: There was a palpable difference, presumably, and not just in terms of the physical environment.

MS: It didn't always go the way you thought it would go. We were very naïve and idealistic. In workingmen's clubs they were still playing the fruit machines whilst we were doing the show, and they wanted to pay us off halfway through because they wanted to get on to the bingo. And then you'd play Bretton Hall, which was full of students, and they'd think it was the most fantastic thing they'd seen ever. People still come up to me from that night saying, 'I've never forgotten'. When we played Castlemilk Community Centre outside Glasgow, there were signs outside asking if anyone knew anything about the body of a baby that had been found in a dustbin, and yet the show seemed likely to take the roof off. That was with Brecht, not with the material that the company had made themselves. He's a fantastic and humorous and passionate storyteller about the bravery of ordinary people, and that's what comes through. People came up afterwards and said, 'That was great. A really great night.' Those were the times that made you think 'Ah, this is right'.

CC: Did you ever go back there with another show?

MS: I never went back there.

CC: Building on that kind of response must have been critical, though, for groups like Belt and Braces.

MS: 7:84 is the company that did this the most. Especially in Scotland they had a whole series of places that they went back to, show after show.

CC: They invented their own route, with occasional forays to enemy territory like the Royal Court. The Scottish company weren't seen as one of those student outfits from down south 'telling us what to do'. They overcame the understandable wariness about political theatre groups with their 'message'.

MS: I think that was why the work had to be so robust, and the humour had to be on the front foot. I don't mean that it was coarse, but we had to be very sharp and truthful.

CC: I remember that seeing shows by companies like Belt and Braces, Red Ladder or 7:84 in a community context was a very different experience from theatre-going in conventional spaces. If you saw 7:84 on one of their visits to the Royal Court, it was very different from seeing a Royal Court production there and very different from seeing them on the road. Regardless of the auditorium they would play out-front, like a pop concert.

MS: Like playing in front of a band, on the front foot.

CC: They would perform out to the audience. They were acting with and to the audience more than with and to each other. Often the audience is the classic fourth wall and the actors don't show any knowledge that the audience exists. With 7:84 and the other groups it was the opposite—they wanted interaction. At the Royal Court they didn't get that. Everyone sat back politely, judging the performance and placing it away in one of their compartments, perhaps with the label interesting, or maybe crude, political theatre. If you saw 7:84 in Scotland it was completely different. The audience would be more voluble, they would shout back.

MS: Part of the point was to be moved, not just in terms of being amused.

CC: Sometimes the sheer exhilaration became achievement enough and confused the important debate within the political theatre movement about the role of aesthetics. How much should it be 'good theatre' and how much 'good politics'. I always thought there shouldn't be a contradiction between the two. It's related to what we were talking about earlier about craft. If you want a popular audience you have to do the thing as well as you could do it.

MS: Absolutely, and in the end Belt and Braces captured its vast audience by going into the West End, with Dario Fo's *The Accidental Death of an Anarchist*. That paid off the deficit, but then the grant was cut and that spelled the end of Belt and Braces really.

CC: In a slightly different way, this happened to Joan Littlewood and Theatre Workshop with their earlier attempts to create a popular theatre. They reached a point where they went into the West End and were doing long runs. They couldn't get the support they needed from the Arts Council, so it was important, but it undermined the attempt to run an ensemble back at their 'HQ' in Stratford East, which had been the basis for their success in the first place. The treadmill finished them off. Did Belt and Braces see going into the West End as a victory?

MS: It was a decision that was taken after a show called *A Day in the Life of the World*, the rock musical that emptied theatres the length and breadth of England. Yet when we toured it to Sweden, it won acclaim among audiences and theatre groups there.

CC: Why didn't it work here?

MS: It wasn't like the old agitprop that you could do in a pub room. It was a big, technical show and the sort of spaces that we needed to play it in we couldn't fill.

CC: What happened then?

MS: We said, 'We can't go on like this. How are we going to get a mass audience?' There were all sorts of notions of maybe one day being able to do something like we had seen in Sweden—about forty groups had got together and toured in a large tent spending two weeks in each town with families and caravans and dancing and music. It was marvellous and very well organized. Meanwhile, Rob Walker had done Fo's *Can't Pay, Won't Pay* at the Half Moon and we thought Dario Fo is the answer to everyone's dream. We seemed to be the last country in Europe to have discovered him.

CC: It was a conscious choice to choose a Fo and to aim for the West End?

MS: It was a conscious decision by the whole company. All the women put themselves out of work because there was only one woman's part in it.

CC: Was there the expectation that if it worked it would bring new life to the company and you'd all be back in it afterwards?

MS: Yes.

CC: And was going to the West End seen as a financial or a political act?

MS: Political, because you get a mass audience.

CC: And conquer foreign territory?

MS: It did. Thousands of people saw *Accidental Death*.

CC: But you paid a heavier price.

MS: It paid off the overdraft and so the Arts Council took us off the revenue grant . . .

CC: Because in theory you didn't need that level of subsidy . . .

MS: . . . and put us onto project grants, limited from project to project.

CC: So you couldn't build a company?

MS: Yes. It fell apart.

CC: And presumably this grant decision was seen as a political act.

MS: Oh yes. I think it was.

CC: There was much argument at the time about the ethics of the state paying people to attack the state, and after Thatcher came to power the political groups and Theatre-in-Education were butchered, the movement as a whole was decimated.

MS: Everything was being cut. Everything.

CC: What happened to you after *Accidental Death*?

MS: I got myself a career. (*Laughs.*)

CC: Out of need.

MS: Out of need. I went to work with Rob Walker at the Half Moon and bullied him to give me a job. I played about six different men in *Arturo Ui*. We did *The Machine Wreckers* and then I did *Guys and Dolls* and from that I got myself an agent and a career, completely unexpectedly as I was devoted to Belt and Braces. Ironically, whilst they were playing at the Albery Theatre I found myself performing opposite Fred Molina in a new production of *Can't Pay, Won't Pay* at the Criterion in Piccadilly Circus.

CC: Going to the Half Moon was staying in the same world as Belt and Braces. The alternative political theatre, like the RSC, had created its own diaspora, and you could go from one company to another and meet like-minded people.

MS: Yes, you could. Loads of people did—Harriet Walter, Fred Pearson, Kenny Ireland, lots.

CC: There was an infrastructure, the organisations, the conferences . . .

MS: With great disagreements about what the true way was. For instance, some people thought Joint Stock were so prissy. There were ridiculous disagreements going on, but it was possible to work and be creative.

CC: What do you think you had learned as an actor? It obviously changed you completely. You weren't recognisable as the graduate of the Bristol Old Vic?

MS: The notion that it's not something separate is really important. I think that's what Brecht was talking about, when he talked about your objective reality. For example, when I was in *Can't Pay, Won't Pay*—a wonderfully well created farce about a working-class Italian woman who can't pay the bills and invents all sorts of things to get herself through—I remember one afternoon when the audience was rolling with laughter and in the last scene, when she's desperately trying to think of yet more ways to lie to her law-abiding Communist Party husband, there was a woman in the front row who just brought the show to a halt. She was beside herself with identification. She was calling out, 'You tell him, you tell him. I know what it's like. I've been in that state.' I had to include her in the performance.

CC: What did you do?

MS: I paid tribute to her. I put my hand out to her and she got a round of applause. One of the things about doing this kind of work is that you have to enable the audience to feel that they're included and that, should they wish to, it was possible to intervene like that. It's to do with the content of the work—the play's about all our lives, with the juxtaposition of love, death and money.

CC: And performed in a style that makes the audience feel they are part of the experience and not just observing it, so it's built into the very way in which the play is presented.

MS: Performing in a way that takes that for granted.

CC: Did you find that when you went on into the rest of the theatre world you carried all that with you? Did you find you were generally accepted or were you treated as an oddball?

MS: There were pockets where it was accepted, and that's much more the case now. For instance, there have been all those actors coming out of the Anna Scher drama school who are used to improvising their authentic experiences and they have an authenticity. And it's true in a cinema as well.

CC: You could say it was beginning to happen even in the mid–1950s, with,

say, the plays of Arnold Wesker which were premièred at Coventry.

MS: Yes indeed.

CC: People despised technique as 'being RADA' and tied up with learning to speak Received Pronunciation—the idea that you hung yourself up on the dressing room door when you went on stage and became something different that was called an actor, with a certain way of thinking as an actor. The other side of the coin in rejecting technique was a self-indulgence, where subjectivity became everything, which can be anti-political although people thought they were being terribly liberal.

MS: Yes.

CC: There must have been conflicts for you as you discovered this unexpected career?

MS: Oh yes, and even now there's a conflict between my brain and my heart about doing some television, and then trying to make the television into something it isn't. But one of the ways I tried to cope was to do cabaret. It was very interesting. The Comedy Store was just starting so quite a number of us did stand-up and toured around. We formed a group called Alternative Cabaret. Tony Allen, who was a well-known anarchist comedian, invented the phrase. If you could make the gig you did, and if not, because of your other work, somebody else would do it.

CC: Did you write the material yourself?

MS: Yes. I was utterly terrified but it was very exciting.

CC: Did it develop out of the musical theatre companies like Belt and Braces were doing?

MS: Yes. For instance, in *Not So Green As Its Cabbage* it was all stand-up stuff.

CC: How did you feel when you did your first major television, *Shine on Harvey Moon*?

MS: It turned out it was quite possible to do all sorts of things with the show: develop the characters and write our own scenes.

CC: Was that built in or did you just bring that to it?

MS: We just did it.

CC: Were the authors happy? Did they know?

MS: I've never been able to tell whether they knew or not. They wrote the lot and then we rewrote as we rehearsed. Loads of stuff was put in, loads of jokes. And it was vindicated because it was terribly popular. People loved it. It was a long way away from political theatre.

CC: That was disappearing.

MS: I had left it in a sense and I felt some relief, because it had been very hard going. I didn't think of returning to it, but I went on to work with Edward Bond.

CC: That was in *The War Plays* at the RSC. Had you thought of joining the RSC before?

MS: Yes, but I'd always been a bit frightened of it.

CC: It was not for you?

MS: I've never been good at big institutions. I don't feel comfortable.

CC: How do you think it was seen amongst your peers?

MS: Oh despised, and the National.

CC: Because they were crap?

MS: Yes—bourgeois crap. These were terribly reductive opinions, and, in retrospect, that didn't help our work at all. But we had to see ourselves as a vanguard.

CC: Now people laugh because Gavin went to *EastEnders*, but that's a popular form. Was it Edward Bond who won you rather than the RSC?

MS: Yes. The chance to work with him was unmissable.

CC: Doing plays by Edward Bond is one of the ways the RSC can justify itself. You don't do classics in a vacuum; you do them along with new writing. The two are supposed to feed each other. That didn't always work, but it was a litmus test, to see if the big national companies still had any point, to be able to stage productions like *The War Plays*. The experience is interesting from that point of view. It was pretty painful for a lot of people.

MS: It was very difficult. I had a big part in it, so in a sense I had to keep my head down to do it. I suffered less because of that. Other people who had less to do suffered more. And also the people who were in the company. I was brought in from outside and that was all I had to do, but people who were in *Richard III* or *Golden Girls* or something else in that London season had a tougher time, because Edward blamed them for the problems we faced.

CC: He has a low opinion of the RSC and of what happens to the actors who work there.

MS: The fact that you were doing two evenings' ambitious, difficult new work about the nuclear desert that would take six hours to perform, and were having to argue about whether or not an actor was available because they had a fight call elsewhere, was beyond the pale to him.

CC: The institution didn't help.

MS: No. The institution got in the way, over and over. He should have had exclusive call on his actors' time. Peter Brook would have had it.

CC: All the actors were committed to the project. It was like working with Peter Brook. This was the chance of a lifetime. I still remember them as extraordinary pieces, yet it led to a lot of bad feeling and Edward leaving half way through.

MS: I remember when he told me he was going to go that I said, 'All right. You can leave, but you can't leave me. You have to phone me everyday.' And he went 'alright', and he kept his promise. He left in order to get the last play on. He didn't want to walk away from his play.

CC: In those big companies, for good reason, he's always keeping his end up.

MS: He has to maintain himself as the outsider.

CC: He battles in order to define himself. I think it's a pity the actors got in the crossfire, and were very unhappy. He has the reputation of not knowing how to work with actors.

MS: He uses a language that some actors are unfamiliar with and talks in images that are sometimes difficult to grasp.

CC: He wants you to come to him. He doesn't go to the actors. He knows exactly what he wants, and you have to discover that. But you stayed with the RSC.

MS: I did the Howard Barker season in The Pit, and that has a line through from my earlier work.

CC: His writing is about things being real, but not in a naturalistic sense. There's a way in which the stuff of life—the muscles and blood as well as the imagination—comes through, like Lucien Freud or Frances Bacon, but it's not a photographic representation.

MS: Yet everyone recognizes the truth of it.

CC: With the best writers you get that with the imagery, the strength of the language, the vocabulary. As in Shakespeare. He is the great popular writer. It's just a shame that so much of what is done with him is poor. That's the irony for us. He is both so popular and yet has more bad productions done of his work than anybody else. When was your first Shakespeare?

MS: That was some time after the Barkers—though I made a great mistake. I was offered a season in Stratford, including Paulina in *A Winter's Tale*, immediately on the back of the Bonds and the Barkers, and I still to this day don't know why I didn't do it. I was very frightened. That's what I wake up in a cold sweat about.

CC: Perhaps it was to do with what you'd been through. Maybe it was the institution.

MS: Maybe it was.

CC: In Stratford you're with the RSC all the time, it's like a campus.

MS: I know and I don't like that. I didn't like it when I got there.

CC: What was your first Shakespeare?

MS: I played Gertrude on the RSC's small-scale tour of *Hamlet* directed by Roger Michell.

CC: Did you think, 'It's a tour, I can cope with that', or did you think it would lead you back into the company?

MS: It was just a tour and I really liked the idea of that, being on the road again, and it was one of the happiest jobs of my life. You are playing all over the country, in great big spaces, but instead of being like Belt and Braces, loading the van yourself, you've got wonderful facilities, and the audiences really want you to come and they have a good time, and they're very grateful.

CC: I suppose *Hamlet* on tour was a continuation of the sort of commitment you had to popular theatre

MS: Yes.

CC: You are going out to places where people don't have regular theatre and the prices are not so steep.

MS: And they are seeing really good work.

CC: You finally went to Stratford for *Much Ado About Nothing*.

MS: Yes, and it was very badly received. So were the other opening shows that season, including a revival of Adrian Noble's production of *Macbeth*. Adrian was running Stratford and a group of us went to see him. We told him he had a company of the walking wounded who needed attention and his response was along the lines of, 'I don't bother with what the critics say. I'll answer them with my next production.'

CC: It was not the response you had expected or sought.

MS: I'm afraid it proved my prejudice. I didn't want to go to Stratford thinking I was the best thing in the world, yet everyone was encouraged by the RSC to think that they were, that this was the pinnacle of everything. But when you hit trouble you were left stranded.

CC: They couldn't just get on with the work. There was always that sense of trying to talk it all up.

MS: It was a hothouse. I've not worked there since.

CC: But you've worked with Bond again.

MS: I've done a Bond on television and one on radio.

CC: There aren't so many opportunities now for you to do that kind of work. I do think we've lost something because of the decline of political theatre. I don't want to make it sound as if it was all wonderful back then—we all saw some awful stuff—but it did make the blood go round quicker. There was an interaction, something electric in the air; they engaged you and you came out feeling 'I'm glad to have been part of that.'

MS: It was visceral.

CC: Nowadays, you don't generally get that connection, although I think there are groups still able to hit the button. And they've built on the legacy of that political theatre. It fed into the broader theatre, because most people from those groups remained active, even though they were not able to do the things they might have been able to do. It's had quite an effect on the theatre, right up to Sir David Hare of Portable fame. People have made great efforts to open theatre up so that it's much less of a club. Money is still a problem, but theatre is not quite so forbidding now. It may not be part of popular culture, as we wished, but that is a different problem.

MS: What is a popular audience? I think it's wishful thinking. Well, Stratford East has it. I would say a popular audience is an audience from the community.

CC: The Hackney Empire has popular audiences, with its black audiences and Turkish audiences, and so forth, and that came out of political theatre, out of CAST.

MS: Theatre doesn't go to so many places now. I toured a Robert Holman play with the Oxford Stage Company a couple of years ago, and I thought I was watching the demise of regional theatre everywhere we went.

CC: Nobody turning up?

MS: Very small audiences, no passion around, no follow up. We went to the Liverpool Everyman. There's no company there. There's a head of department for bringing shows in, but they hadn't done any publicity. We had reviews you could die for and it still said 'Coming Next Week' on the front of the theatre.

CC: So now they all come down in busloads to see *Les Misérables*.

MS: They would have been doing that anyway.

CC: But they might also have seen something else. But that something else isn't available and it will take some effort to get it back again.

MS: I do think it's to do with funding, which has been taken away.

CC: The government needs to say, 'This is important. Here's a strategy for rebuilding theatre out there, up and down the country.'

MS: You would have places you would key into, as Belt and Braces did, like the old Liverpool Everyman.

CC: You have to relearn again a whole other way of acting that reconnects with the audience, but of course it's all linked with the material.

MS: Yes. For example, it seems as though Brecht has got rather a bad name now.

CC: When those alternative companies disappeared hardly anybody else was doing him, except for a handful of his best-known plays. The big companies thought he was bad box-office but they rarely did him well anyway. They didn't understand what he was about. They were trying to accommodate him. He was seen as a classic playwright so that's how they did him. The British have still hardly seen any of his plays if you look at the total output. Perhaps we're paying the price for having had all that political theatre you were involved in—everybody's saying, 'We've done all that'.

MS: It's more than that. It's the whole thing about socialism, which has a bad name. 'We beat the communists so what's the point of putting their plays on?'

CC: That'll change at some point. But you need resources to do many of Brecht's plays.

MS: You certainly need resources to do *Mother Courage*. I did it a few years ago at the Lyceum in Edinburgh with Kenny Ireland, and it was after a long time of not having done that kind of work. I had to do an awful lot more work than I ever did when working on *The Mother*. I read up about it and about Helene Weigel's original performance. I had a book of photographs of that first production and Brecht's notes about how you direct a scene and the way a scene was laid out on the stage, figuratively, so that you could get from this moment to the next moment. That was completely fascinating, and that's when I realized that he's just not done properly. What we see has been made either respectable or milky.

CC: Just as Shakespeare has been made deadly.

MS: It seemed, looking back, that the work we were doing in the 1970s was on the right footing.

CC: You got an audience, so he's not that bad at the box office.

MS: We certainly got an audience at the Lyceum, and they laughed a lot and were very moved. We used the David Hare adaptation, which was very good. It was quite a traditional production, I suppose because of Kenny and me. I lifted stuff from Weigel, like the way she always clicked her handbag and the business with the coins at the end, when she gives money for her daughter's burial and then takes one coin back. I needed the sort of energy that we had to use in Belt and Braces, that being on the front foot and being a survivor— it was like survivor's theatre, wasn't it? That was exactly what was needed to perform the play, and to keep it alive, because she's so full of life. She has to be full of life right to the end even though she's exhausted. What we were doing in Edinburgh was very much in line with what we were doing in Belt and Braces.

CHAPTER FOURTEEN

Working Wonders

Mark Rylance at the New Globe

Martin White

There's great acting; there's very great acting; and then there's what Mark Rylance does on top of that. (Paul Taylor, *The Independent*, 1994)

The new Globe Theatre stands on the South Bank of the Thames, a short distance from the site of the original playhouse, alongside Tate Modern and reached across the Thames by the Millennium Bridge. The wood-framed, plastered building—evocatively described by Peter Thomson as nestling 'amid concrete like a spilled heirloom'[1]—was the brainchild of American actor Sam Wanamaker (who died before it opened). It opened in 1995 with a workshop season, and then presented a prologue season in 1996 and its first full season the following year. In 1991, a 32-year-old actor and director, Mark Rylance, had been invited to join the Artistic Directorate, and subsequently, in 1995, became its first Artistic Director. It was an inspired choice.

Brought up in Chicago, the son of British parents who worked as teachers in America, Rylance had returned to England in 1978 to train at the Royal Academy of Dramatic Art (RADA). Following his first season with the Royal Shakespeare Company (RSC) in 1983–84 (playing Peter Pan and being nominated for an award for his performance as Michael in *Arden of Faversham*), he decided he wanted 'to explore other ways of communicating Shakespeare', including working without a director, and formed the London Theatre of the Imagination which in turn became the company Phoebus Cart. With this company he presented a number of Shakespeare plays, often in non-traditional venues such as the Rollright Stone Circle in Warwickshire or in Heaven, then a leading London gay club, his own roles including Iago and—in a production of *The Tempest* in the unfinished Globe—Prospero. But he kept links with more mainstream theatre and by the early 1990s Rylance was established as one of the finest classical actors of his generation, his reputation enhanced by a universally acclaimed performance in Ron Daniels's RSC production of *Hamlet* (a production that included, at Rylance's suggestion, Broadmoor secure hospital in its itinerary),[2] and an Olivier award as Best Actor for Benedick in Matthew Warchus's production of *Much Ado About Nothing* in 1994.

These experiences ensured that Rylance—a natural non-conformist—brought to his role at the Globe a crucible of talents and an openness of imagination that the project needed. And he brought, too, a resilience that soon proved vital as he and the new theatre were buffeted from all sides. The project became, in Peter Thomson's words, 'an open invitation to academic assertiveness'[3] and Rylance initially found what he terms 'a style of academic certainty' disconcerting: 'It took me a while to realize that in the academic world criticism is an expression of love', he says.[4] Although he now believes the relationship between the Globe and scholars is on the whole strong, some academics were, and some remain, sceptical, especially of its claims to be seeking a level of 'authenticity' in its productions. Others raised more serious (and perhaps more seriously held) issues concerning the architectural choices and the interpretation of the evidence on which they were made. It was, however, the theatre community that Rylance found the least interested in and challenged by the project. Some fellow professionals saw it as quaint and regressive, and the aim to re-think the role of the director was widely—and damagingly—misinterpreted to reflect an 'anti-director' stance. When Rylance was appointed, Robert Hewison wrote in the *Sunday Times* that the new director 'will have to steer carefully between the pedants and the tourists'. And so it proved, as from all sides came criticism of the project as 'theme park Shakespeare', 'commodified heritage' theatre, 'cultural tourism' or what Disney executives call 'edutainment'.[5]

At the centre of the storm was Rylance, who appropriately often draws on nautical images in discussing experiences at the Globe (he talks, for example, of actors learning to 'sail' the audience). A slightly built man, with a light, beautifully modulated voice and an expression and manner of inquisitiveness, Rylance has determinedly led his company from the front, one of the few artistic directors also to appear in his own and other directors' productions. While the choice of *Two Gentlemen of Verona* as the main production in the prologue season may have seemed odd to many critics (the play was neither written for nor possibly ever performed at the original Globe), the part he played—Proteus—was entirely apt. For Proteus—the water spirit of Roman mythology who could shape-shift at will—was frequently employed by Elizabethans as a positive image of the actor. Indeed, it was precisely this analogy that Richard Flecknoe invoked when seeking to describe the talents of the King's Men's and the Globe's first leading actor (the first to play roles such as Hamlet, Lear, Macbeth, Leontes)—Richard Burbage. It is an equally appropriate image for Burbage's successor, Mark Rylance.

'Plays depend on the imagination of the audience; they don't happen otherwise' (*Mark Rylance*)

In the final chapter of his book *On Actors and Acting*, a chapter titled 'The New Globe: monument or portent', Peter Thomson examines a number of issues concerning the historical 'accuracy' of the building, sympathetically testing it against his experience of working there with his MA students. At the close of the chapter he moves to a discussion of the opportunities and challenges it presents to actors and audiences. It demonstrates, he says, that 'on an empty, unlit stage, it is only the story that stands between the actor and a mass exodus of onlookers'.[6]

In September 2002, as the season was nearing its end, I talked with Mark Rylance about his work as an actor and at the Globe in particular. His roles in the season had been Olivia in *Twelfth Night* and the lead in Peter Oswald's new play, *The Golden Ass*. I should note, though, that the transcription of our conversation cannot capture its performative nature, as Rylance regularly illustrates his points with short, physical demonstrations.

We began our discussion on this particular topic of the 'story'.

MR: It's first of all very important here at the Globe, in a way that I never realized before I came here, that the actors are aware of the story. My image is that the story is like a boat that is cutting through the water, or ice or whatever. The audience's imagination is cutting through time and space and there's a kind of prow, a front of the story, which is where the particular question of what's going to happen next is. And it's often between two people, or between one person and him or her self or sometimes a whole group. But generally it passes as if it was a ball, it passes from different players to players. And it's very important for the audience that the actors give that front of the story a sharpness by their attention to it, by their need to know whether it's going to cut through the water or not and what it's going to find, whether it's going to hit an iceberg or not. If they don't give their attention to what's just in front of the boat—the story—then it's hard to ask the audience to. It can be useful at times of course to throw the attention all around and for the audience to go into a feeling of 'Oh, I know what's happening here', and then suddenly bring it in. But we do this very much with the focus of our imagination and the expression of that through stillness. Stillness in the creation of silence for speaking, and the creation of stillness for someone to move into—the polarity of those is very important: actors give focus to their fellow actors, and take focus, through the use of stillness and movement.

MW: Though when the theatre opened everyone seemed to think that the actors would need to move about a lot.

MR: I remember the stage seeming very huge at first, and actually I wasn't confident I could master it. But every year it's got smaller, and it now seems very intimate to me. At times I can be very still, can speak very quietly, and it's exactly right. Whereas at the beginning it felt like we were going to have to reach out so much to get people's attention, now we realize there's the alternative magnetic force of creating a vacuum inside, and drawing people towards us.

There's a moment in *Twelfth Night*, for example, when the twins meet in Act V and embrace each other, knowing each other, and the audience is focused on that. And then they look up to the immediate beneficiaries of this revelation, Orsino and Olivia. And Orsino and I were always turning on that revelation that Viola is, in fact, a woman, and looking at each other. And we would draw the audience's attention and they would laugh, and the laugh would dissipate the build-up of tension that two twins had been working on. Now, both of us stay watching Viola, so though we are playing the reality of realizing what's happened, we don't take focus, we keep giving the focus there, on the twins. It's much better, there is no laugh when that happens and the audience stays with the twins until they embrace. Then they turn to us, so there is a kind of paragraphing; before, we were slipping in a sentence from a later paragraph into an earlier paragraph and it wasn't right. So there is a sense of keeping still and taking the ball when it's the right time in the text to take it, and it's difficult to learn those things. It is just very telling in the stillness. If everyone was moving around a lot, if everyone played individual realities, no matter they might be true to the character, they are not true to the service of the story, the rhythm of the story and the exquisite hiding and revealing which makes this play so fantastic.

I didn't really know before I came here how much you can work with a story, how much a story is like a great spotlight or a great microphone to events. There are places in the story where you are building up the audience's attention and involvement and those need to have a lot of stuff to keep them attractive. But then there are certain moments in a story, such as before King Lear leaves and goes out into the heath, where maybe five or six spotlights are on Lear, and it's as if microphones have come up close to him because everyone wants to know what he is going to do now. And the actor can hold that moment, wait until there is a silence, and speak in the tiniest voice or do the tiniest thing, and the audience's imagination and the player's imagination will make it totally expressive. But the actors must be aware of the dynamics of the story.

MW: Part of telling the story must involve the arts of Shakespeare's language, especially as in a theatre like the Globe not all of the audience can see the action all of the time and have to rely on what they hear. How has working here affected that part of your work?

MR: I think before I came to the Globe I had always felt very repressed and unhappy and didn't think the results of the big verse workers, such as Peter Hall, were particularly good. I really didn't have much care for it at all and had always kind of just flung by, by finding the truth of the line and playing from the truth of motivation and letting the verse land.

MW: Adrian Noble has a good phrase about actors in Shakespeare needing to make the language sound 'as if it's the only language they can speak', which is easier said than done. You have that ability. Is it from an embedded desire for the language plus experience?

MR: Experience must come into it. Perhaps I had a particular need to speak because I couldn't be understood until I was six or seven. Only my brother could understand what I was saying, so I needed a lot of help with language. It didn't come easily to me expressing myself to other people, so play-acting gave me wonderful things to say that made sense to me, but which I could never find the words to express. So I leapt at the opportunity to say these things in the beautiful ways Shakespeare had said them.

MW: Do you mean that you found learning to talk difficult, or that you just spoke a language that was your own?

MR: I think I spoke without consonants, I think I would say 'eeeaaauuooooaaa', very, very fast. My father says he used to sit on trains with me and I would be jabbering on about things outside the window, and everybody would be looking. I was sent to a therapist about it, so maybe that has something to do with it. I was never really taught how to speak verse until I met Giles Block[7] here at the Globe. He's very attentive to the text, but he believes that Shakespeare is trying to capture—more in verse than in prose—the way that people speak, the way that they suspend a sentence only when there's a question hanging in the air. He is using the technique of verse speaking to support what I've always wanted, which is for it to sound natural, that it doesn't need to be unnatural to be beautifully spoken. The speaking of it should not draw your attention to the speaker, it shouldn't be that kind of vanity. The speaking of it should reveal the character, you should never think 'Oh, that's very well spoken', it should try to be natural. It should be spoken quicker; I think most of the time the main area that we fail in is that we don't speak as quickly, or with as much variety and discovery as people do when they speak normally. There are so many things in parentheses, so many leapings of full stops when people speak, and jumps, and things that. People use different tones, and they organize what they are saying in all kinds of wonderful ways when they speak on the street. Beautiful verse speaking tends to level it out. There is actually more beauty, more vitality to be found by listening to the way people actually speak.

In fact, much as companies like Théâtre de Complicité have helped rede-
fine the parameters of the physical expression of a story in the theatre, there's
a whole area of re-discovery to be made about the sound, the tunability of a
company of actors. That's one of the main things that's become of interest to
me here.

'Authenticity should be in mind rather than practice'[8]

From the outset, following Sam Wanamaker's requirement that at least one
production per season should be as 'authentic' as possible, the Globe has
aimed to explore aspects of original staging practices. Among the most contro-
versial has been the decision to perform with all-male casts.

We know little of the young men—those 'careless boys' as one opponent
of the theatre described them in 1574—who played the female roles on the
Elizabethan and Jacobean stage.[9] Among the records of over 700 actors who
worked in London from the opening to the closing of the playhouses, only a
few are clearly identified as having played the female roles. The young actors,
some—but not all—of whom progressed to adult roles, remain mainly names,
with occasionally a snippet of some circumstantial detail that throws them into
sharper, but still brief, focus: the record of a part played; Ben Jonson's report
that Richard Robinson, who married Winifred Burbage, Richard's widow,
was able, in Jonson's words, to 'set the table in a roar' by his female impersonation; the bodice needed for the actor who played Alice in the Admiral's
Men's lost play *Pierce of Winchester*, listed, like the 'red suit of cloth' worn by
William Pig, Alleyn's apprentice, in Henslowe's 1598 inventory.

Alexander Goffe was unequivocally such a player, called the 'Woman
Actor' by John Wright in *Historia Histrionica*, but I still find it problematic
when I consider that his first recorded—perhaps, even, his first ever—role,
when only twelve, was to play Caenis in the 1626 production of Massinger's
The Roman Actor. What's especially intriguing is that Caenis is evidently the
oldest female character in that play, the concubine of the deceased emperor
Vespasian. The surviving cast list names other 'women actors'. William Trigg
played Julia; John Honyman, aged 14, played Domitilla (with a number of
references being made in the play to his short stature); and, with perhaps the
most taxing role of all in terms of its emotional range, John Thompson,
possibly about 16, played Domitia.

In an essay some years ago, Stephen Orgel asked an obvious (and therefore rather difficult to answer) question: 'Why did the Elizabethans take boys
for women?'[10] Well, partly convention, of course; partly because their status
was in many ways equivalent to that of women outside the theatre, allowing
their 'otherness' from the adult actors to be distinct; partly, perhaps, because
their looks allowed it; but also, of course, because they were good at it. It's

inconceivable that any dramatist, knowing exactly where, by whom and to whom his play would be performed, would set his young actors impossible targets. And it's equally inconceivable that actors such as Burbage, Lowin or Taylor were going to be satisfied with make-weights in the female roles. The RSC performed *The Roman Actor* in its 2002 Swan season (seen subsequently in London, at the Gielgud Theatre),[11] and seeing the scenes between Domitia and Domitian, or Domitia and Paris, only strengthened my admiration for John Thompson and his fellows.

For me, therefore, this question of the performance of the female roles remains one of the most elusive aspects of contemporary theatre practice, alongside, for some of the same reasons, the work of the children's companies. Despite the considerable range of critical and theoretical standpoints on the implications of youths playing women, viewed from medieval, sixteenth century and modern perspectives, a sense of how young (and possibly older) male actors could meet the challenges of roles that have taxed the greatest actresses of succeeding generations remains unresolved.

But are there ways that modern theatre can explore this phenomenon? Cross-gender casting within productions of Shakespeare in the last couple of centuries is not new, though (apart from Glasgow Citizens, for example) this has tended more to take the form of performances of male roles by female performers. Madame Vestris played Ariel in 1840 (setting a trend followed until the First World War), Sarah Bernhardt (1899), Judith Anderson (1971, aged 73), Frances de la Tour (1979) and Angela Winkler (1999) have played the more obviously masculine role of Hamlet, while Fiona Shaw took the part of Richard II at the National Theatre in 1995. Kathryn Hunter has played a clutch of male roles for Théâtre de Complicité, her most striking being King Lear in 1997, a part also played by European actresses Marianne Hoppe and Maria Casares. In 2000, Vanessa Redgrave played Prospero at the Globe.

All-male productions are less common. A production of *As You Like It* in 1920 gave not 'the slightest cause for offence . . . in attire [or] in tone', and in more recent times there have been all-male productions of *As You Like It* (National Theatre 1967, revived 1974) and *Hamlet* (Glasgow Citizens), while Cheek by Jowl had considerable success with their 1991 (revived 1995) production of *As You Like It*.

'Give me a man's face, a boy's face is not worth a hair' (*Conceits, Clinches, Flashes and Whimzies*, 1639)

In 1997 Rylance played the title role in an all-male *Henry V*; in 1999 he directed an all-male production of *Julius Caesar* and played Cleopatra in the same season. In 2002 he took on the role of Olivia in *Twelfth Night*, first at Middle Temple (where the play had been first performed in February 1602), then at the Globe. The term 'transvestite' commonly employed to describe these performances is misleading, as it tends to make what was then a convention into a theme. Watching the male actors perform female roles I've been struck by how swiftly I forget the sexuality of the player until the story requires the actor to call my attention to it, an effect only possible once I have accepted the convention. When playing Cleopatra, Rylance notes, the audience sometimes reacted the first time he spoke, but very quickly accepted the convention.

Laurence Senelick observes, in his recent, robust discussion of 'playboys and boy players', that:

> Shakespeare's Cleopatra has been the stumbling block for many scholars in imagining the efficacy of the boy player. Loath to grant that unfledged striplings could convey all the complexities of Shakespeare's mature female characters, they have hypothesized men being cast in these parts.[12]

Well, it's a hypothesis not to be summarily dismissed. Scholars of medieval theatre practice (where males played women) have underlined that many of these actors' voices did not break until much later than today, there is evidence of men in their late twenties playing female roles on the Jacobean stage, and one contemporary refers specifically to both men and boys playing these parts.[13] Rylance himself argues that 'these parts were played by strong young actors, not boys with unbroken voices . . . the boy actors played women long after their voices had broken'—but not, he admits, alluding to himself, 'pushing forty'. Crucially, however, Rylance sees his decision to play a female role not so much as an exercise in 'authenticity', but as a further test of the imaginative leaps ('jumps of faith' he calls them) that both actors and audiences can—indeed, must—make at the Globe. His audiences are, he says, his 'co-creators'. How then, did he approach this acting task?

MR: There were things that playing Cleopatra confirmed to me. For example, I was very concerned to try to look like a woman as much as I could, certainly up until Act V, and so the wig was a very expensive human hair wig. I realized at the end of Act V when I took the wig off—and I'd cut my hair to look as if she had pulled her hair out—that the audience didn't lose belief because of that. All I had on was just a cotton nightdress and yet I'd done enough. If you do enough initially to convince, the audience will stay with you; you can actually strip things away.

And so when Jenny Tiramani [the Globe's Head of Design] said that she'd like to explore this more rigorously with Olivia—that they didn't have human hair wigs but just had silk wigs, that sat on like hats and are not so realistic— I was more comfortable to agree, to see how little we can do, to trust the audience's imagination even more. I was also quite keen to do something that was a little more restrained than Cleopatra. I remember that Claire [van

Kampen, Director of Globe Music] used to go out in the auditorium during the show and hear conversations, and she came upon a couple and the wife said in the interval, 'Well, what do you think of it?' He said, 'Who is that playing Cleopatra, I thinks she's playing the sexy side a bit strong', and his wife said, 'Look, you do realize it's a man?', and Claire said his ears went bright red. But I did feel that in my nervousness to convince, I had focused on that side of the character, so with Olivia I wanted to play a more 'restrained' role.

Also it's quite natural for me as artistic director to take a central kind of authoritative position in the story—as the head of Olivia's household, which is what the tiring-house and stage are during most of the play. My position amongst the actors supports that place.

MW: Your physical performance and your white-face make-up were presumably inspired by Japanese theatre, which I know you admire.

MR: I have always loved Japanese culture and the connections that the Globe has brought for me with the Kabuki tradition which, though it's had innovations and renovations, has lasted more strongly than ours.[14] So I think there is a lot to be found there. And the *onagatta* [the mature male Kabuki actors who play the female roles] are very wonderful at contrast which I think is such a key with Shakespeare. They move very smoothly and then they do these wonderful broken movements [Rylance is up on his feet doing this while he talks]. And they are so economic with their facial expression. You have a limited amount of space and time to tell the story in the theatre, so it's a lot about revealing something at the right moment and not before that moment, and discovering something at the right moment, not discovering it in bits and pieces.

MW: It's interesting what you say about wanting to play a more restrained role in Olivia. Although I could see the influence of your interest in the Japanese theatre—the way you move, the small foot movements . . .

MR: And contrasting later on, with how she has to run round, with the spear and then fainting . . .

MW: And with that blank face, looking a bit like Queen Victoria, herself a bit of a professional mourner, there was a rather nice mix of things going on there I thought. But, at other stages in the performance it seemed to me the most liberated performance of Olivia that I had ever seen.

MR: It's got more and more liberated as it's gone on.

MW: I've never seen Olivia throw things at people, or come on with a huge pike staff and try to defend Cesario. Is there any sense in which—because you are a man playing a woman—you are in some way liberated about the part, not so conditioned by notions of how women ought to behave?

MR: People often say that to me about me playing a woman, that a woman couldn't have played it that way.

MW: I don't mean a woman couldn't, but that a woman might not be encouraged to play in that way.

MR: I think probably a woman would come to those parts—Cleopatra and Olivia—with very different pressures than I do. They certainly don't come with any pressure to convince people that they are a woman, which is a pressure I have to deal with. I think at my best I come up with surprising manifestations of any part, male parts as well. They don't always work, but they are often unusual, so I don't know if it's the fact I am playing a woman.

MW: Has your experience of playing these female roles opened up any discoveries for you as an actor, not necessarily about Elizabethan acting, but in general? Or is it—to put it bluntly—just another part?

MR: It's just another part I think really. I suppose it's a little less easy for me to project myself, my own experiences as a man, onto them. I have to be a bit more careful about that. Playing Henry V was in some ways more difficult for me, because I have had the experiences of love with women, and felt more masculine or feminine depending on the strength of the woman. But experiences of war and leading men to war were further away from my own experience of life.

MW: You mention *Henry V*, a production which famously had the actors in authentic underwear. What are you wearing for Olivia?

MR: I have nothing that Jenny hasn't made for me. In fact I have even longer cotton white pants than the other actors. They come down to my knees because she was concerned when I fainted that if my dress ever went up she felt my legs should be covered, and she even went to the trouble of putting lace at the bottom of it, which none of the men have. I think often men keep their own underwear on, but I very much like to wear the whole thing.

MW: Are you building her from the moment you start dressing?

MR: Yes. I mean, if the underwear didn't come some day or I ripped it and I had to wear my own underwear it wouldn't ruin for me, I would be okay. I like the story of the Italian director, Visconti, whom I admired so much, who, if there was a chest or trunk on the set, would make sure there were very expensive things in there, even if they never opened it.

Grounding yourself and giving yourself a very grounded reality helps I think to come to those other things which are claiming their right to the reality of the moment, but you have to feel really confident that mind reality is the dominant one.

MW: So did you do particular research into kind of the roles and habits of women in 1600?

MR: To a certain degree. The actor Robert de Niro said a great thing about research: that the research should never show. He does it to make him feel that when he comes out onto the set in front of the camera, it's as if there is no one in the entire world that has more right to be that person at that moment than him. He said if he could feel that without doing any research, then he wouldn't do any, but he needs the research to feel absolutely confident that he has the right to play this part and for people to watch it. I agree with that.

Preparing for *Twelfth Night* we visited Hatfield House two times, and meeting Lady Salisbury and her lady-in-waiting, who showed us around the house, was very informative. I recorded them speaking on a little tape recorder, and I have also recorded Judi Dench speaking some stuff. I have found for a number of years now that that is the best thing for me, to have a little tape recorder and I just listen to a voice for a little bit, back stage in the tiring house, after I've got dressed and I'm sitting waiting to go on.

MW: And do you do that with other parts?

MR: I'm getting a bit superstitious. I feel like when I do do that it always works out better than when I don't. For instance, I had a wonderful recording of Oswald Mosley's son speaking. I heard him in the morning on Radio 4 and rushed and recorded it when I was playing Cloten [in *Cymbeline* at the Globe, 2001, a part he doubled with Posthumus]. Cloten never sounded exactly like him, but listening to that and imitating it would move me to a certain place with Cloten—it was a trigger. And my tape recorder and the tape got stolen and I was nervous for five months about going to New York and thought I must write to the BBC and get a copy of this and I never did. Indeed in New York I didn't ever feel that the character came to me again in the same way. He changed and he didn't anchor in the same way.

'Mark Rylance plays Shakespeare like Shakespeare wrote it for him the night before' (*Al Pacino*)

MW: How do you square being an actor living in the same moment as the audience with performing in a playhouse which is in a sense recalling another period?

MR: As an actor, there's an enormous amount of expressing the griefs or joys of my own life, that come out through characters. There's a lot of personal stuff that goes on inside to fill the role out, to make it hopefully as real as possible. The important thing is that *you* are playing it and you are not to copy a tradition but really try to come to it with your own experience of life. I remember when I got cast as Hamlet at the RSC, going to an old friend and saying 'I can't meet you this weekend. I've got to go up to Stratford and read all the prompt books, and find out what everyone has done so far in this great oak tree of Hamlet performances and see where my branch can add a bit more, and I'll use some and reject things.' He said, 'You fool, why are you doing that? It's a crazy idea. You are the one who is lucky enough to be asked to play it. You live now in the same time as the audience, and the ones that you speak about admiring, like David Warner, they were great because of their relationship to the time. So all you need to do is understand it as fully as you can and bring as much of your own physical, emotional, mental and soulful life to the part. But going and finding how other people did it, is not necessarily going to help you at all, that may just actually distance you from it.'

So within all these things about the collective consciousness of the story and the technical things of stillness and movement, the basic premise is that there is a part of me that is very subjective and thinking what part of myself can I use to do this. And sometimes I actually feel ashamed about it. Sometimes if I am grieving for someone who has died and who I feel I didn't really properly look after in my life, I sometimes think where the soul of that person is, as they see me again dredging up the grief about them to make a living, to tell a story of something else. I hope they forgive me for doing it, because it's a recycling of and using things, I think many people would think that's a bit cruel.

I feel the fact that the Globe is being rebuilt at this moment is very, very telling. It's exactly the right tool for the present moment. We're learning as actors here. We are learning naturally. Actors are learning again about gesture, but it's more about the antithesis and contrast in a good gesture rather than just hand signals for things or just largeness for largeness's sake. It's the marrying of contrast and the enjoyment of changes and rhythm, those things. In fact, I think most of my profession haven't woken up to it, in a way that could massively help their own theatres, in terms of its regard for an audience and its celebration of the social nature of going out. Why go out and sit isolated in darkness in cramped places, when that's what you are getting at home? To go out and feel in a crowd, it's very difficult to do that unless you are a football supporter or go to rock concerts or something like that, and even then the people are very far away or dark. Here, everyone's present and I don't feel it's an old fashioned space at all. I feel I am in the most modern theatre there is.

Notes on Contributors

MARTIN BANHAM is Emeritus Professor of Drama and Theatre Studies at the University of Leeds. He is editor of *The Cambridge Guide to Theatre* (Cambridge: Cambridge University Press, 1995) and co-editor of the annual book/journal *African Theatre*. For Cambridge University Press he is at the moment preparing *The Cambridge History of Theatre in Africa*. African theatre has been his major scholarly interest and is an area where he has published widely, but publications in other fields include monographs on John Osborne, the Victorian playwright Tom Taylor and the uses of drama in education (with the late John Hodgson).

RICHARD BOON is Professor of Performance Studies at the University of Leeds. His research interests lie primarily in the theoretical and practical investigation of political theatre (especially British political theatre of the twentieth century), multicultural theatre and the uses of theatre as a tool for conscientization and empowerment. He has published extensively on the work of Howard Brenton, *Brenton the Playwright* (London: Methuen, 1991) and is completing *About Hare* (London: Faber, 2004) for new series on post-war British and Irish playwrights, edited with Philip Roberts. He co-edited, with Jane Plastow, *Theatre Matters: Performance and Culture on the World Stage* (Cambridge: Cambridge University Press, 1998), and is currently completing a follow-up volume, *Theatre and Empowerment*.

COLIN CHAMBERS is Senior Research Fellow in Theatre at De Montfort University. Before that he was a journalist, critic and Literary Manager of the Royal Shakespeare Company (1981–97). His books include *Other Spaces: New Theatre and the RSC* (London: Eyre Methuen, 1980), *The Story of Unity Theatre* (London: Lawrence and Wishart, 1989), and the award-winning *Peggy: The Life of Margaret Ramsay, Play Agent* (London: Nick Hern, 1997). He also edited *The Continuum Companion to Twentieth Century Theatre* (London: Continuum, 2002) and writes stage adaptations and plays. He is working on another book about the RSC, one on political commitment and performance, and a play about London.

CHRISTINE DYMKOWSKI is Reader in Drama and Theatre at Royal Holloway, University of London. She is the author of *Harley Granville Barker:*

A Preface to Modern Shakespeare (Washington: Folger Shakespeare Library, 1986) and the theatre history edition of *The Tempest* in the Shakespeare in Production series (Cambridge: Cambridge University Press, 2000); she has also written articles and papers on Lena Ashwell, Edy Craig, Cicely Hamilton, Susan Glaspell, Caryl Churchill, Sarah Daniels and Timberlake Wertenbaker, as well as introductions to thirteen plays by Eugene O'Neill (London: Nick Hern, 1991–95). She is currently a member of the editorial team, led by Andrew Gurr, preparing the New Variorum edition of *The Tempest*.

GER FITZGIBBON lectures in the English Department, University College, Cork, and is Chair of the university's Board of Drama and Theatre Studies and programme director of the university's undergraduate and post-graduate programmes in drama and theatre studies. He has lectured and published on the work of Brian Friel, Tom Murphy, Frank McGuinness and Sebastian Barry, was a contributing editor to *The Cambridge Guide to Theatre* and *The Concise Cambridge Guide to Theatre*, and has recently co-edited a book of interviews *Theatre Talk: Voices of Irish Theatre Practitioners* (Dublin: Carysfort, 2001). He is a founder-member and currently Chair of Graffiti Theatre Company, Ireland's leading theatre-in-education company. He has written a number of plays, including *The Rock Station* (first produced 1992), *Sca* (1999) and *Ice Soon* (2002).

VIV GARDNER is Professor of Theatre Studies at the University of Manchester. Her research interests include women in British theatre, partic-ularly contemporary theatre; the iconography of the New Woman, 1890–1914; women managers before 1914; twentieth-century German theatre, particularly Brecht. Her publications include, with Linda Fitzsimmons, *New Woman Plays* (London: Methuen, 1991); with Susan Rutherford, *The New Woman and Her Sisters: Feminism and the Theatre 1850–1914* (London: Harvester Wheatsheaf, 1992) and with Peter Thomson, *Brecht: Mother Courage and her Children* (Cambridge: Cambridge University Press, 1997). She is editor of the journal *Nineteenth-Century Theatre and Film*.

BAZ KERSHAW trained and worked as a design engineer before reading English and Philosophy at Manchester University. He has extensive experi-ence as a director, devisor and writer in experimental, radical and community-based theatre, including productions at the legendary Drury Lane Arts Lab in London. He has published many articles in international journals, and is the author of *The Politics of Performance: Radical Theatre as Cultural Intervention* (London: Routledge, 1992) and *The Radical in Performance: Between Brecht and Baudrillard* (London: Routledge, 1999); and co-author of *Engineers of the Imagination: The Welfare State Handbook* (London: Methuen, 1990). He is currently Chair of Drama at the University of Bristol, and Director of PARIP (Practice as Research in Performance).

ALEXANDER LEGGATT is Professor of English at the University of Toronto. He has published widely on English drama, citizen comedy, Jacobean public theatre and Shakespeare's plays. His most recent publications include *English Stage Comedy 1490–1990* (London: Routledge, 1998) and *Introduction to English Renaissance Comedy* (Manchester: Manchester University Press, 1999). He is editor of *The Cambridge Companion to Shakespearean Comedy* (Cambridge: Cambridge University Press, 2002).

CHRISTOPHER McCULLOUGH is Professor of Theatre and Head of the School of Performance Arts at the University of Exeter. He has worked frequently as a visiting professor and director in Italy, the United States and Brazil. He has published widely on the contemporary mediation of Elizabethan theatre and early twentieth-century political theatre in Europe, including *Theatre and Europe 1957–95* (Exeter: Intellect, 1996). His current research focuses on the cultural politics of the theatrical adaptations of Gothic novels in the nineteenth and twentieth centuries.

JAN McDONALD is James Arnott Professor of Drama at the University of Glasgow. Research interests include nineteenth- and early twentieth-century British theatre and contemporary Scottish theatre. Her first article on Webster's *Taming of the Shrew* (1843) was included in *Nineteenth-Century British Theatre*, edited by Kenneth Richards and Peter Thomson (London: Methuen, 1971), and a happy association with Peter has now continued through the Standing Committee of University Departments of Drama, external examining, and, most recently, co-membership of the Arts and Humanities Research Board's Panel for Research in Music and the Performing Arts. Jan McDonald is currently working on the Scots dramatist and founder of the Citizens' Theatre, James Bridie.

JANE MILLING is Lecturer in Drama at the University of Exeter. She has written several articles on Restoration performers and early female playwrights, including contributions to the *New Dictionary of National Biography*. She is author, with Graham Ley, of *Modern Theories of Performance: From Stanislavski to Boal* (London: Macmillan, 2000). She is a contributing co-editor, with Peter Thomson, of Volume 1 of the forthcoming *Cambridge History of British Theatre*. She is currently working on a study of the early eighteenth-century playwright Susanna Centlivre.

JOEL SCHECHTER is Professor of Theatre Arts at San Francisco State University. His books include *Durov's Pig: Clowns, Politics and Theatre* (New York: Theatre Communications Group, 1985), *Satiric Impersonations: The*

Congress of Clowns (Carbondale: Southern Illinois University Press, 1998), *The Pickle Clowns: New American Circus Comedy* (Carbondale: Southern Illinois University Press, 2001) and *Popular Theatre: A Sourcebook* (London: Routledge, 2003). He served as editor of the journal *Theater* at the Yale School of Drama for fifteen years, and recently staged several Yiddish plays in new translations.

LAURENCE SENELICK is Fletcher Professor of Drama at Tufts University and Honorary Curator of Russian Theatre at the Harvard Theatre Collection. His latest books are *The Chekhov Theatre: A Century of the Plays in Performance* (Cambridge: Cambridge University Press, 1997), which won the Barnard Hewitt Award of the American Society for Theatre Research; and *The Changing Room: Sex, Drag and Theatre*, which won the George Jean Nathan Award as best book on drama published in 2000. He is currently working on a documentary history of Soviet theatre.

MARTIN WHITE is Professor of Theatre at the University of Bristol. Much of his work focuses on the less-well-known plays and playwrights of the Elizabethan and Jacobean period, and on the performance of those plays in their own playhouses and our own. He works closely with the Globe in London, and has created in Bristol a full-scale candle-lit reconstruction of a playhouse based on drawings by Inigo Jones. His publications include *Middleton and Tourneur* (London: Macmillan, 1992) and *Renaissance Drama in Action* (London: Routlege, 1998). He is currently preparing an edition of Massinger's *The Roman Actor* for the Revels series.

DON B. WILMETH is the Asa Messer Professor at Brown University. He is co-editor with Christopher Bigsby of the award-winning three-volume *Cambridge History of American Theatre* (Cambridge: Cambridge University Press, 1998–2000), editor of the *Cambridge Guide to American Theatre* (Cambridge: Cambridge University Press, 1996), and series editor for Cambridge's Studies in American Theatre and Drama. He authored the award-winning *George Frederick Cooke: Machiavel of the Stage* (Westport, Conn.: Greenwood Press, 1980). A recipient of the Anthony Denning Award from the British Society for Theatre Research, he has been honoured with career achievement awards by the Association for Theatre in Higher Education and the American Society for Theatre Research. He worked with Peter Thomson as an editorial advisor to Martin Banham's *Cambridge Guide to Theatre* and on his series (co-edited with Martin Banham) of nineteenth-century plays.

Notes

Preface
1   Leslie du S. Read, 'Acting', in Martin Banham, ed., *The Cambridge Guide to World Theatre* (Cambridge: Cambridge University Press, 1988; repr. 1992, 1995, 2000).
2   Peter Thomson, *On Actors and Acting* (Exeter: University of Exeter Press, 2000).
3   *Shakespeare's Professional Career* (Cambridge: Cambridge University Press, 1992; repr. 1994, 1999).
4   Peter Thomson and Gamini Salgado, eds, *The Everyman Companion to the Theatre* (London: Dent & Sons, 1985).

Section One: The Idea of Acting
Introduction
1   Michael Bristol, 'Theatre and popular culture', in J.D. Cox and D.S. Kastan, eds, *A New History of Early English Drama* (New York: Columbia University Press, 1997), 248.
2   Thomas Heywood, *An Apology for Actors* (London, 1612), E2v.
3   Cited in Lesley Wade Soule, *Actor as Anti-Character* (Westport, Conn.: Greenwood Press, 2000), 125.
4   Jonas Barish, *The Antitheatrical Prejudice* (Berkeley: University of California Press, 1981).
5   J. Gailhard, *The Compleat Gentleman, or Directions for the Education of Youth* (1678), I, 94.
6   Cited in Matthew Wikander, *Fangs of Malice: Hypocrisy, Sincerity and Acting* (Iowa City: University of Iowa Press, 2002), 67.
7   Jean-Jacques Rousseau, *Politics and the Arts: Letter to M. d'Alembert on the Theatre*, trans. and ed. Allan Bloom (Ithaca, N.Y.: Cornell University Press, 1968).
8   Soule, *Actor as Anti-Character*, 125.
9   Peter Thomson, *On Actors and Acting* (Exeter: University of Exeter Press, 2000), 9.
10 Kristina Straub, *Sexual Suspects* (Princeton, N.J.: Princeton University Press, 1992).

Chapter One
1   *On Actors and Acting* (Exeter: University of Exeter Press, 2000), xii.
2   'On the Death of the Famous Actor R. Burbage', quoted from C.M. Ingleby, *Occasional Papers on Shakespeare: Being the Second Part of Shakespeare the Man and the Book* (London: Trübner & Co., 1881), 178. The elegy exists in several versions, one of which seems to have been expanded by the eminent scholar-forger John Payne Collier to include a list of parts Burbage almost certainly did not act (the plays in question belonged to other companies). Ingleby surveys the controversy over the elegy (169–77) and prints two versions from a manuscript then in the possession of A. Huth. Unless otherwise specified, I am quoting from the first version. Page references for future quotations will be given in the text; here and elsewhere, spelling and punctuation have been modernized.
3   *New Shreds of the Old Snare* (1624), quoted from G.E. Bentley, *The Jacobean and Caroline Stage*, 7 vols (Oxford: Clarendon Press, 1941; repr. 1966), II, 396–97.
4   Revels edition, ed. E.A. Horsman (London: Methuen, 1960), V iii 79–81.
5   Quoted from Edwin Nungezer, *A Dictionary of Actors and of Other Persons Associated with the Public Representation of Plays in England before 1642* (New Haven: Yale University Press, 1929), 73.
6   Bentley, *Jacobean and Caroline Stage*, II, 396.
7   Quoted from E.K. Chambers, *The Elizabethan Stage*, 4 vols (Oxford: Clarendon Press,

1923; repr. 1951), II, 308.
8   Nungezer, *Dictionary*, 77.
9   Robert Parker Sorlien, ed., *The Diary of John Manningham of the Middle Temple 1602–1603* (Hanover, N.H.: University Press of New England, 1976), 75.
10   Nungezer, *Dictionary*, 78.
11   All references to Shakespeare are to Stephen Greenblatt (general editor), *The Norton Shakespeare* (New York: W.W. Norton, 1997). References to *King Lear* will be to the Folio version.
12   Thomson, *On Actors and Acting*, 11.
13   All references to *The Duchess of Malfi* are to the Revels edition, ed. John Russell Brown (London: Methuen, 1964).
14   Ralph Richardson also specialized in stage falls, a gift put to use in Pinter's *No Man's Land*.
15   Chambers, *Elizabethan Stage*, IV, 256.
16   Thomson, *On Actors and Acting*, 85. Thomson notes that Garrick was not always consistent on this point (85–86).
17   Nungezer, *Dictionary*, 67–68.

Chapter Two
1   Joel Schechter, ed., *Popular Theatre: A Sourcebook* (London: Routledge, 2003), 1.
2   Thomas Betterton [Edmund Curll], *The History of the English Stage from the Restauration to the Present Times* (London, 1741), 5.
3   Anthony Aston, *A Brief Supplement to Colley Cibber Esq, his lives of the famous actors and actresses* (London, 1747), 3.
4   Joseph Roach, *The Player's Passion* (Ann Arbor: University of Michigan Press, 1993), 55.
5   Samuel Pepys, *The Diary of Samuel Pepys: A New and Complete Transcription*, ed. Robert Latham and William Matthews (London: Bell & Hyman, 1985), 4 November 1661.
6   Ibid., 19 March 1661; 24 August 1661: 'To the Opera and there saw *Hamlet, Prince of Denmark*, done with Scenes very well. But above all, Batterton did the Prince's part beyond imagination.' When Betterton was ill for almost the whole of the 1667–68 season, Pepys records his absence from familiar roles and the stage with great sadness.
7   Pepys, *Diary*, 24 February 1668.
8   *Tatler* 169, 2–4 May 1709.
9   Judith Milhous, 'An annotated census of Thomas Betterton's roles 1659–1710', *Theatre Notebook* 29:1 (1975), 33–42.
10   *Tatler* 169, 2–4 May 1709.
11   This was in part a parody of Delarivière Manley's *The Royal Mischief*, in which Betterton starred as Osman, the prime Vizier, who is married to, or in love with, every woman in the play.
12   Colley Cibber, *Apology for the Life of Mr Colley Cibber*, 2 vols, ed. R.W. Lowe (London: John Nimmo, 1889), I, 103.
13   Aston goes on to praise Betterton for another clichéd tribute to his acting, that of staying focused on his character during his performance, a truism that Alexander Leggatt comments on in relation to Burbage, elsewhere in this volume: '*Betterton*, from the Time he was dress'd to the End of the Play, kept his Mind in the same Temperament and Adaptness, as the present Character required' (Aston, *A Brief Supplement*, 5).
14   Judith Milhous and Robert Hume, eds, *Roscius Anglicanus* (London: Society for Theatre Research, 1987), 78.
15   *The Dictionary of Thieving Slang* (London, 1737) tells us that Whetstone's Park was a lane between Holborn and Lincoln's Inn Fields, 'a noted Nest for Whores'.
16   Anon., *A Comparison between Two Stages* (London, 1702), 199.
17   Montague Summers, *Restoration Theatre* (London: Kegan Paul, Trench, Trubner, 1934), 101. Betterton had masterminded Shadwell's *Psyche* to the stage in February 1675, and continued with his own opera *The Prophetess* (1690) and *King Arthur* (1691) among others. Roger North, writing in 1726, notes that Betterton 'contrived a sort of plays, which were called Opera, but had been more properly styled Semioperas, for they consisted of half Musick, and half Drama . . . Mr Betterton whose talent was speaking and not singing, was pleased to say, that 2 good dishes were better than one' (P. Highfill et al., *A Biographical Dictionary of Actors, Actresses etc.*, 16 vols, (Carbondale: Southern Illinois University Press, 1973–93), I, 83). Betterton had been influenced by French stage design and French performers, for example bringing over Msr Grabut for the ill-fated *Albion and Albanius* in

1685.

18   Summers, *Restoration Theatre*, 228.
19   Summers, *Restoration Theatre*, 275
20   Highfill, *Biographical Dictionary*, I, 77.
21   Some commentators estimate his investment in the East India Company at £2,000 and a return, had the cargo survived, of £120,000. This staggering profit, although to be shared with fellow adventurer Sir Francis Watson, would have taken Betterton firmly up the social scale. His earnings as a shareholder in the Duke's Company might have been approximately £50 a share, Milhous estimates, making more than £150 a year, along with extra income for 'maintenance' of the actresses, training for the women and junior members, and his benefit night. With the United Company, his demotion to a three-quarters shareholder yielded poor returns and meant he was better off on salary income.
22   Anon., *Comparison*, 7.
23   P. Holland, *The Ornament of Action* (Cambridge: Cambridge University Press, 1979), 76. Dryden wrote to Tonson in August 1684:

> For the Actors in the two plays which are to be acted of mine, this winter, I had spoken with Mr Betterton by chance at the Coffee house the afternoon before I came away: & I believe that the persons were all agreed on, to be just the same you mention'd. Only Octavia was to be Mrs Buttler, in case Mrs Cooke were not on the Stage. And I know not whether Mrs Percivall who is a Comedian, will do so well for Benzayda.

John Dryden, *Letters,* ed. C.E. Ward, (New York: AMS Press, 1965), 23–4.
24   John Dennis, Preface to *Liberty Asserted*, in *Works*, ed. E.N. Hooker (Baltimore: Johns Hopkins University Press, 1943), I, 324.
25   *The Causes of the Decay and Defects of Dramatick Poetry* in Dennis, *Works*, II, 277–78. Gould's satire on the playhouse tasks Betterton for his aspirations to literary significance:

> No Parts, no Learning, Sense or Breeding, yet
> He sets up for th'only Judge of *Wit*.
> If all cou'd judge of *Wit* that think they can,
> The arrant'st Ass wou'd be the Wittiest Man.
> In what e'r Company he does engage,
> He is as formal as upon the *Stage*,
> Dotard! And thinks his stiff comportment *there*
> A Rule for his Behaviour *every where*.

Likewise *A Comparison Between Two Stages* only lets him off the hook for writing because he has not published, and the earlier poem *Session of the Poets* mockingly suggests him for the next laureate.
26   Anon., *A Satyr on The Players* (*c.*1682–85) MS 'Satyrs and Lampoons', BL Harley 7317, 96–102.
27   Gould in *Poems, chiefly consisting of satyrs and satyrical epistles* (London, 1689), 183.
28   Tiffany Stern, *Rehearsal from Shakespeare to Sheridan* (Oxford: Oxford University Press, 2000), 151 n99, discusses Powell's mimicry of Betterton as Heartwell and uses Thomas Davies's assertion that Powell played Falstaff, with 'those acute pains of gout' which sometimes 'surprised' Betterton in performance, cited in *Dramatic Miscellanies*, 3 vols (London, 1784), I, 138.
29   Farquhar, *Works*, 2 vols, ed. Shirley Strum Kenny (Oxford: Clarendon Press, 1988), II, 341.
30   *A Satyr on The Players*, see note 26.
31   Summers, *Restoration Theatre*, 319, 321.
32   *A Satyr on The Players*; Farquhar, Preface, *Love and Honour* (1702); Tom Brown dubs Betterton 'his gravity', more perhaps for his managerial attitude than his acting. In *Amusements* (*c.*1695), and in his *Letters from the Dead*, Brown has Joseph Haines on a tour of the underworld guided by Mr Nokes, encounter Sir Thomas Pilkington, who asks 'and pray sir, how doth Mr Betterton's lungs hold out?' (1703), 25.
33   *Reply of the patentees* (1694) cited in Allardyce Niccoll, *History of English Drama* (Cambridge: Cambridge University Press, 1959), 376.
34   He had played men far older than his age in his younger years, though, like Colonel Jolly or Sir Salomon, and his new roles in the early eighteenth century tended to be fathers or older statesmen.

35   *Tatler* 169, 2–4 May 1710.
36   Charles Johnson, *The Force of Friendship* (1709), Preface.
37   Charles Gildon, *The Life of Mr Thomas Betterton, the Late Eminent Tragedian* (London: Robert Gosling, 1710).
38   Ibid., 16.
39   Pepys, *Diary*, 24 August 1661.

Chapter Three
1   Vs. Vsevolodsky-Gerngross, *Istoriya russkogo teatra* (Leningrad and Moscow: Tea-Kino-Pechat, 1929), I, 335.
2   Among others, Ettore Lo Gatto, 'La Commedia dell'arte in Russia', *Rivista di studi teatrali* 9:10 (1954), 176–81.
3   L.M. Starikova, *Moskva starodavnyaya. Geroi zhizni i stseny* (Moscow: Artist-Rezhisser-Teatr, 2000), 148–49, 152–53. Italian biographies of Sacchi which have him arriving in Russia in 1742 will now have to be corrected.
4   The most up-to-date source on this subject is L.M. Starikova, ed., *Teatral'naya zhizn' Rossii v époxy Anny Ioannovny. Dokumental'naya khronika 1730–1740 vypusk 1* (Moscow: Radiks, 1995), 27–8. It transcribes the original archival material.
5   The original source of the scripts may have been the French publications, *Le théâtre italien de Gherardi* (1701) and *Comédies diverses* (1730s). V.N. Peretts, 'Ital'yanskaya intermediya 1730-kh godov, v stikhotvornom perevode', in *Starinnyy teatr v Rossii XVII-XVIII vv. Sbornik statey*, ed. V.N. Peretts (St Petersburg: Academia, 1923), 144–45, 148.
6   The text can be found in V.N. Peretts, *Italianskiya komedii i intermedii predstavlennyya pri dvore Imperatritsy Anny Ioannovny v" 1733–1735 gg. Tektsy* (Petrograd: Imperatorskaya Akademiya Nauk, 1917), 205–15.
7   Starikova, *Teatral'naya zhizn'*, 61.
8   Journal of the Senate, 12 September 1750, quoted in Malcolm Burgess, 'Fairs and entertainers in 18th-century Russia', *Slavonic and East European Review* 38: 90 (December 1959), 101–2.
9   See G.P. Fedotov, *The Russian Religious Mind*, 2 vols (Cambridge, Mass.: Harvard University Press, 1946), II, 316–43. Pushkin's *Boris Godunov* originated a number of the modern preconceptions of the *yurodivy*.
10   The standard works in Russian are A. Famintsyn, *Skomorokhi na Rusi* (St Petersburg, 1889) and A.A. Belkin, *Russkie skomorokhi* (Moscow: Nauka, 1975); in English, Russell Zguta, *Russian Minstrels: A History of the Skomorokhi* (n.p.: University of Pennsylvania Press, 1978).
11   Sandra Billington, *A Social History of the Fool* (Brighton: Harvester Press, 1984), 16; and Martin Steens and James Paxson, 'The fool in the Wakefield plays', *Studies in Iconography* 13 (1989–90), 67. For images of the fool as a persecutor of Christ, see James H. Marrow, *Passion Iconography in Northern European Art of the Late Middle Ages and Early Renaissance: A Study of the Transformation of Sacred Metaphor into Descriptive Narrative* (Kortrijk: Van Ghemmert, 1979), Pl. X, XIII, XIV.
12   Dianne Ecklund Farrell, 'Popular prints in the cultural history of eighteenth-century Russia' (Ph.D. dissertation, University of Wisconsin-Madison, 1980), 127–30.
13   Ivan Aleksandrovich Balakirev (b.1699) was a military officer who had been exiled under Peter, but recalled and promoted by his widow Catherine I. After her death, he remained at court as a kind of official fool. A 'Collection of Anecdotes of Balakirev', published by K.A. Polevoy in 1830, attributed to him a wide range of traditional jokes and sayings. P. Kallinikov and I. Korneeva, eds, *Russkiy biograficheskiy slovar' v dvadtsati tomakh* (Moscow: Terra, 1998), II, 61.
14   Both anecdotes come from K.G. Manshteyn [Munstein], *Zapiski o Rossii* (Derpt, 1810), quoted in Starikova, *Teatral'naya zhizn'*, 90.
15   Lacosta, correctly D'Acosta, was a Portuguese Jew brought to Russia from Hamburg; master of several languages and well-read in Holy Writ, he often debated religion with Peter the Great, who dubbed him 'King of the Samoyeds' and bestowed on him an unpopulated island in the Gulf of Finland. Kallinikov and Korneeva, *Russkiy biograficheskiy slovar'*, IX, 217.
16   The pioneering work on the *lubok* is Dmitry A. Rovinsky, *Russkie narodnye kartinki*, 5 vols of text, 4 vols of illustrations (St Petersburg, 1887); a facsimile edition was published in 2001. All later writers draw both their examples and their conclusions from this progenitor. An important recent collection is N.E. Danilova, ed., *Mir narodnoy kartinki* (Moscow: Progress-Traditsiya, 1999). In other languages see Alla Sytova, *The Lubok: Russian Folk*

Prints 17th to 19th Century, trans. Alex Miller (Leningrad: Aurora Art, 1984) and Wolfgang Till, ed., *Lubok. Der russische Volksbilderbogen* (Munich: Münchner Stadtmuseum, 1985).

17   Catherine Claudon-Adhémar, *Populäre Druckgrafik Europas. Russland vom 16. bis zum Beginn des 20. Jahrhunderts,* trans. Ragni Maria Gschwend (Munich: Georg D.W. Callwey, 1975), 31.

18   Pierre-Louis Duchartre, *L'Imagerie populaire russe et les livrets gravés 1629–1885* (Paris: Gründ, 1961), 153.

19   Wilhelm Fraenger, 'Deutsche Vorlagen zu russischen Volksbilderbogen der XVIII. Jahrhunderts', *Jahrbuch für historische Volkskunde,* Vol. II: *Von Wesen der Volkskunst* (Berlin, 1926), 126–73; repr. in *Von Bosch bis Beckmann. Ausgewählte Schriften* (Dresden: Fundus-Bücher, 1977).

20   S.N. Shoubinsky, 'Court jesters and their weddings', in H.C. Romanoff, ed., *Historical Narratives from the Russian* (London: Rivingtons, 1871), 12–17.

21   Erika Tietze-Conrat, *Dwarfs and Jesters in Art,* trans. Elizabeth Osborn (New York: Phaidon Publishers, 1957), 75. Catherine the Great had adapted *Merry Wives of Windsor* as a comedy called *Thus 'Tis to Have Buck-baskets and Linen* (1786).

22   For engravings of the 1702 wedding of the fool Shpansky and the 1710 wedding of Peter's dwarf, see Starikova, *Moskva starodavnyaya,* 77–79.

23   Ibid., 81–82. Women seem to have been introduced on the Russian public stage in the person of Johann Kunst's wife. This innovation chimed in with the growing participation of women in the social life of court circles, but it is clear from contemporary records that the off-stage behaviour of Kunst's players resembled that of the characters in Scarron's *Roman comique.* See N. Popov, 'Materialy dlya istoriya russkago teatra. Vyezzhie komedianty pri Petre', *Bibliographicheskiya zapiski* 14 (1861), 417–18.

24   See Stephen V. Dock, 'Problems in Molière iconography: the Sganarelle costumes revisited', *Theatre History Studies* 19 (June 1999), 81–107.

25   Duchartre claims that Yeryoma means tow or oakum (which it doesn't), because the clown swallows flaming tow (as well as pulling endless snakes out of his mouth). He also states without any proof that Foma is a derivative of Gian-Farina. In general, Duchartre seems to have gleaned his highly unreliable information from the first wave of post-Revolutionary Russian émigrés to Paris, and taken what they told him on trust.

26   Rovinsky, *Russkie narodnye kartinki,* V, 272.

27   European commentators like to see the name Farnos as a distortion of the Italian Gian-Farina, but *farnosy* is simply an archaic word for snub-nosed. Duchartre's assertion that Pedrillo is the direct prototype of Farnos cannot be demonstrated either.

28   At the end of the eighteenth century the folk comic is called Petrushka-farnos, but in her book on the Russian puppet-theatre, Catriona Kelly discounts the idea that there is any direct connection between the puppet Petrushka and Pedrolino, Petrillo or Pulcinella; in her opinion, the similarity of names is coincidental. Catriona Kelly, *Petrushka: The Russian Carnival Puppet Theatre* (Cambridge: Cambridge University Press, 1990), 125–28.

Section Two: The Celebrated Actor as Cultural Icon
Introduction

1   Josephine Harrop, *Victorian Portable Theatres* (London: Society for Theatre Research, 1989); Paul Sheridan, *Penny Theatres of Victorian London* (London: Dennis Dobson, 1981); Marvin Carlson, 'The Golden Age of the Boulevard', in J. Schechter, ed., *Popular Theatre* (London: Routledge, 2003), 22–34; M. Booth, *Theatre in the Victorian Age* (Cambridge: Cambridge University Press, 1991).

2   Tracy C. Davies, 'Edwardian management and the structures of industrial capitalism', in M. Booth and J. Kaplan, eds, *The Edwardian Theatre: Essays on Performance and the Stage* (Cambridge: Cambridge University Press, 1996).

3   Laurence Senelick, *National Theatres of Northern and Eastern Europe 1746–1900* (Cambridge: Cambridge University Press, 1991), 2.

Chapter Four

1   Mrs Clement Parsons, *The Incomparable Siddons* (London: Methuen, 1909), 12. 'Acting and the austere joys of motherhood were the all sufficient emotional outlets for this rarely constituted woman-artist.'

2   Ann Catherine Holbrook, *The Dramatist, or Memoirs of the Stage* (Birmingham: Martin and

Hunter, 1809), 60.

3   Sarah Kemble married William Siddons, a young actor in her parents' touring company, in 1773, and in the course of the next twenty years she gave birth to seven children, five of whom survived to maturity, but only two of them outlived their mother. They were Henry (1774–1815), Sarah or Sally (1775–1803), Maria (1779–1798), George (1785–?) and Cecilia (1794–1868).

4   Thomas Campbell, *The Life of Mrs Siddons*, 2 vols (London: Effingham and Wilson, 1834), I, 211.

5   James Boaden, *Memoirs of Mrs Siddons*, 2 vols (London: Henry Colburn, 1827), II, 261.

6   Campbell, *Life*, II, 18.

7   Boaden, *Memoirs*, II, 137.

8   Boaden, *Memoirs*, I, 290.

9   Boaden, *Memoirs*, II, 73.

10   Quoted in Naomi Royde-Smith, *The Private Life of Mrs Siddons: A Psychological Investigation* (London: Gollanz, 1933), 204.

11   Campbell, *Life*, I, 173.

12   Boaden, *Memoirs*, II, 62.

13   Katharine C. Balderston, ed., *Thraliana: The Diary of Mrs Hester Lynch Thrale (Later Mrs Piozzi)*, 2 vols (Oxford: Clarendon Press, 1942), 693.

14   Letter from Sarah Siddons to Mr Whalley, quoted in Yvonne Ffrench, *Mrs Siddons: Tragic Actress* (London: Vershoyle, 1954), 136.

15   Boaden, *Memoirs*, II, 289.

16   Quoted in Royde-Smith, *Private Life*,180.

17   Quoted in Ffrench, *Mrs Siddons*,192.

18   Parsons, *Incomparable*, 197.

19   Quoted in Parsons, *Incomparable*, 197.

20   Letters from Mrs Siddons to Mr Whalley, quoted in Parsons, *Incomparable*, 201; Oswald G. Knapp, ed., *The Intimate Letters of Hester Piozzi and Penelope Pennington, 1788–1821* (London: Bodley Head, 1969), 167.

21   Campbell, *Life*, II, 360.

22   Quoted in Royde-Smith [my italics], *Private Life*, 204.

23   Knapp, *Piozzi/Pennington Letters*, 220.

24   James Boaden, *Memoirs of Mrs. Inchbald*, 2 vols (London: R. Blentley, 1833), I, 71.

25   Quoted in Roger Manvell, *Sarah Siddons: Portrait of an Actress* (London: Heinemann, 1970), 141.

26   Balderston, *Thraliana*, 876.

27   Quoted in Ffrench, *Mrs Siddons*, 155.

28   William van Lennep, ed., *The Reminiscences of Sarah Kemble Siddons* (Cambridge: Printed at the Widener Library, 1942), 6–7.

29   Quoted in Campbell, *Life*, I, 92.

30   Van Lennep, *Reminiscences*, 31. An interesting gloss on this incident and how it framed her subsequent performance as Mrs Beverley in *The Gamester*, another example of a mother abandoned with her child as the result of an errant husband, is given in Ellen Donkin's chapter 'Mrs Siddons looks back in anger' in Janelle G. Reinelt and Joseph R. Roach, eds, *Critical Theory and Performance* (Ann Arbor: University of Michigan Press, 1992), 276–90.

31   Quoted in Campbell, *Life*, II, 263.

32   Tate Wilkinson, *The Wandering Patentee*, 4 vols (York: Printed for the Author, 1795), I, 256.

33   Balderston, *Thraliana*, 877.

34   Campbell, *Life*, I, 133–34.

35   Kalmin A. Burnim, ed., *Letters of Sarah and William Siddons to Hester Lynch Piozzi* (Manchester: John Rylands Library, 1959), 62.

36   Quoted in Ffrench, *Mrs Siddons*, 143.

37   Balderston, *Thraliana*, 867.

38   Quoted in Ffrench, *Mrs Siddons*, 189.

39   Campbell, *Life*, II, 357.

40   Adrienne Rich, 'Of Woman born: motherhood as experience and institution', in Maggie Humm, ed., *Feminisms: A Reader* (London: Wheatsheaf, 1992), 275.

41   Mrs Galindo wrote in her abusive 'open letter', 'What sort of a Mother lingers on in dalliance while her supposedly beloved daughter coughs her life away?' *Mrs Galindo's Letter to Mrs*

Siddons (London: privately printed, 1809).

42   Quoted in Oswald Knapp, ed., *An Artist's Love Story, Told in the Letters of Sir Thomas Lawrence, Mrs Siddons and her Daughters* (London: George Allen, 1904), 152.
43   Ibid., 176.
44   Ibid., 212.
45   Ibid., 213.
46   Manvell, *Sarah Siddons*, 256.
47   Boaden, *Memoirs*, I, 311.
48   Van Lennep, *Reminiscences*, 1.

Chapter Five

1   In addition to Nightingale's piece, there was a similar assessment of the American invasion by Mark Shenton in the theatre trade paper *Back Stage*, 7 June 2002. This apparent reversal of a long-established pattern should not suggest that American audiences are any less enamoured of British plays and actors than they have ever been. Over the years British actors, in particular, have been recipients of major recognitions for appearances in New York. Recently, for example, the outstanding actor Tony awards for 2001−2 went to Alan Bates in *Fortune's Fool* and Lindsay Duncan in *Private Lives*. Coward's comedy, which transferred virtually intact from the West End where it had been directed by Howard Davies and with Alan Rickman and Duncan in the leads, was honoured by the Tonys as best play revival.
2   There are scattered records of professional actors in the US or in the West Indies between 1703 and the appearance of Hallam's company, but none of these were of great significance as actors, regardless of their historical importance. In addition, there is a fascinating history of amateur theatre as early as 1665. A recently published calendar of colonial theatre indicates that up to the closing of theatres at the outbreak of the War of Independence in October 1774 there were more professional companies than usually noted (at least sixteen), and thus more actors than previously suggested, some professional and some amateur, fleshing out these companies. See Odai Johnson and William J. Burling, *The Colonial American Stage, 1665−1774: A Documentary Calender* (Cranbury, N.J.: Associated University Presses, 2001).
3   For the most recent history of American theatre, see the three-volume *The Cambridge History of American Theatre*, edited by Don B. Wilmeth and Christopher Bigsby (Cambridge: Cambridge University Press, 1998−2000) and in particular Volume I, *Beginnings to 1870* (1998). Although not always factually reliable, nonetheless still a unique early and often first-hand history is William Dunlap's *History of the American Theatre* (New York: J. & J. Harper, 1832). Dunlap, a playwright and manager, is often called 'The Father of American Drama'. The definitive history of colonial theatre remains Hugh F. Rankin, *The Theater in Colonial America* (Chapel Hill: University of North Carolina Press, 1965), although its coverage of the Hallam company and its convoluted history has been superseded by the following: Philip Highfill, 'The British background of the American Hallams', *Theatre Survey* 11 (May 1970), 1−35, and the Hallam entry in Philip Highfill, Kalman Burnim and Edward Langhans, eds, *A Biographical Dictionary of Actors, Actresses, Musicians, Dancers, Managers, and Other Stage Personnel in London, 1660−1800*, 16 vols (Carbondale: Southern Illinois University Press, 1973−93), VII, 29−51. This is an excellent source for information on the careers of most significant actors of the eighteenth century who also appeared in America. For corrections to Rankin and Highfill and new information on the Hallam family tree, see Robert J. Myers and Joyce Brodowski, 'Rewriting the Hallams: research in 18th century British and American theatre', *Theatre Survey* 41:1 (May 2000), 1−22. For more succinct entries on actors and other topics relevant to this essay, see also Don B. Wilmeth, ed., with Tice L. Miller, *Cambridge Guide to American Theatre*, corrected and expanded edition (Cambridge: Cambridge University Press, 1996).
4   This included Lewis Hallam Snr, his wife, and three children, including twelve-year-old Lewis Hallam Jnr. Significantly, one daughter, Isabella, stayed behind and as Mrs Mattocks became a famous actor on the British stage.
5   J.B. Booth's career is recounted in Stephen M. Archer, *Junius Brutus Booth, Theatrical Prometheus* (Carbondale: Southern Illinois University Press, 1992). A scholarly biography of his son Edwin is being written by Daniel Watermeier.
6   See Don B. Wilmeth, *George Frederick Cooke: Machiavel of the Stage* (Westport, Conn.: Greenwood Press, 1980) and Wilmeth's essay, 'Cooke among the Yankee Doodles', *Theatre Survey* 14:2 (November 1973), 1−32. Prior to my biography, where I demonstrated otherwise, it had been suggested that Cooke did not intend to return to England. A letter recently

purchased by Special Collections, Brown University Library, written by the British actor Joseph George Holman to the writer John Taylor on 26 September 1812, the day of Cooke's death, confirms that Cooke was expected back at Covent Garden. Both an embargo, the result of the War of 1812, and of course his death prevented this from happening.

7   The most reliable documented biography of Kean remains Harold N. Hillebrand's *Edmund Kean* (New York: Columbia University Press, 1933), especially on Kean's American tours.

8   This fact is more significant than it might appear, for St Paul's is located near the site of the World Trade Twin Tower tragedy of 11 September 2001 at Broadway and Fulton; yet the church and its immediate surroundings were largely undamaged and became a relief site for those involved with the search and rescue operation.

9   See Errol Hill, *The Jamaican Theatre, 1655–1900: Profile of a Colonial Theatre* (Amherst: University of Massachusetts Press, 1992).

10   'International stars and companies', in Wilmeth, *Cambridge Guide to American Theatre*, 205–7.

11   See Jonas Barish, *The Anti-Theatrical Prejudice* (Berkeley: University of California, 1981) and the forthcoming book by John Houchin on censorship of the American stage to be published by Cambridge University Press (2003).

12   Not, however, as the great moral influence it often claimed. See Rankin, *Theater in Colonial America*, 190.

13   See Jared Brown, *The Theatre in America During the Revolution* (Cambridge: Cambridge University Press, 1995).

14   Barish, *Anti-Theatrical*, 296.

15   The most complete biography of Holland is David Rinear's '"Innocent and heart merriment": the life and work of George Holland', *Theatre History Studies* 12 (1992), 157–71; 161. See also 'Notable players of the past and present: George Holland' (No. 26), *New York Clipper*, 25 June 1910.

16   See Joseph Jefferson, *The Autobiography of Joseph Jefferson,* ed. Alan S. Downer (Cambridge, Mass.: Belknap Press of Harvard University Press, 1964 [first published in 1890]), 152–53. E.M. Holland confirms the veracity of Jefferson's reportage and acknowledges that, although Jefferson does not mention him by name, he was the son of George with Jefferson at the meeting with Sabine. This information is in the undated holograph draft of a letter in my possession written by Edmund to a Philadelphia newspaper. Details on the 'Little Church around the Corner' have been drawn from Suzette G. Stuart, *Guidebook of Church of the Transfiguration* (New York: Published by the Church, 1951).

17   Like St Paul's Church in London's Covent Garden, it is also known as the Actors' Church, with a series of memorial bronze tablets to other notables of the theatrical profession, ranging from humourist Will Rogers, to actors Otis Skinner and Minnie Maddern Fiske, and manager Ben Greet. Memorial windows are dedicated to actors Richard Mansfield, Mary Shaw and Joseph Jefferson III, among others. Other members of Holland's family were buried at 'The Little Church around the Corner', including his sons E.M. (died in 1912) and Joseph Jefferson Holland (died in 1926).

18   Arthur Bloom, *Joseph Jefferson: Dean of the American Theatre* (Savannah, Ga.: Frederic C. Beil, 2000), 238.

19   See Wilmeth, *George Frederick Cooke*, 275–86; the story is also found in my essay, 'The posthumous career of George Frederick Cooke', *Theatre Notebook* 24:2 (Winter 1969–70), 68–74.

20   See Francis Hodge, *Yankee Theatre: The Image of America on the Stage, 1825–1850* (Austin: University of Texas Press, 1964).

21   See Gresdna Doty, *The Career of Mrs. Anne Brunton Merry in the American Theatre* (Baton Rouge: Louisiana State University Press, 1971).

22   For the most complete explications of the Drew-Barrymore family tree, see Carol Stein Hoffman, *The Barrymores* (Lexington: University Press of Kentucky, 2001) and Mary Ann Jensen, 'From strolling players to Steven Spielberg: two hundred years of a theatrical family', in Barbara Naomi Cohen-Stratyner, ed., *The Drews and the Barrymores: A Dynasty of Actors* (New York: Theatre Library Association, 1988), 16–28. In the latter collection I explored in more detail 'American acting dynasties' (1–15).

23   Henry John also had two lesser-known sisters who were actresses: Mary (Mrs Stanley) and Elizabeth (Mrs Pincott). The latter was mother of actress Leonora, later known as Mrs Alfred Wigan.

24   Roach, 'The emergence of the American actor', in Wilmeth and Bigsby, *Cambridge History*,

I, 361–62; Roach also provides the salient details of the Farren Riots of 1834, a precursor of those at the Astor Place Opera House; the most detailed account of the latter riot is Richard Moody, *The Astor Place Riot* (Bloomington: Indiana University Press, 1955). Simon Williams, 'European actors and the star system in the American theatre, 1752–1870', also in Wilmeth and Bigsby, provides another perspective on the Astor Place riot.

Chapter Six

1   Standard versions would include Augusta Gregory, *Our Irish Theatre* (Dublin: Putnam, 1913); Hugh Hunt, *The Abbey: Ireland's National Theatre 1904–1978* (Dublin: Gill & Macmillan, 1979); Lennox Robinson, *Ireland's Abbey Theatre: A History 1899–1951* (London: Sedgwick & Jackson, 1951); Robert Welch, *The Abbey Theatre 1899–1999: Form and Pressure* (Oxford: Oxford University Press, 1999).

2   Hunt, *The Abbey*, 18. For fuller consideration see Robert Hogan and James Kilroy, *The Irish Literary Theatre 1899–1901* (Dublin: Dolmen, 1975).

3   W.G. Fay and C. Carswell, *The Fays of the Abbey Theatre* (London: Rich & Lowan, 1935), 118.

4   Fay and Carswell, *Fays of the Abbey Theatre*, 152.

5   W.G. Fay's own account is in Fay and Carswell, *The Fays of the Abbey Theatre*, but see also copy of a letter from Brigit Fay to the *Irish Independent*, dated 3 March 1933, in Ms 2652, National Library of Ireland, where she says 'my husband's stage experience previous to his association with the Abbey Theatre was of about nine years . . . during which time he toured Ireland, Scotland, England and Wales with various theatrical companies'.

6   Gerard Fay, *The Abbey Theatre: Cradle of Genius* (Dublin: Clonmore & Reynolds, 1958), 27–30.

7   Quoted in Hogan and Kilroy, *The Irish Literary Theatre*, 106.

8   Fay and Carswell, *Fays of the Abbey Theatre*, 115.

9   M. Nic Shiubhlaigh, *The Splendid Years: Recollections of Maire Nic Shiubhlaigh; as told to Edward Kenny* (Dublin: Duffy & Co, 1955), 19.

10   Fay and Carswell, *Fays of the Abbey Theatre*, 157.

11   Adrian Frazier, *Behind the Scenes: Yeats, Horniman, and the Struggle for the Abbey Theatre* (Berkeley: University of California Press, 1990), 238. See also James W. Flannery's *Miss Annie F. Horniman and the Abbey Theatre* (Dublin: Dolmen, 1970) and Sheila Gooddie's *Annie Horniman: A Pioneer in the Theatre* (London: Methuen, 1990).

12   See Frazier, *Behind the Scenes*, 176–79. Frazier finds neurotic sexual elements in Horniman's behaviour, but other evidence suggests a more rational explanation. It appears that the Abbey was not progressing as she had envisaged and she was trying to persuade Yeats to leave the Abbey and pursue his own style of theatre in London.

13   See Frazier, *Behind the Scenes*, 182–84. Frazier gives a colourful but compelling account of the complex class politics of the company.

14   Fay papers, Ms 5977, National Library of Ireland.

15   Fay and Carswell, *Fays of the Abbey Theatre*, 208.

16   Ibid.

17   Ibid., 32–36.

18   Gabriel Fallon, 'The Abbey Theatre acting tradition', in Sean McCann, ed., *The Story of the Abbey Theatre* (London: New English Library, 1967), 115.

19   Holloway papers, Ms 1803–1, National Library of Ireland.

20   Ibid.

21   Ibid.

22   Ibid.

23   Ibid.

24   Ibid.

25   Ibid.

26   Ibid.

27   Fallon, 'Abbey Theatre acting', 111.

28   See Fallon, *passim*.

29   Holloway papers, Ms 1803–1, National Library of Ireland (7 October 1905)

30   Ibid.

31   See, for example, Nic Shiubhlaigh, *The Splendid Years*, 22–26.

32   Quoted in Hogan and Kilroy, *Laying the Foundations*, 10.

33   Ibid., 10–11.

34 Holloway papers, Ms 1802–1, National Library of Ireland.
35 Fay papers, Ms 5975, National Library of Ireland.
36 Ibid.
37 Ibid.
38 Robert Hogan and Michael J. O'Neill, eds, *Joseph Holloway's Abbey Theatre: A Selection from his Unpublished Journal, 'Impressions of a Dublin Playgoer'* (Carbondale: Southern Illinois University Press, 1967), 102.
39 Quoted in Robert Hogan and Richard Burnham, *The Art of the Amateur 1916–1920* (Dublin: Dolmen, 1984), 24.
40 Letter dated 22 April 1911, Fay papers, Ms 22,404 iv, National Library of Ireland.
41 Undated letter, ibid.
42 Letter, ibid.
43 Hogan and Burnham, *The Art of the Amateur*, 85.
44 Letter to Dudley Digges, dated 15 November 1918, quoted in Hogan and Burnham, *The Art of the Amateur*, 172.
45 W.G. Fay and Nora Robinson, *On the Road to Cork* (London: Samuel French, 1930). This one-act comedy was first produced at the Royal Court Theatre, 29 March 1914. It contains a number of ironic moments which may reflect Willie's history or current situation. The main butt of the play is a cigarette-smoking, snobbish Englishwoman who is easily duped into buying fake antiques by the wily Irish characters.
46 W.G. Fay, *Merely Players*, with preface by Sir Barry Jackson (London: Rich & Cowan, 1932). Other publications mentioned are *A Short Glossary of Theatrical Terms* (London: Samuel French, 1930) and *How to Make a Simple Stage and the Scenery For It* (London: Samuel French, 1931).
47 Details taken from Fay papers, Ms 10951 (4), National Library of Ireland.

Chapter Seven
1   Headline, *Daily Express*, 30 January 1907.
2   *The Times*, 30 January 1907.
3   Francesco Alberoni, 'L'Elite irresponsible: théorie et recherché sociologique sur *le divismo*', cited in Richard Dyer, *Stars* (London: BFI Publishing, 1998), 7.
4   Dyer, *Stars*, 9–10.
5   In fairness to Dyer's and other books on Hollywood stars, they sometimes do draw attention to a pre-history, or interrelated history of theatre and early film celebrity. See, for example, Christine Gledhill, ed., *Stardom: Industry of Desire* (London: Routledge, 1991).
6   Dyer, *Stars*, 10. I think this is different in film where the performance remained, and remains, a significant part of that symbiosis.
7   *Daily Mirror*, 30 January 1907. The previous day Gertie Millar was reported by the *Daily Mirror* as 'being snugly stowed away in a very ample, though perfectly fitting, fur jacket. On her head was the most piquant of fur toques. Her beauty shone demurely through a dainty veil.' The *Daily Express*, 30 January 1907, records her as 'dressed tastefully in velvet, with white headdress, collar and cuffs'.
8   *The Times*, 29 January 1907.
9   *Daily Express*, 29 January 1907.
10 *The Times*, 29 January 1907. Monckton had also originally trained for the Bar. One wonders about the labyrinth of connections here.
11 Ibid.
12 *Daily Mirror*, 30 January 1907.
13 *The Times*, 30 January 1907.
14 Ibid.
15 *Picture Postcard and Collectors' Chronicle* 8:80 (February 1907), 7.
16 Peter Bailey, 'Naughty but nice: musical comedy and the rhetoric of the girl, 1892–1914', in M. Booth and J. Kaplan, eds, *The Edwardian Theatre* (Cambridge: Cambridge University Press, 1995), 39.
17 Gerald Bordman, *American Musical Comedy: From Adonis to Dreamgirl* (Oxford: Oxford University Press, 1982), 7.
18 Cited in ibid., 51.
19 *The Times*, 30 January 1907.
20 'Musical Comedy', song from *Sergeant Brue*, cited in Bordman, *American Musical Comedy*, 85.

21 Cited in Richard Carline, *Pictures in the Post: The Story of the Picture Postcard and its Place in Popular Art* (London: Gordon Fraser, 1971), 55.
22 *The Times*, 30 January 1907; *Manchester Guardian*, 30 January 1907.
23 I have no evidence of this, but cannot imagine that the theatres would not, in some way, have taken advantage of both the profit and the publicity that would accrue through sales in the theatre.
24 Carline, *Pictures*, 45.
25 *Picture Postcard and Collectors' Chronicle* 8:84 (July 1907), 218.
26 Carline, *Pictures*, 100. It is reported on several occasions that Post Office workers had complained that the 'glitter' and jewelling was 'injurious to the health of the officials', and restrictions were put in place by the Postmaster-General. *Picture Postcard and Collectors' Chronicle* 8:84 (July 1907), 198.
27 'Plate-sunk cards are quite the thing of the hour in the world of photographic cartophily.' *Picture Postcard and Collectors' Chronicle* 8:83 (May–June 1907), 139.
28 *Punch*, 21 August 1907, 131.
29 *Punch*, 20 November 1907, 368.
30 There may be a problem here, as in the case of the Gaiety performers the costumes were often contemporary and the line between costume and fashion a fine one. As Peter Bailey notes: 'musical comedy's use of the vernacular was . . . very selective, constituting a distinctly stylised form of naturalism . . . its resort to modern dress heavily favoured high fashion, as part of the intense glamorisation of women, both stars and the reconfigured dance chorus.' Bailey, 'Naughty but nice', 37.
31 *The Times*, 29 January 1907.
32 Laurence Senelick, 'Eroticism in early theatrical photography', *Theatre History Studies* 11 (1991), 2.
33 Interestingly both these cards were clearly sent for that very 'naughty' quality as they are inscribed by the senders: 'Saucy, is she not?' and 'Rather saucy. Nicht wahr', and both were sent to a woman from a woman.
34 *The Times*, 30 January 1907.
35 See Bram Djikstra, *Idols of Perversity* (Oxford: Oxford University Press, 1986).
36 Raymond Mander and Joe Mitchenson, *Musical Comedy: A Story in Pictures* (London: Peter Davies, 1969), 19.
37 Monckton is also credited with, Pygmalion-like, helping her lose her strong Bradford accent. See Alan Hyman, *The Gaiety Years* (London: Cassell, 1975), 119.
38 I have yet to uncover the research that tells us the origins of the striped bathing trunks as 'the ordinary costume for the Negro'. Interestingly again, Rotary had issued a copy of the 'spider' card themselves by July 1907, if the franking on my 'plain card' can be cited as evidence.
39 *Daily Mirror*, 30 January 1907; *Daily Express*, 30 January 1907.
40 Carline, *Pictures*, 164.
41 *The Times*, 30 January 1907.
42 Walter Benjamin, 'Unpacking my library: a talk about book collecting', in *Illuminations: Essays and Reflections*, ed. and intro. Hannah Arendt (London: Harper Collins, 1992), 68–9.
43 Roland Barthes, *Camera Lucida* (London: Vintage Classics, 1993), 3.
44 Ibid., 32.
45 Walter Benjamin, 'The work of art in the age of mechanical reproduction', in *Illuminations*, 214–15.
46 Jackie Stacey, *Star Gazing: Hollywood Cinema and Female Spectatorship* (London: Routledge, 1994), 30.
47 *Picture Postcard and Collectors' Chronicle* 8:80 (February 1907), 7.

Section Three: Extraordinary Acting for Popular Audiences
Introduction
1 John McGrath, *A Good Night Out* (London: Eyre Methuen, 1981).

Chapter Eight
1 See, for example, Julie Holledge, *Innocent Flowers: Women in the Edwardian Theatre* (London: Virago, 1981), 41–43, 44, 73–75, 77, 97–99; Claire Hirshfield, 'The actress as social activist: the case of Lena Ashwell', in Ronald Dotterer and Susan Bowers, eds, *Politics,*

Gender and the Arts: Women, the Arts, and Society (London: Associated University Presses, 1992), 72–86; Elizabeth Schafer, *Ms-Directing Shakespeare: Women Direct Shakespeare* (London: Women's Press, 1998), 212–15, 259, and 'Daughters of Ben', in Richard Cave, Elizabeth Schafer and Brian Woolland, eds, *Ben Jonson and Theatre: Performance, Practice and Theory* (London: Routledge, 1999), 155–59, 176; Christine Dymkowski, *'Diana of Dobson's*: Marriage as a trade-off', in *The Cambridge History of British Theatre, Volume 3: Since 1895*, ed. Baz Kershaw (Cambridge: Cambridge University Press, forthcoming 2004). The fullest account of Ashwell's career, meticulously documented, is to be found in Margaret Leask's unpublished Ph.D. thesis: 'Lena Ashwell, 1869–1957: "actress, patriot, pioneer"', University of Sydney, 2000.

2   For example, Simon Trussler's *The Cambridge Illustrated History of British Theatre* (Cambridge: Cambridge University Press, 1994), 265, simply notes in passing her management of the Kingsway Theatre, while a distinguished reference work like *The Cambridge Guide to Theatre*, ed. Martin Banham (Cambridge: Cambridge University Press, 1995) contains no entry for her at all. Nor does her work at the Century Theatre during 1924–29 figure in J.P. Wearing's invaluable resource, *The London Stage 1920–1929*, 3 vols (Metuchen, N.J.: Scarecrow Press, 1984).

3   My interest in Ashwell's career is long-standing. Having directed *Diana of Dobson's*, a role Ashwell originated, in March 1987, in 1999 I wrote a case study of the original production of the play for *The Cambridge History of British Theatre* (forthcoming, see note 1); in the meantime, I had become intrigued by the Lena Ashwell Players' production of *The Tempest* while researching the play's theatre history for my 'Shakespeare in Production' edition (Cambridge: Cambridge University Press, 2000). My various researches uncovered much material about the Players, the history of which I had planned to document fully in the present article. However, half-way through my research, I discovered Margaret Leask's comprehensive account of Ashwell's career as actress, manager and campaigner (see note 1), which can be consulted on-line at http://setis.library.usyd.edu.au/adt/public.html. As her comprehensive documentation of Ashwell's work with the Players does not allow her space for detailed consideration of individual productions, I have re-shaped my topic to complement her work. Where I have relied on Leask for information, I have of course acknowledged my debt; in other places my own research duplicates hers.

4   Leask, 'Lena Ashwell', 1, 18–21. Ashwell was born in Britain but raised in Canada between the ages of 8 and 19; having matriculated at the University of Toronto and studied for a time in Lausanne, Switzerland, she enrolled at the Royal Academy of Music in London, where Ellen Terry's response to her performance of a speech from *Richard II* encouraged her to abandon singing for the theatre. See Leask, 'Lena Ashwell', vi, 1.

5   Lena Ashwell, *Myself a Player* (London: Michael Joseph, 1936), 131.

6   G. Spencer Edwards, 'Miss Ashwell's new departure', *Illustrated Sporting and Dramatic News*, 3 September 1904, quoted in Leask, 'Lena Ashwell', 42–43.

7   See Ashwell, *Myself a Player*, 131, 137, and Leask, 'Lena Ashwell', 41–42, 47–48, 54, 64.

8   Ashwell, *Myself a Player*, 147, and Kingsway Theatre policy pamphlet, 9 October 1907, Theatre Museum, London.

9   For more information about Ashwell's management of the Kingsway, see Dymkowski, *'Diana of Dobson's'*.

10   For example, *Musical Standard*, 1 February 1908, I, 180; *Varsity*, 20 February 1908, I, 209; *Planet*, 22 February 1908, I, 211; *Bristol Times & Mirror*, 20 March 1908, I, 247; *Westminster Gazette*, 21 March 1908, I, 252; *The Times of India* [April 1908?], I, 274 (quoted from press clippings in two of Lena Ashwell's paginated scrapbooks (1907–April 1908 and 1908, identified respectively as I and II), now in the Theatre Museum, London). The *Nation* recognized Ashwell's attempt 'to found a repertoire theatre on the same plan as the old Court', but thought her likely to 'fall a victim to the long run' (7 March 1908, I, 236). In reality, Ashwell fell between the two stools, allowing a long run of successful pieces but replacing them before they had exhausted their potential audiences.

11   See Ashwell, *Myself a Player*, 145–48, 154–55.

12   Ibid., 156.

13   Ibid., 158. Ashwell further explains that she 'began to discover that the world of the theatre was not the only world, and that there were movements going on; for the seeds of revolution were germinating. There was much in the world that needed to be put right, and I became immersed in the suffrage movement and the position of women' (163). Unfortunately, lack of space does not allow me to document her extensive work in this area;

readers should consult Holledge, *Innocent Flowers*; Hirshfield, 'The actress', 77–81; and
Leask, 'Lena Ashwell', 129–50.

14 See Lena Ashwell, *The Stage* (London: Geoffrey Bles, 1929), 141–51, and *Myself a Player*,
194–222 (quotation from 194); Ashwell also published a book about the 'Concerts at the
Front', called *Modern Troubadours* (London: Gyldendal, 1922). Programmes for the
1923–24 season of the Lena Ashwell Players, now in the Theatre Museum, note that in
1914–15 they played in France; in 1915–1917 in France, Egypt, Malta, and for the Adriatic
fleet; in 1917–19 in Palestine, Egypt, France, Belgium and Germany; and in 1920–23 in
London and the provinces.

15 Ashwell, *The Stage*, 141. For a full account of Ashwell's musical, theatrical and campaigning
activities during the war, see Leask, 'Lena Ashwell', 150–215.

16 Quotations from, respectively, Ashwell, *The Stage*, 151, and *Myself a Player*, 237–38.

17 See Ashwell, *The Stage*, 151–52, and *Myself a Player*, 238–39. Later, as Prime Minister in
the post-war Labour government (1945–51), Attlee established the welfare state.

18 Ashwell, *The Stage*, 153, with interpolations from *Myself a Player*, 239.

19 Ashwell, *Myself a Player*, 240.

20 Ibid., 215, 237.

21 Ibid., 283–84; at the Town Halls of Fulham, Battersea and Shoreditch on Mondays,
Tuesdays and Fridays respectively, and on Saturdays at the Church Street Baths in
Camberwell, 283.

22 On Mondays at Ealing's Longfield Hall and Winchmore Hill's St Paul's Institute; Tuesdays
at Battersea's Town Hall and Dulwich's Public Baths; Wednesdays at Canning Town's
Public Hall; Thursdays at Deptford's Borough Hall and Harrow's Victoria Hall; Friday at
Greenwich's Borough Hall and Sutton's Public Hall; Saturdays at Camberwell's Old Kent
Road Baths and Watford's St John's Hall. *Candida* programme, 13 December 1920, Theatre
Museum, London.

23 Ashwell, *Myself a Player*, 240.

24 Ashwell, *The Stage*, 157.

25 Leask, 'Lena Ashwell', 275.

26 Ibid., 274. Ashwell, *The Stage*, 163, notes that 'every season a reduced Company went to
York and Bath for long summer seasons of repertory. All profits on these commercial under-
takings were used for the reduction of the [Players'] debt. Alas! These profits were small.'

27 Ashwell, *The Stage*, 159–60.

28 Ronald Mayes, 'The romance of London theatres. No. 129. The Century Theatre,
Bayswater', *The Magazine Programme*, unidentified clipping, Theatre Museum, London.

29 Ashwell, *Myself a Player*, 248.

30 'Recreation for the people', undated appeal leaflet (1924?), Theatre Museum, London.

31 Ashwell, *The Stage*, 160; she notes that it helped Leslie Banks, Frederick Leister and Esmé
Church into West End work.

32 Unidentified article, 1924, Century Theatre file, Theatre Museum, London, corroborated
by numerous newspaper reviews. The same article notes the theatre's capacity as about 400.

33 Theatre Museum, London. At this time, the 'A' circuit comprised venues in Sutton,
Battersea, Holloway, Beckenham, Greenwich and Watford, and the 'B' venues in
Winchmore Hill, Ilford, Edmonton, Hounslow, Streatham and Staines. The venues and the
days of the week on which the company played there correspond to those listed for 1927–28
and 1928–29 in the Appendix to Ashwell, *Myself a Player*, 284.

34 *Leah Kleschna* programme, 1922–23 season; Announcement for the Century Theatre,
Autumn Programme, 1925, Theatre Museum, London.

35 Sources for these figures are, respectively, 'Recreation for the people' undated appeal leaflet
(1924?), *Leah Kleschna* programme (1922–23 season), and announcement for the Century
Theatre, Autumn Programme, 1925, Theatre Museum, London. The *Leah Kleschna*
programme notes the middle price at touring venues as 1s 3d (£1.73 in today's terms; see
note below). Maggie Gale, *West End Women: Women and the London Stage 1918–1962*
(London: Routledge, 1996), 45, explains that 'In 1924 the [entertainment tax] . . . was abolished on all seats under the price of 1s 3d but this was more beneficial to the cinema than
to the theatre'. Her comment not only makes clear that Ashwell's lower-priced tickets were
set competitively with those for films, but also suggests why the 1922–23 1s 3d ticket price
was lowered by a penny in 1925: the seat cost the theatregoer less, while the company lost
none of the price to tax. (1924 programmes for Somerset Maugham's *Caroline* and *Caesar's
Wife* give the Century's top tax-inclusive price as 5s and lowest as 1s 3d; the announcement

for the 1926 winter programme notes that reserved seats could be bought for 5s 9d, 3s 6d and 2s 4d, while unreserved seats cost 1s 2d.)

36   The Bank of England gives the equivalent purchasing power of £1.00 in 1925 as £27.72 today (12 August 2002); the information comes from the Bank's public enquiries telephone service, but the calculations are my own. Edith Shackleton's contemporaneous article in *The Queen: The Lady's Newspaper and Court Chronicle*, 21 January 1925, 7, complains about both 'the cost of stalls in London theatres and the queue system' for seats in the pit, arguing that people could not easily afford 12s 6d for the former or two hours to spare for the latter; her complaints highlight Ashwell's considerate setting of prices and allowance of reservations in the pit.

37   *John Glayde's Honour*, by Alfred Sutro. 'Tell me a story' pamphlet/programme for the Lena Ashwell Once-a-Week Players, Theatre Museum, London.

38   Review of *Enemy of the People*, which opened the week beginning 9 November 1925, unidentified clipping, Theatre Museum, London.

39   Announcement for the Century Theatre, Autumn Programme, 1925, Theatre Museum, London. Ervine notes that Walbrook's was a new play.

40   Norman MacDermott, *Everymania: The History of The Everyman Theatre 1920–1926* (London: The Society for Theatre Research, 1975), 12.

41   Ashwell, *The Stage*, 172. As mentioned above, the Players also produced other classics, such as *She Stoops to Conquer* (16 January 1922), *The Rivals* (12 March 1923) and *The Country Wife* (14 January 1924), the latter adapted by Beatrice Wilson.

42   Ibid., 173.

43   Ibid., 173.

44   David Thomson, *England in the Twentieth Century: 1914–63* (Harmondsworth: Penguin, 1965), 91, 93, 95–98.

45   Margaret Morris, ed., *The General Strike* (Harmondsworth: Penguin, 1976), 46–47, 162–63.

46   Rodney Mace, 'The strike in the regions: Battersea, London', in Morris, ed., *The General Strike*, 379–93.

47   'The Lena Ashwell Players' leaflet, Theatre Museum, London.

48   Leask, 'Lena Ashwell', 301.

49   Ashwell, *Myself a Player*, 248. In her *Reflections from Shakespeare: A Series of Lectures*, ed. Roger Pocock (London: Hutchinson, [1926]), 16, Ashwell records that the Players 'always [produced] at least two [Shakespeare plays] set down by the University and Scholastic Boards for their Examinations'.

50   The term 'directed' is anachronous; programmes note the person who 'produced' the play. Although early Players' programmes sometimes lack this information, the director can be ascertained by those for revivals of productions. Although Ashwell appears to scathe 'producers' in *Myself a Player*, she makes clear that her target is 'direction imposed from without', which treats actors as 'automata on parade' (259 and 264): 'Only the stage-trained producer can encourage imagination and emotion, leaving the actor free to work out the scenes before he begins to suggest, to prune down, to explain the impression created, and so polish the general effect' (264–65).

51   Christopher Innes, 'People's National Theatre', in Banham, ed., *Cambridge Guide to Theatre*, 844.

52   Her obituary in the *Stage*, 28 January 1943, notes her teaching activities as well as her productions of *Alien Corn* at the Westminster in 1934 and *Busman's Honeymoon* at the Comedy in 1936.

53   Ashwell, *Myself a Player*, 240.

54   *Much Ado* (17 October 1921) had two short intervals, one after the first arbour scene and the other after the church scene, while *Othello* (14 February 1924) had a five-minute interval after the Senate scene and a three-minute one after the 'Willow Scene'; Dr Charles Beard designed costumes and fights for the latter.

55   Programme for *As You Like It*, 26 January 1925.

56   See Christine Dymkowski, *The Tempest*, Shakespeare in Production (Cambridge: Cambridge University Press, 2000), 39–40, 96. Ashwell, *Reflections from Shakespeare*, 220, clearly recognized the importance of the play's opening scene, lamenting that 'it is usual to present the shipwreck so darkly that nobody can see, and so noisily that nobody can hear'; she might have added that often there was very little *to* hear, as the scene was usually so drastically cut.

57   Quotation from Ashwell, *Reflections from Shakespeare*, 227; see Dymkowski, *Tempest*, 40ff.,

for the evolution of Ariel's theatrical presentation.

58 London and Bath: Mendip Press, n.d. (Ashwell, *Myself a Player*, 245, dates the preface from 1926.)

59 The review praises other actors besides Church, who was a mainstay of the Players throughout virtually all of its life, acting major roles and directing many productions. She left to become a 'leading lady' at the Old Vic, then turned to direction and management before returning to the Old Vic in 1936 'as head of the School of Acting'. She was also director of the children's theatre Young Vic 9 and in 1944 became director of the Bradford Civic Playhouse (obituary in *The Times*, 1 June 1972).

60 Unidentified clipping, Theatre Museum, London.

61 Unidentified clipping, Theatre Museum, London.

62 Unidentified clipping, Theatre Museum, London.

63 Programme for *Good Friday*, 6 April 1925. Wilson also includes a note explaining that Herod wears the costume of the 'Provincial Grecian' period, as he was 'an enthusiastic Grecophile and leader of the movement for Hellenising the Jews', and that Pilate's reed pen, inkpot and writing block are copied from originals in the British Museum—details that suggest the care taken with costumes and props even though money could not be lavished on scenery.

64 Unidentified clippings, Theatre Museum, London.

65 *Observer* clipping, 1 March 1925, Theatre Museum, London.

66 Leask, 'Lena Ashwell', Appendix 6, 38.

67 *Observer* clipping, 1 March 1925, Theatre Museum, London.

68 Review in the *Stage*, undated clipping, Theatre Museum, London.

69 The play was performed there on 8, 9, and 10 January, but the production had already been touring to the outlying boroughs from late December 1924.

70 The *Daily Express*, 7, gives the figure of nine years, and the *Daily Herald*, 5, that of ten (both 9 January 1925). In order to analyse critical response, I have consulted notices in twenty-five national and London newspapers and periodicals and in four suburban newspapers; I am grateful to Margaret Leask for providing me with dates of reviews in the latter.

71 Ashwell, *Myself a Player*, 248.

72 Leask, 'Lena Ashwell', 289 n.13, records that Ashwell did return to the professional stage one last time, in December 1928, for a special matinée performance of a one-act play to raise funds for the Lifeboat Service; in 1950 and 1951 she also appeared in a Moral Re-Armament play in Switzerland and the US (Leask, 364).

73 St John G. Ervine, *The Ship: A Play in Three Acts* (London: George Allen & Unwin, 1922); further references are to this edition and appear in the text. Ervine specifies the characters' respective ages as 83, 62, 42, 21 and 19.

74 Hubert Griffith, 'The week's theatres', *Observer*, 11 January 1925, 11.

75 Mr Gossip, 'Echoes of the town', *Daily Sketch*, 10 January 1925, 5; the critic nevertheless thought it 'very well worth seeing'.

76 Hubert Griffith, 'The week's theatres', *Observer*, 11 January 1925, 11. In fact, another reviewer was even able to describe it as 'full of fun but with a serious undercurrent and a touch of tragedy' (*Sutton Advertiser and Surrey County Reporter*, 1 January 1925, 5).

77 One review betrays a kind of defensiveness, admiring *The Ship* as 'a clever play, logical, well-written, interesting, and with the tense and realistic domesticity of the repertory system, including the father and son controversy, without which a play is dismissed in certain quarters as mere commercial drama' (P.P., 'Stage & Screen', *Sunday Express*, 11 January 1925, 5).

78 'Criticisms in cameo', *Sketch*, 21 January 1925, 122.

79 *Observer*, 11 January 1925, 11; Griffith was probably also 'H.G.' writing in the *Daily Chronicle*, 9 January 1925, 7, which is similar to the *Observer* review.

80 E.S.H., 9 January 1925, 3. Similarly, the *Illustrated London News*, 17 January 1925, 112, thought it 'the most interesting play given for some months past in London', and the *Daily Telegraph*, 9 January 1925, 4, judged it 'easily the most interesting new serious play that we have seen for some time'; see also *Weekly Dispatch*, 11 January 1925, 7.

81 See *Illustrated London News*, 17 January 1925, 112; Griffith, *Observer*, 11 January 1925, 11; Carados, 'Dramatic gossip', *Bystander*, 11 January 1925, 3. In fact, apart from the Players' own revival some months later (see below), the play was next seen in London in Malcolm Morley's 1929 production at the Everyman (John Oliver, 'Malcolm Morley at the Everyman 1927–1931', supplement to MacDermott, *Everymania*, 5).

82 'In the limelight', *Sunday Pictorial*, 11 January 1925, 9.

83 E.A.B., *Daily News*, 9 January 1925, 7. The critic added that the 'acting . . . itself made amends for several heavy nights recently spent in West End theatres'.

84 See *Illustrated London News*, 17 January 1925, 112; Griffith, *Observer*, 11 January 1925, 11; Grein, *Sketch*, 21 January 1925, 122; *The Times*, 9 January 1925, 10.

85 Respectively 4, 8, 7; for other favourable reviews of the acting, see also *Stage*, 15 January 1925, 18; M. E., *Daily Herald*, 5; *Daily Mail*, 14; *Daily Mirror*, 14; P.P., 'Stage & Screen', *Sunday Express*, 11 January 1925, 5; E.S.H., *Evening Standard*, 3; *Sutton Advertiser and Surrey County Reporter*, 1 January 1925, 5; Sheridan, *Ilford Recorder and South Essex News*, 7; *Enfield Gazette & Observer*, 25; *Kentish Mercury*, 13 (all 9 January 1925 unless otherwise noted). The one demurral came from Carados, who thought that when the play 'soon reach[ed] some leading West-end theatre . . . it [would] receive more adequate casting and production than could be expected from this roving repertory company' (*Bystander*, 11 January 1925, 3).

86 *Sunday Express*, 11 January 1925, 5; in James Agate's opinion, it was, 'for an accomplished actress, easier than tumbling off a tree' (*Sunday Times*, 11 January 1925, 4).

87 Respectively, *Queen*, 14 January 1925, 8; *Sketch*, 21 January 1925, 122; *Daily News*, 9 January 1925, 7. This praise for Ashwell's voice and delivery is somewhat ironic, given some criticisms levelled at her earlier in her career. Reviewing *Diana of Dobson's* in 1908, for example, the *Musical Standard*, 22 February 1908, I, 23, thought her voice sometimes too high and her articulation poor; the *Clarion*, however, dismissed the criticism, arguing that Ashwell's 'slight tripping over words' when excited is 'all the more natural' than the 'assumed and forced voices' usually heard on stage (24 February 1908, I, 220). Athene Seyler, in a posthumous appreciation, singled out 'the high, sweet, sometimes nasal quality of [Ashwell's] voice; the reed-like sound of it had a peculiar fascination impossible to explain'. She also admired 'the quiet intensity of thought and feeling, unaided by gesture or great variety of expression, which gripped and moved one by its deep sincerity', adding that, when as a girl she saw Ashwell play *Madame X* in 1909, 'at the end of the performance I was in a fainting condition, so powerfully did Lena's interpretation move me' (*Drama: The Quarterly Theatre Review* (Summer 1957), 35–36).

88 Similarly, the *Stage*, commenting that she 'played it exquisitely, without the slightest exertion', wished that our young actresses would master the technique of acting with a maximum of effect and a minimum of effort, as Miss Ashwell has done' (15 January 1925, 18).

89 *Daily Sketch*, 10 January 1925, 5; the *Daily Mail*, 9 January 1925, 10, similarly notes the 'delicate beauty' of her portrayal.

90 *Evening* Standard, 9 January 1925, 3. Shackleton, mentioning his 'strangely belated attack of Ruskinitis', complains that 'giving him such out-of-date theories on the simple life and the mechanical age' robs him 'of some sympathy' (*Queen*, 14 January 1925, 8).

91 *Time & Tide*, 23 January 1925, 82.

92 *Illustrated London News*, 17 January 1925, 112.

93 Respectively, Sheridan, *Ilford Recorder*, 9 January 1925, 7, and *Daily Mail*, 9 January 1925, 10.

94 Respectively, *Daily News*, 9 January 1925, 7, and *Observer*, 11 January 1925, 11.

95 Respectively, *Sutton Advertiser*, 1 January 1925, 5; *Illustrated London News*, 17 January 1925, 112; *Morning Post*, 9 January 1925, 8; Agate, *Sunday Times*, 11 January 1925, 4. Agate's comment made Ervine break with protocol and address his criticism: 'I deny that there is anything fundamentally "nasty" in his character, and I assert that the man who says there is . . . is incapable of forming a just opinion on the character of any man. I take it that Mr. Agate does not deny the verity of this character, but merely insists that he is "nasty". But if he does . . . then . . . his experiences in the war passed off him like water off a duck's back' (*Sunday Times*, 18 January 1925, 4).

96 Respectively, *Daily Mirror*, 14; *Kentish Mercury*, 13; *Enfield Gazette*, 5; *Enfield Gazette*, 5 (all 9 January 1925).

97 M. E., 9 January 1925, 5. Hamilton, *Time & Tide*, 23 January 1925, 82, noted that 'the character of Cornelius, "broke in our wars", by itself would make *The Ship* noteworthy'.

98 Respectively, *Sutton Advertiser*, 1 January 1925, 5; *Kentish Mercury*, 9 January 1925, 13.

99 Mr Gossip, *Daily Sketch*, 10 January 1925, 5; the reviewer's comment that the 'despotic father' looked 'startlingly like the late Lord Kitchener' further suggests how large the war still loomed to audiences of the play.

100 *Daily Telegraph*, 9 January 1925, 4. The reviewer continues, 'Mr. Reeves's little scene wherein, only half-released by a couple of tots of whisky from the Englishman's terror of

being "sloppy", he relates how he once heard a lark singing in a lull between bombardments, is superb.'

101 *Weekly Dispatch*, 11 January 1925, 7; the reviewer also compares his discovery to Cooper's.

102 *The Times*, 9 January 1925, 10. Hamilton, *Time & Tide*, 82, similarly remarked that such applause, though interrupting the action and perhaps annoying the other actors on stage, was 'spontaneous and inevitable'.

103 E.S.H., *Evening Standard*, 9 January 1925, 3.

104 *Queen*, 14 January 1925, 8.

105 *Time & Tide*, 23 January 1925, 82. The lack of scenery similarly appears not to have bothered Grein, who commented that 'it is all to the credit of Miss Lena Ashwell and her Players that they have produced [*The Ship*] so excellently' (*Sketch*, 21 January 1925, 122).

106 *The Era*, 9 May 1925, 8. *Weekly Westminster*, 25 April 1925, 765, announced the revival's opening.

107 Of the three extant programmes in the Theatre Museum, London, that name Leister as the play's producer, one credits him with playing John and two credit Frederick Victor, so there must have been a further change of actors during the revival. Different actors also took the part of George Norwood, John's employee and Hester's fiancé, in the original production and the revival.

108 Ashwell, *Myself a Player*, 248.

109 Ibid., 244.

110 Gale, *West End Women*, 45.

111 Respectively, *Myself a Player*, 244, and *The Stage*, 162–63.

112 Ashwell, *The Stage*, 162.

113 Ashwell, *Myself a Player*, 250. Ashwell's husband was eminent gynaecologist Henry Simson.

114 Ashwell, *The Stage*, 161–62.

115 See her *Daily Telegraph* obituary 15 March 1957, Phyllis Whitworth's appreciation in *Drama* (Summer 1957), 35, and Leask, 'Lena Ashwell', 245–47, 357–66; the latter, 366, noting that Ashwell's public involvement with the MRA ended in July 1953, contradicts information in the obituary.

116 22 September 1952 report of the unveiling of a bust of Ashwell at the British Drama League, Theatre Museum, London.

Chapter Nine

1 Kenneth Tynan, review of *Zip Goes a Million* for the *Evening Standard*, October 1951, quoted in David Bret, *George Formby: A Troubled Genius* (London: Robson Books, 2001), 190. Much of the biographical information used in this chapter is drawn from Bret's book.

2 Formby is often said to have played a ukelele, which is a small guitar-shaped instrument invented in Hawaii in the late nineteenth century. The instrument that made him famous, though, was a banjulele—a small four-string banjo invented by the American Alvin Keech in the early twentieth century.

3 'In the general election of February 1950, the great and growing gulf between the regions and classes of the land became more apparent.' Kenneth O. Morgan, *The People's Peace: British History 1945–1990* (Oxford: Oxford University Press, 1992), 83.

4 Bret, *George Formby*, 110.

5 The George Formby Society and fan club can be found at http://www.georgeformby.com.

6 Raphael Samuel reports a telling example from the 1985 revival of the 1937 musical *Me and My Girl*, which included the Formby song 'Leaning on a lamp post' not in the original production. Raphael Samuel, *Theatres of Memory—Volume 1: Past and Present in Contemporary Culture* (London: Verso, 1994), 398.

7 Patrick Hughes and George Brecht, *Vicious Circles and Infinity: An Anthology of Paradoxes* (Harmondsworth: Penguin, 1978), 75.

8 Jacques Derrida, *Archive Fever: A Freudian Impression*, trans. Eric Prenowitz (Chicago: University of Chicago Press, 1996), 100. This chapter draws on Derrida's lecture more than there is space to acknowledge; I recommend it, especially to readers interested in sub-textuality.

9 Hughes and Brecht, *Vicious Circles*, 54.

10 Slavoj Žižek, *The Sublime Object of Ideology* (London: Verso, 1989). As with Derrida, I draw on Žižek more than there is space to acknowledge, especially his Chapter 6. Their two books together, for some of my purposes here, constitute a very significant 'dialogue' regarding Lacan and Freud.

11 Žižek, *Sublime Object*, 203–6.
12 John Fisher, *George Formby* (London: Woburn-Futura, 1975), 80; *ITMA* (*It's That Man Again*) 'attracted up to 16 million listeners', Andrew Davies, *Other Theatres: The Development of Alternative and Experimental Theatre in Britain* (London: Methuen, 1987), 196; for Mass Observation, see http://www.sussex.ac.uk/library/massobs/
13 Fisher, *George Formby*, 14.
14 George Orwell, *The Road to Wigan Pier* (Harmondsworth: Penguin, 1962), 66.
15 Robert Hewison, *The Heritage Industry: Britain in a Climate of Decline* (London: Methuen, 1987), 16.
16 Bret, *George Formby*, 223.
17 Ibid., 229.
18 Žižek, *Sublime Object*, 212.
19 Bret, *George Formby*, 193.
20 Fisher, *George Formby*, 53.
21 See, for example: Iain Chambers, *Popular Culture: The Metropolitan Experience* (London: Methuen, 1986); John Fiske, *Understanding Popular Culture* (Boston: Unwin Hyman, 1989); Richard Dyer, *Only Entertainment* (London: Routledge, 2002).
22 Leonard Wallace, 'Introducing George Formby', *Film Weekly*, 6 November 1937, quoted in Bret, *George Formby*, 72, emphasis in original.
23 Roland Barthes, *Mythologies* (London: Granada, 1973), 56; see also Bert States, 'The phenomenological attitude', in Janelle G. Reinelt and Joseph R. Roach, eds, *Critical Theory and Performance* (Ann Arbor: University of Michigan Press, 1992), 376–77.
24 Robert Pogue Harrison, *Forests: The Shadow of Civilisation* (Chicago: University of Chicago Press, 1992).
25 Bret, *George Formby*, 66–67.
26 In the archive this negative impression of Beryl is remarkably pervasive, so much so that to say a 'good word for her', as some do, always risks confirming the power of the negative through exception, producing a doubled stamp of condemnation. Such automatic collusions create paradoxes in the gendering of archives that are, for example, intensified by other stories surrounding *Keep Fit*: as Formby was sleeping with Walsh, so, allegedly, was Beryl with Gavin Gordon, a young actor in the film who, allegedly, recently had 'bedded Garbo and Dietrich' (Bret, *George Formby*, 68). Who is worse shod than the shoemaker's wife? Unfortunately, further exploration of this fascinating but all too intractable territory must await another occasion.
27 Žižek, *Sublime Object*, 207.
28 Bret, *George Formby*, 97.
29 Geoff J. Mellor, *They Made Us Laugh: A Compendium of Comedians Whose Memories Remain Alive* (Littleborough: George Kelsall, 1982), 30.
30 Hughes and Brecht, *Vicious Circles*, 47.
31 Derrida, *Archive Fever*, 91.
32 Hughes and Brecht, *Vicious Circle*, 56.
33 Bret, *George Formby*, 56.

Chapter Ten
1 Herman Yablokoff, *Der Payatz: Around the World with Yiddish Theater*, trans. Bella Mysell Yablokoff (Silver Spring, Md.: Bartleby Press, 1995), 365.
2 Henry Sapoznik, *Klezmer!* (New York: Schrimer Books, 1999), 84.
3 Nahma Sandrow, *Vagabond Stars: A World History of Yiddish Theater* (New York: Harper and Row, 1977), 127.
4 Ibid., 288.
5 Richard Shepard, untitled review in *New York Times*, 21 October 1963, 39. As this review hints, Leo Fuchs also performed comic tricks with his fiddle; he played it while holding the instrument behind his back, for example. I learned this from his former stage colleague, the Yiddish actress Frances Wagenfeld (now known as Robin Tigelbaum), in a conversation in 2002.
6 Irving Howe, *World of Our Fathers* (New York: Simon and Schuster, 1876), 464.
7 Hutchins Hapgood, *The Spririt of the Ghetto*, ed. Moses Rischin (Cambridge, Mass.: Belknap Press of Harvard University Press, 1967), 174.
8 These lines and others quoted later from the film *I Want to Be a Boarder* are taken from the subtitles in the version released by the National Center for Jewish Film at Brandeis University

of Massachusetts. The film, directed by Joseph Seiden, was completed in 1937 and is available in videotape form.

9   Yablokoff, *Der Payatz*, 360.

10   Anna Deavere Smith, *Fires in the Mirror* (New York: Anchor Doubleday, 1993), xxxiii.

11   The song can be heard on the audiotape *Leo Fuchs Sings Yiddish Theatre Favorites*, released by the Greater Recording Company of Brooklyn, New York, in 1973.

12   Howe, *World of Our Fathers*, 558.

13   Judith Goldberg, *Laughter Through Tears* (Rutherford, N.J.: Associated University Presses, 1983), 93.

14   Richard Shepard and Vicki Gold, *Live and Be Well: A Celebration of Yiddish Culture in America* (New York: Ballantine Books, 1982), 26.

15   Walter Benjamin, 'Surrealism', in *Selected Writings*, 3 vols, trans. Rodney Livingston et al. (Cambridge, Mass.: Belknap Press of Harvard University Press, 1996–2002), II, 217–18.

16   Howe, *World of Our Fathers*, 567.

17   Leo Rosten, *The Joys of Yiddish* (New York: Simon and Schuster Pocket Books, 1970), 348.

18   Walter Benjamin, 'Ibizan sequence', in *Selected Writings*, II, 590. Leo Fuchs wanted to perform another great schlemiel role, Gimpel the Fool, in his own adaptation of I.B. Singer's story *Gimpel the Fool*. Yiddish actress Frances Wagenfeld told me in 2002 that Fuchs wanted her to play the role of Gimpel's wife, but the production was never realized.

19   Sapoznik, *Klezmer!*, 33.

20   For this vision of *Yiddishkeit* I am indebted to Paul Buhle's essay, 'Tikkun—Shadows of empire, hopes of redemption', *Tikkun* 17:1 (2002), 58.

21   For this observation I am indebted to my colleague Laurence Senelick, private correspondence, 2002. Another comic dance by Fuchs was described to me by Yiddish actress Frances Wagenfeld, who performed the dance with him. In a parody of traditional dance partnerships, at a point where the audience expected the actress to leap gracefully into Fuchs's arms, he would jump into hers. Wagenfeld, who first performed in Yiddish theatre at the age of 10, and often portrayed young boys (as did Molly Picon), told me about this act and others in 2002, and I am grateful to her for all her information.

22   Yablokoff, *Der Paysatz*, 379.

23   Peter Thomson, *Shakespeare's Professional Career* (Cambridge: Cambridge University Press, 1991), 116, 139.

24   J. Hoberman, *Bridge of Light: Yiddish Film Between Two Worlds* (New York: Schocken Books and Museum of Modern Art, 1991), 219. Both Hoberman and critic Judith Goldberg note that film director Joseph Seiden created *I Want to Be a Boarder* by using outtakes from his film *I Want to Be a Mother*; I do not think this genesis of the film in any way reduces its comedy or its impact.

25   'Leo Fuchs hit of production—musical comedy opens at the public theatre', review (signed by W.S.) in *New York Times*, 2 December 1936, 19.

26   'Musical show on Second Ave.', review (signed by W.S.) in *New York Times*, 4 October 1937, 17.

27   Dialogue excerpted from the film *Avalon*, directed by Barry Levinson (1990).

28   For this information I am indebted to Hoberman, *Bridge of Light*, 321.

29   Richard Shepard, untitled review in the *New York Times*, 29 October 1962, 36.

30   S.J. Perelman, 'The sweet chick gone', in *Chicken Inspector No. 23* (New York: Simon and Schuster, 1966), 129. Here I have resisted adding that Fuchs achieved these heights without too much *schmaltz* (*schmaltz* being a Yiddish term for both chicken fat and sentimentality).

Chapter Eleven

1   Bertolt Brecht, 'Alienation effects in the narrative pictures of the Elder Brueghel', in John Willett, ed. and trans., *Brecht on Theatre* (London: Methuen, 1978), 157–59.

2   Bertolt Brecht, *The Swamp*, in John Willett and Ralph Manheim, eds, *Bertolt Brecht Poems 1913–1956*, trans. Naomi Replansky (London: Methuen, 1976), 381.

3   James K. Lyon, *Bertolt Brecht in America* (London: Methuen, 1982), 213.

4   Bertolt Brecht, 'The question of criteria for judging acting (Notes to *Mann ist Mann*)', in Willett, *Brecht on Theatre*, 53–57.

5   Graham Holderness, 'Introduction', in Graham Holderness, ed., *The Politics of Theatre and Drama* (Basingstoke: Macmillan, 1992), 2.

6   Brecht, 'Criteria for judging acting', 57.

7   Ibid., 54.

8   Ibid., 55.
9   Ibid.
10   My main reference points are Sergei Eisenstein (*Battleship Potemkin*), the early Cubist paint-
     ings of George Braque and Pablo Picasso. Reference may also be made to Walter Benjamin,
     in particular the collection of essays under the title of *Illuminations* (London: Jonathan Cape,
     1970).
11   Brecht, 'Criteria for judging acting', 56.
12   Joel Schechter, 'Brecht's clowns: *Man is Man* and after', in Peter Thomson and Glendyr
     Sacks, eds, *The Cambridge Companion to Brecht* (Cambridge: Cambridge University Press,
     1994), 68–78.
13   Ibid., 68.
14   Bertolt Brecht, *The Messingkauf Dialogues*, trans. John Willett (London: Methuen, 1965).
15   The hearts and susceptibilities of Edwardian audiences were stirred by recitations of *The
     Green Eye of the Yellow God* by J. Milton Hayes (1911).
16   Christopher McCullough, 'Building a dramatic vocabulary', in David Hornbrook, ed., *On
     the Subject of Drama* (London: Routledge, 1998), 169–84.
17   Brecht, 'A radio speech' in Willett, *Brecht on Theatre*, 19; Joel Schechter, 'Brecht's clowns',
     68.
18   Brecht's involvement with film was limited to two significant ventures. In 1931, the film
     version of *The Threepenny Opera* (*Die Dreigroschenoper*) was a personal disaster for Brecht,
     but *Kuhle Wampe* (the name of a camp for the dispossessed), the only film for which Brecht
     gained a screenplay credit, demonstrated the possibilities for Brecht's work to be dissemi-
     nated through the medium of film. This is particularly true of the final sequence set in a
     train when the young people are travelling back to Berlin and engage in a lively debate about
     world economic affairs.
19   Lee Baxandall, 'Brecht in America, 1935', *Drama Review* 12:1 (1967), 69–87.
20   Ibid., 76.
21   Stephen D. Youngkin, James Bigwood and Raymond Cabana Jnr, 'Introduction', in *The
     Films of Peter Lorre* (Secaucus, N.J.: Citadel Press, 1982), 25.
22   Ibid., 30. The grammar of this quotation is somewhat eccentric, but is a direct quotation
     from the given source.
23   Ibid., 37.
24   Ibid., 43.
25   Ibid., 35.
26   Bela Lugosi, another middle European émigré, is best remembered for his screen portrayal
     of Count Dracula. Amazon.com website http://uk.imdb.com/Bio, Lorre+Peter.
27   Youngkin et al., *The Films of Peter Lorre*, 62.
28   Peter Thomson's recent volume, *On Actors and Acting* (Exeter: University of Exeter Press,
     2000), argues the perceived move in playing from 'representation' to a notion of 'person-
     ation', 9. It is an argument, given time and space, that may offer much to any consideration
     of Peter Lorre's acting and the move from Europe to America.
29   John Willett, *Brecht in Context* (London: Methuen, 1986), 41.

Chapter Twelve
1   The royal family is said to have delayed dinner to watch to the end of the seventy-minute
     programme. It was also likely to have been enjoyed by the tall, balding Major-General Yuri
     Kobaladze and the short Colonel Oleg Tsarev, two high-ranking British-based KGB agents
     known to their colleagues (by dint of their enthusiasm for the act and their similar physical
     appearance) as 'Morecambe' and 'Wise'. See Graham McCann, *Morecambe and Wise*
     (London: Fourth Estate, 1998), 238. Various compilations from the television shows are
     available on video. A useful selection includes, *The Morecambe and Wise Show Christmas
     Cracker* (Quantum Leap Group, Ref: QLG5020), *Classic Morecambe and Wise* (Vols 1–5:
     Quantum Leap Group, Ref: QLG5021–25), *Eric and Ernie Live* (Polygram, Ref:
     CFV11222; the only record of the live stage show generally available).
2   Quoted in Paul Taylor, 'Some new jokes what I wrote . . .', *Independent Wednesday Review*,
     7 November 2001, 11. Some Eddie Braben material is collected in his *The Best of Morecambe
     and Wise* (London: Woburn Press, 1974).
3   Quoted in McCann, *Morecambe and Wise*, 313–14.
4   Quoted in ibid., 140.
5   Kenneth Bailey, *People*, 25 April 1954, 8.

6   Eric Midwinter, *Make 'Em Laugh: Famous Comedians and their Worlds* (London: Allen and Unwin, 1979), 163–64.
7   A useful description of the routine is to be found in McCann, *Morecambe and Wise*, 233–35.
8   Ernie Wise, with Trevor Barnes, *Still on My Way to Hollywood* (London: Duckworth, 1990). Morecambe and Wise made several attempts to 'crack' America later in their careers, but failed to do so; conventional wisdom puts them in that long line of British comics the nature of whose humour has failed to engage with American audiences, but in fact their appearances on the *Ed Sullivan Show*, which numbered nearly twenty, seem to have been received reasonably well. A likelier reason for their failure was a lack of sufficient effort, arising from Morecambe's anxiety about compromising their British success and his fear of flying. See McCann, *Morecambe and Wise*, 158ff.
9   *Abbott and Costello Meet Frankenstein* (1948, U-I, Robert Arthur).
10   Midwinter, *Make 'Em Laugh*, 170.
11   John Fisher, *Funny Way to be a Hero* (London: Frederick Muller, 1973), 291.
12   Kenneth Tynan, 'The top joker', *Observer Magazine*, 9 September 1973, 20–23; 20.
13   Quoted in McCann, *Morecambe and Wise*, 229.
14   Tynan, 'The top joker', 23.
15   Ibid., 21.
16   Quoted in Midwinter, *Make 'Em Laugh*, 164.
17   Quoted in McCann, *Morecambe and Wise*, 216.
18   Ibid., 214.
19   Tynan, 'The top joker', 23.
20   McCann, *Morecambe and Wise*, 215–16. *A Chump at Oxford* (1940, Hal Roach).
21   Eric Morecambe, *Mr Lonely* (London: Methuen, 1981).
22   Following Morecambe's death, Wise confessed to a 'terrifying and unworthy' thought: 'How could he do this to me?' (Wise, *Still on My Way to Hollywood*, 166), and to feeling 'like there's a cold draught down one side of me where Eric should be' (*Daily Star*, 29 May 1984, 15).
23   Fisher, *Funny Way to be a Hero*, 295.

Chapter Fourteen
1   Peter Thomson, *On Actors and Acting* (Exeter: University of Exeter Press, 2000), 189.
2   'Hamlet and Romeo', Mark Rylance interviewed by Rob Ferris, in Murray Cox, ed., *Shakespeare Comes to Broadmoor* (London: J. Kingsley, 1992).
3   Thomson, *On Actors*, 188.
4   In an interview with Sue Parrish for the Directors Guild of Great Britain, 1999.
5   Dennis Kennedy's essay, 'Shakespeare and cultural tourism', in Edward J. Esche, ed., *Shakespeare and his Contemporaries in Performance* (Aldershot: Ashgate, 2000), 3–20, is the most thorough exploration of the Globe in this context.
6   Thomson, *On Actors*, 200.
7   The Globe's Master of Verse.
8   No. 18 of 40 'principles' for using the Globe, drawn up at the review of the 1997 season. These principles reveal the Globe to be much more open in its approaches to 'original practices' than its critics allow—or perhaps understand.
9   Geoffrey Fenton, quoted in Glynne Wickham, Herbert Berry and William Ingram, eds, *English Professional Theatre 1530–1660* (Cambridge: Cambridge University Press, 2000), 159.
10   Stephen Orgel, 'Nobody's perfect: or, why did the English stage take boys for women?', *South Atlantic Quarterly* 88:1 (1989), 7–29.
11   Directed by Sean Holmes, its first performance was on 22 May 2000.
12   Laurence Senelick, *The Changing Room* (New York: Routledge, 2000), 131.
13   See Richard Rastall, 'Female roles in all-male casts', *Medieval Theatre Studies* 7:1 (1985), 25–50; Martin White, *Renaissance Drama in Action* (London: Routledge, 1997).
14   The Globe has also hosted a visit by a Japanese Kyogen company.

Index

Abbey Theatre, Dublin 84, 88, 90, 94, 95, 127
Abbott and Costello 178, 182, 183
acrobatics 44
acting style 5, 6, 11, 12, 27, 32, 73–7, 83, 88–93, 127, 166–75, 192, 194, 201, 208–9, 218–20
action 5, 6, 11, 22, 23, 30, 34, 58, 213, actor
    actor's body 21, 22, 29, 31, 32, 33, 138, 139, 141, 142, 149, 174
    actor's eyes 12, 14, 22, 26, 99, 144–5, 147
    actor's movement 13–15, 23–7, 58, 212, 221
actor-manager 21, 32, 72, 74, 80, 120,
actors, child 15, 66, 80, 181, 215–20
Actors' Company 23, 24, 30, 32, 33
actress 6, 7, 27, 56, 57–70, 97–112, 117–19, 120–34, 191–209
Adler, Jacob 154
Admiral's Men 215
advertisement 48, 104, 175
African-American performers 155, 159, 160
agit-prop 172, 199
Alexander Leggatt xi, 6–20
Alleyn, Edward 11
Alleyn, John 20
alternative theatre companies 196–9, 208
amateur performers 38, 85, 91, 92, 95, 127, 128, 229
America 55, 56, 71–82, 86, 94, 165, 210
Anna Ioannovna, Empress 37, 39, 40–3
Anne of Denmark 9
anti-theatricality 32, 33, 75, 76
Antoine, André 92

archive 137–44, 147, 149
aristocracy 30, 31, 32, 55, 81
art 6, 34, 35, 91, 92, 136
arts associations 194
arts centres 196
Arts Council 194, 198, 199
Ashwell, Lena 118, 120–34
asides 29, 39
Astaire, Fred 150, 155, 157
Aston, Anthony 22
Astor Place Opera House 81–2
Attlee, Clement 122
audience xi, 5, 6, 10,11,12,14, 18, 22, 27, 28, 29, 30, 32, 33, 36–8, 42, 58, 61, 87, 92, 94, 120, 122, 124–5, 127–9, 133–4, 143, 146–7, 152–4, 156, 158, 164, 168, 171, 179, 180, 182, 183, 184, 186, 189, 201, 211, 212–13, 217–18, 221–2
    American 73, 79, 82
    popular 21, 50, 119, 135, 194, 196–9, 207–9
    provincial 55, 63, 132
audition 19, 193
auditorium 87, 186, 218
authenticity 82, 95, 201, 211, 212
autobiography 58, 84, 95, 112

ballet dancing 37
Banham, Martin xi–xii
banjulele 135, 141, 143, 239
Barker, Howard 205
Barrington, Rutland 12
Barthes, Roland 110, 144
Bartley, George 74
Bath 63, 64
bathos 60, 87
baths, swimming 121, 122